W9-CEE-127

Unruly Women

Gender & American Culture

Victoria E. Bynum

The University of North Carolina Press

Chapel Hill and London

Unruly Women

The Politics of
Social and Sexual
Control in the
Old South

Manufactured in the United States of America
99 98 97 96 95 7 6 5 4 3

Library of Congress Cataloging-in-Publication Data
Bynum, Victoria E.
Unruly women : the politics of social and sexual control in the old South / by Victoria E. Bynum.
p. cm. — (Gender & American culture)
Includes bibliographical references (p.) and index.
ISBN 0-8078-2016-4 (cloth : alk. paper). —
ISBN 0-8078-4361-X (pbk. : alk. paper)
1. Women—North Carolina—History—19th century. 2. Deviant behavior—History—19th century. 3. Female offenders—North Carolina—History—19th century. 4. Social control—History—19th century. 5. North Carolina—Race relations.
I. Title. II. Series.
HQ1438.N6B96 1992
305.4'09756—dc20 91-33851
CIP

The paper in this book meets the guidelines for permanence and durability of the Committee on Production Guidelines for Book Longevity of the Council on Library Resources.

An earlier version of Chapter 6 appeared as "'War within a War': Women's Participation in the Revolt of the North Carolina Piedmont, 1863–65," *Frontiers: A Journal of Women Studies* 9, no. 3 (1987): 43–49. Portions of Chapter 4 and the Epilogue appeared as "The Lowest Rung: Court Control over Poor White and Free Black Women," *Southern Exposure* 12 (November–December 1984): 40–44.

For Gregg

Contents

Tables, Charts, & Maps

Tables

Charts

Maps

Acknowledgments

Many people have assisted me in my work on this book. I wish to thank Thomas Dublin for encouraging my insights and seriousness of purpose as this study evolved into an analysis of disparate groups of unruly women and their relationship to the political economy of nineteenth-century North Carolina. I benefited from discussing history with Harry Scheiber and with Kathleen Berkeley, Stephen Hahn, Earl Pomeroy, Edward Reynolds, and Robert Ritchie. I am deeply indebted to Dolores Janiewski, who provided crucial intellectual stimulation and moral support for my ideas.

Friends like Lucy Duvall, Ann Elwood, Adrienne Hood, Richard Hunt, Colleen O'Connor, and Kristin Webb shared my high moments in graduate school and made more bearable the hard times. Charlene Borga, Laurie Fellwock, and my children, Randy and Erika Pierce, helped me not to lose sight of the bigger picture in life.

I would like to thank the fine staffs of the North Carolina Department of Archives and History, the Special Collections Department of Duke University, and the Southern Historical Collection of the University of North Carolina, Chapel Hill, for their cooperation and courtesy during the year I spent in North Carolina researching this book. A fellowship from the Business and Professional Women's Foundation in 1984 allowed me to return to the East Coast for additional research. Stephen Hahn and Ira Berlin made it possible for me to sift through the files of the Freedmen and Southern Society Project at the University of Maryland.

Several scholars and students of North Carolina history have shared their time and ideas with me. I owe thanks especially to William Auman, John Inscoe, LuAnn Jones, Anne Firor Scott, Harry Watson, and Peter Wood. I am particularly grateful to Marjoleine Kars for sharing my enthusiasm for North Carolina's unruly women and for extending numerous courtesies to my daughter and me during our stay in North Carolina.

I have profited from discussions with students of women's history at Southwest Texas State University. Lisa-Marie Coppoletta and Jonnie Wilson, in particular, have shared important insights about the convergence of race, class, and gender. These insights have enriched this book.

I want to thank Iris Tillman Hill, former editor-in-chief at the University of North Carolina Press, for soliciting my manuscript. I am equally fortunate that her successor, Kate Torrey, worked patiently with me to produce this book. Likewise, managing editor Sandra Eisdorfer and copyeditor Trudie Calvert sharpened my prose and saved me from embarrassing textual errors. I also wish to thank Nell Painter and Colin Palmer for challenging me to expand my study and sharpen my analysis.

I would like to thank the following people who have chaired or commented on conference papers that I have given as this book took shape: Kathleen Berkeley, Catherine Clinton, Suzanne Lebsock, George Rable, LeeAnn Whites, Carol Berkin, and Harold Woodman.

I regret that my father, Stanley Bynum, did not live to see my book in print, especially since his rural Mississippi roots provided much of the initial inspiration for my work. I owe my mother, Margaret Bynum, special thanks for encouraging me always to value ideas over objects and for providing financial assistance during the final critical years of this study.

Finally, I dedicate this book to my husband, Gregg Andrews. Although a relative newcomer to the evolution of this book, he has read and discussed it with me over the past three years as it moved toward its final form. His superb intellectual, editing, and typing skills contributed immeasurably to the final product.

Unruly Women

Introduction

Who were the unruly women of antebellum and Civil War North Carolina, and what did they do that marked them as deviant or disorderly? Why should historians interested in the dynamics of power and politics in the antebellum South investigate this politically powerless minority of women? This book addresses these questions by examining three broad categories of women who behaved in atypical fashion. First, it studies women who, strictly speaking, did not misbehave by challenging the rules or the bases of power in North Carolina society. Rather, these women publicly complained about misbehaving husbands or other male household members whom they accused of abusing male prerogatives of power. Such complaints usually singled out men who exhibited physical and mental cruelty toward women. The second category of unruly women includes those who defied the rules of society by engaging in forbidden social and sexual behavior. Finally, this study examines a third category of women who implicitly or explicitly defied the authority of the Confederate state during the Civil War.[1]

By focusing on women from these three categories, we can better grasp the impact of race and class on southern women's behavior, and we can deepen our understanding of the connections between the private world of home and family and the public world of commerce and politics. Thus we not only identify the ways in which gender, race, and class generated profoundly different experiences among women and between women and men but also the ways in which power flowed between the private and public spheres of society.[2]

Studying discontented and disorderly women within and outside the household setting sheds light on the centrality of marriage and slavery to the patriarchal structure in the antebellum South. For example, marriage as an ideal social institution promised white women love, honor, and protection; yet the North Carolina Supreme Court routinely denied legal separations and divorces to women trapped in abusive, degrading marriages. Moreover, the harsh punishment meted out to sexually active unmarried free women suggests that marriage functioned primarily as a mechanism for appropriating women's reproductive behavior rather than as a means of protecting women. Motherhood, the noblest calling of southern white women, became the most appalling symbol of degradation when it occurred outside marriage.

As members of a biracial slaveholding society, North Carolina leaders exercised more careful and coercive control over white women's sexual behavior than did their northern counterparts. White women were the "carriers" of racial "purity" in the South. Although the studies of antebellum southern law by Michael Hindus, Mark Tushnet, and Edward Ayers do not specifically address gender, they demonstrate that the courts' treatment of women cannot be separated from the boundaries of race and class that helped to form the grid of human relations in the Old South.[3] Michael Grossberg's argument that a "judicial patriarchy" emerged in the United States during the nineteenth century has particular meaning when applied to the antebellum South. Grossberg finds that courts increasingly mediated the "distinction between the male authority to govern the home and the female responsibility to maintain it" as a means of strengthening the republican family (and thus the republic).[4] This trend had added force in the South, where slavery remained embedded in the household.

This book places unruly women at center stage by showing how they struggled to carve out a space for themselves in a society that condemned and marginalized them. The task of moving subordinate people into the historical limelight without losing sight of the political framework in which they operated is challenging. As Willie Lee Rose has noted, "It challenges the historian's ingenuity . . . to make participants who did not dominate the story dominate the frame of reference." Broadening our concept of what constitutes power begins the task. If we view power only in the context of a person's ability to dominate and control another, then subordinate people appear as little more than inert masses. By the same token, people from dominant classes appear, in the words of Arthur Brittan and Mary Maynard, as "clockwork" oppressors "wound up by some inexorable determining mechanism which resides in the system."[5] Human agency and resistance fade from view when we rivet attention solely on sexual, racial, and economic forces and exclude the people who wield and respond to those forces.

As Linda Gordon has argued, placing subordinate people center stage need not trivialize the effects of institutionalized oppression. Nor should viewing women as active agents of their own lives suggest that they were to blame for their own oppression.[6] Although many of the women studied in this book internalized society's judgment of them as unworthy and degraded, and although they misbehaved in part because it was expected of them, many others resisted society's definition of them and maintained vitality and self-respect through exhibiting unruly behavior. Each expressed a need to experience life as something more than simply being the psychic or material property of another.

Recent scholars have provided excellent models for analyzing the dehumanizing effects of oppression without reducing its subjects to merely passive, interchangeable victims. Many studies of socially and politically marginalized people offer fresh insights into how societies create and maintain power and how marginalized people resist that power. The historiography of slavery is a case in point. Eugene Genovese, John Blassingame, Herbert Gutman, Lawrence Levine, and Paul D. Escott are among those scholars who in the 1970s reshaped our understanding of slavery. Following the example set by W. E. B. Du Bois some seventy years earlier, they mined the folktales, songs, autobiographies, and narratives of former slaves to reconstruct the world of slaves.[7] The slave's world thus became central rather than peripheral to analyses of the antebellum South's political economy.

Treating race relations as central to the formation of southern institutions has also enriched our understanding of white southern culture and ideology. The slaveholding elite's notions about status and honor conformed to the traditional English model, which stressed family lineage, wealth, and, for men, physical prowess, sexual virility, and intellectual leadership.[8] Power and honor went hand in hand; one could hardly achieve one without the other. The southern version of honor was also grounded, however, in the need to maintain racial distinctions within institutions of the family, law, politics, and the economy.

Of course, slavery prevented blacks from obtaining wealth, education, or legally recognized family lines. It was considerably harder, however, to prevent African American men from achieving status through time-honored expressions of "masculine" virility. By endorsing a one-sided exchange of women, the North Carolina ruling class tried to limit the expression of black masculinity. White men had access to black women, but white women were off-limits to black men. Slaveholders devised laws to limit interracial social contact, and the ideology of paternalism posited slavery as the stewardship of infantile, uncivilized blacks by noble, beneficent whites.[9] Paternalist ideology effectively denied adult status to all blacks; it denied the rights of manhood to black men and the rights of womanhood to black women.

By denying to black men the traditional means to achieve honor and power, white men sought to ensure racial control. Try as they might, however, they did not completely "emasculate" black men. Many historians have shown that a rich slave culture and a semi-autonomous slave community that drew on African customs and models of gender relations provided buffers against the harsh pressures of slavery on the identity and self-respect of slaves. African extended kinship systems, women's participation in African agricultural work, and acceptance of premarital sex by certain African societies shaped the response of the slave community.[10]

This book emphasizes that distinctly "masculine" activities were open to enslaved and free black men outside the home setting. Illegal gambling, trafficking in illegal goods, and competing for women provided some black men with a sense of mastery over their own world and sometimes over portions of the world of their masters. Achieving success through underground commerce brought status in African American communities, particularly when it undermined white control. It sometimes even earned the grudging, if hostile, respect of local lawmakers.

A gendered view of slavery that spotlighted slave women appeared in the 1980s. Bettina Aptheker, Angela Davis, bell hooks, Paula Giddings, Deborah Gray White, Jacqueline Jones, and Elizabeth Fox-Genovese produced studies that focused on, or at least included, slave women. They described how black women, whether they adhered to or rejected the imposed images of "Mammy" and "Jezebel," resisted slavery in ways that usually reflected their gender and individual temperament.[11]

Davis, Giddings, White, and Fox-Genovese have noted slave women's propensity for arson, poisoning, the feigning of female illnesses and pregnancies to escape work, and occasional acts of abortion and infanticide. Because of slave women's responsibilities to children and family, they usually resisted enslavement by engaging in acts of individual rather than collective defiance. Whether slave women behaved like Mammies or Jezebels depended on the role imposed on them. Certainly the role of Mammy was safer. Sexless and loyal, according to white images, Mammy inspired the trust of whites and thus usually received better treatment and perhaps greater access to household goods. As Deborah Gray White points out, the role of Jezebel represented the sexually charged, seductive counterimage of the "bad" black woman. In some cases, however, this role brought material rewards from white men, including, on occasion, advantages to the children of interracial liaisons.[12]

The rape of slave women by white men marked the distinct convergence of racial, sexual, and economic systems. The ease with which white owners might rape slave women attested to the brutal display of power invited by the institution of slavery. As Angela Davis has noted, the rape of a slave woman "was not exclusively an attack upon her. Indirectly, its target was also the slave community as a whole." Yet, as Davis points out, rape was an attack on the slave woman *as a woman*.[13]

So embedded were notions of race and gender in nineteenth-century America that the advantages of being free were relative for

African American women. In both the North and South, free black women suffered the dehumanizing effects of racism and sexism. Social and economic segregation served as a means of racial control in the North, where black women were stereotyped as less virtuous and chaste than white women.[14] Free blacks fared even worse in the South, where their mobility was more restricted and they could be compelled at any time to prove they were legally free.[15]

Historians have recently begun to incorporate gender into the study of free blacks before the Civil War. For example, Suzanne Lebsock's pathbreaking study of free black women in antebellum Petersburg, Virginia, emphasizes that black women faced "enormous burdens with pitifully slim resources." Although we must be careful not to overgeneralize from Lebsock's study of an urban area like Petersburg, given that the antebellum South was predominantly rural, she shows that free black women developed creative strategies for survival. Many of Petersburg's free black women defied sexual and racial norms of behavior. If propertied, they sometimes resisted marriage in an effort to maintain economic autonomy.[16]

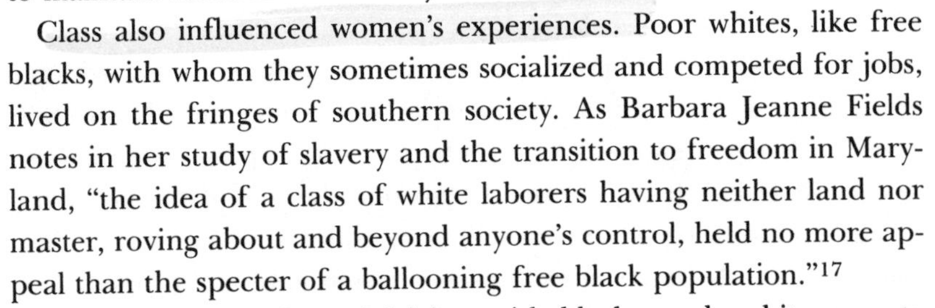

Class also influenced women's experiences. Poor whites, like free blacks, with whom they sometimes socialized and competed for jobs, lived on the fringes of southern society. As Barbara Jeanne Fields notes in her study of slavery and the transition to freedom in Maryland, "the idea of a class of white laborers having neither land nor master, roving about and beyond anyone's control, held no more appeal than the specter of a ballooning free black population."[17]

The association of menial labor with blacks made white poverty even more degrading in the South. To be without property or profession was to be without honor and respectability; it often meant being regarded as a social parasite and a potential threat to social harmony and order. Augustus White Long, commenting on the remarkable spirit of generosity of his forebears, remarked that "no contempt was in their hearts *except* for the shoddy and shiftless." Even many slaves looked down on poor whites.[18]

To be poor was even more shameful for white women because it violated norms of white femininity. A Virginia slaveholder told Frederick Law Olmsted that "white girls" forced to work outside the home were "worse than the [white] men, much worse than the negroes. . . . No girl hereabouts, whose character was good, would ever hire out to do menial service."[19] Poverty defeminized white women much as race defeminized black women.

The loss of innocence, purity, and male protection meant the loss of honor for white women, but poverty did not demasculinize poor men per se, whether they were white or black. The underground subculture in which many poor men and women participated was distinctly masculine. It emphasized illegal gaming, carousing, and frequent fighting. Men's unruly behavior might achieve a measure of distinction, but women who participated in the social underground generally invited further condemnation, even from the men with whom they participated.

Only her labor gave a poor woman in the North who lacked secure family ties any footing in the community. In the rural South, there was little demand for the labor of white women outside the family household. Although many white farm wives worked the family fields, slaves and white males were the primary source when additional labor was needed.[20] Their race and gender dictated that poor white women conform to the wholly domestic image of the true woman, but their class left them without the means to do so.

The almost nonexistent role of poor white or free black women in the antebellum southern economy contrasted with the growing demand for women's labor in the industrializing North. In contrast to the antebellum South, there emerged in the North a more positive image of "working women"—at least white working women. As Thomas Dublin shows, mill owners and mill workers defended the virtues and respectability of the Lowell factory girls, at least until Irish immigrant families replaced native-born, Yankee farm women as workers. Christine Stansell has also found that the "boisterous," "vivacious," and forthright working-class "Bowery Gal" of antebellum New York City emerged as an "alternative mode of feminine self-realization to the bourgeois ideal of true womanhood."[21]

To be poor, female, and without the guardianship of a white male figure was to be without honor or worth in the antebellum South, but class distinctions among white women were based on more than simply property holding. Slaveholding determined a woman's social standing. In the North Carolina Piedmont, however, the religious and ethnic diversity and nascent entrepreneurial outlook of the Whig planter class gave rise to a social ethos distinct from that of the eastern Democratic planter class. In addition, because the region had an equally diverse and relatively large nonslaveholding yeomanry, Whig newspaper editors tended to celebrate the hardworking farmer and farm wife as the social equals (if not superiors) of the eastern aristocratic planter and mistress.[22]

Although Piedmont newspaper editors vigorously promoted what Barbara Welter has termed a "cult of true womanhood," there is little evidence that a middle-class female culture comparable to that in the North emerged among white women in the Piedmont, except perhaps among those of Quaker, Moravian, and Wesleyan Methodist communities. Neither did a women's rights movement take root in North Carolina before the Civil War. As Jean Friedman and Elizabeth Fox-Genovese point out, rural isolation, semifrontier conditions, and slavery delayed the growth of closely knit communities of women like those that accompanied northern industrialization.[23]

In the North, families became increasingly privatized, displaced in the public domain by burgeoning institutional and economic growth. Since men controlled the public world, women became even more empowered to maintain the private sphere. Although southern women were no less relegated to the domain of hearth and family, they were far less empowered to rule over the home. Since southern farms and plantations remained the locus of economic production and labor discipline, patriarchal authority over the home setting remained central. Furthermore, most churches, important examples of "feminization" in the North, remained thoroughly male-dominated in the South because of their close connections to slavery.[24]

Slaveholding women in the North Carolina Piedmont differed somewhat from the typical plantation mistresses described by Anne Scott, Catherine Clinton, and Elizabeth Fox-Genovese. Their plantation mistresses are anchored within an aristocratic cult of ladyhood that, like the southern code of honor, evolved from the medieval code of chivalry. Fox-Genovese further argues that the values of both yeoman and elite southern women were distinct from those of the emergent "true woman" of the North. In the Piedmont, however, where huge plantations with more than twenty slaves were rare, the commitment of Whig slaveholders to commercial diversification and expansion encouraged interest in developing northern ties and included an embrace of the northern middle-class ideal of womanhood.[25]

Notwithstanding the familiar northern images of womanhood in the North Carolina Piedmont, an important aspect of the traditional planter code did remain consistent throughout the South: southern white women must not associate with black men! Maintaining a slave society based on racial distinctions necessitated control over women's sexual behavior and offspring. "Honorable" white women in the antebellum South, besides being expected to embrace the virtues of religious piety, maternal devotion, and moral uprightness, were also to abhor black men.

To link female honor to purity would have proven sexually inconvenient for southern white men, however, had they not bifurcated the sexuality of white and black women. The creation of Jezebel provided the rationale for allowing sexual relations between white men and black women. Southern proslavery ideologue William Harper made no apology for the sexual degrading of black women by white men. He simply extended his theory that "slavery anticipates the benefits of civilization and retards the evils of civilization" into the realm of sexual relations. By regarding black women as a "class of women who set little value on chastity," he argued that slavery protected black women by saving them from the alternative of being cast out of society in the manner "justly and necessarily applied to promiscuous free women." Harper further argued that sexual access to enslaved women discouraged white men from debauching "pure" white women and provided them with "easy gratification" for their "hot passions" without violating the southern code of honor. Finally, he reasoned, such sexual access made white men "less liable to those extraordinary fascinations, with which worthless [white] women sometimes entangle their victims."[26]

The sexual identities assigned to white and black women further rationalized the economic and political ends of their reproductive functions. As John D'Emilio and Estelle Freedman point out, "Systems of sexual regulation, like sexual meanings, have correlated strongly with other forms of social regulation, especially those related to race, class, and gender."[27] Confining white women's sexual and reproductive activities within the institution of marriage and black women's within slavery reinforced the plantation patriarchy. White wives perpetuated the lines of kinship that underlay the wealth and authority of white men, while slave women produced wealth for white men through their productive and reproductive labors.

Although the sexual and economic roles assigned to slaveholding and slave women illuminate the place of gender in North Carolina's political economy, neither slave nor slaveholding women are the central focus of this study of female unruliness. Since their behavior was generally governed privately by masters and husbands, records seldom document their unruliness or resistance to slavery and marriage. Although the wives of masters could certainly file peace warrants, assault and battery charges, and divorce petitions when they could no longer endure marriage, these actions rarely challenged the parameters of power, only men's abuse of power. Disorderly slave women are especially hard to trace in public records because they had virtually no access to the courts. As Fox-Genovese notes, "The records provide, at best, an imperfect guide to the nature, extent, and meaning of slave women's resistance to their enslavement."[28]

Women whose misbehavior was regularly a part of the public record are the primary focus of this book. As marginalized members of society in the North Carolina Piedmont, unmarried free black and poor white women were more likely than married women to violate social taboos and thus face punishment by the courts. If North Carolina lawmakers could have done so legally, they would have rid society altogether of free black and unmarried poor white women. Instead, they enforced laws against fornication, bastardy, and prostitution in an attempt to limit these women's reproduction of the "dangerous classes." They appropriated the rearing and labor of illegitimate children through the apprenticeship system. The courts most frequently prosecuted and bound out the children of women who fraternized with slaves and stepped across racial lines.[29]

Unlike free blacks and poor whites, the yeomanry occupied a respected position in the antebellum North Carolina Piedmont. The Civil War, however, shattered the fragile political consensus of the antebellum years and challenged the validity of southern leaders' claims that the interests of slaveholding and nonslaveholding women were identical. Many white yeoman wives who faced material deprivation and suffering during the war encouraged their menfolk to desert the Confederate army, or they engaged in political protests against the Confederacy. Unruly yeoman farm women thus hastened the collapse of the Confederacy after concluding that they were being asked to shoulder the major burdens of a slaveholders' war.[30]

In the broadest sense, lawmakers' tasks in regard to women were to maintain the authority of husbands, slave masters, and the state. Thus, examining the disparate groups of unruly women enables us to untangle the entwined strands of gender, race, and class that were woven into the fabric of antebellum North Carolina society. An investigation of which women and which behaviors were punished by state and local officials provides vivid insights into how gender arrangements shaped the political economy of North Carolina.

My study focuses on three counties—Granville, Orange, and Montgomery—in the central Piedmont area of North Carolina. Despite their geographic proximity (see Map 1), these counties displayed an economic, demographic, and cultural diversity that mirrored the diversity of the antebellum South as a whole. In some respects, the North Carolina Piedmont was a microcosm of the various permutations of race, class, and gender in the Old South. Certainly, such diversity counters the enduring stereotype of the antebellum South as a land populated primarily by slaves and slaveholders.

The vast majority of white women in North Carolina were wives or daughters of nonslaveholding farmers. Nearly 11 percent of African American women were free. In each of the counties, however, the proportions of women who were white or black, free or slave, rich or poor, varied significantly. In Granville, free black females outnumbered free black males by nearly 4 percent; in Orange County, white females outnumbered white males by more than 2 percent (see Table I.1). Combined, slave and free African American women made up a

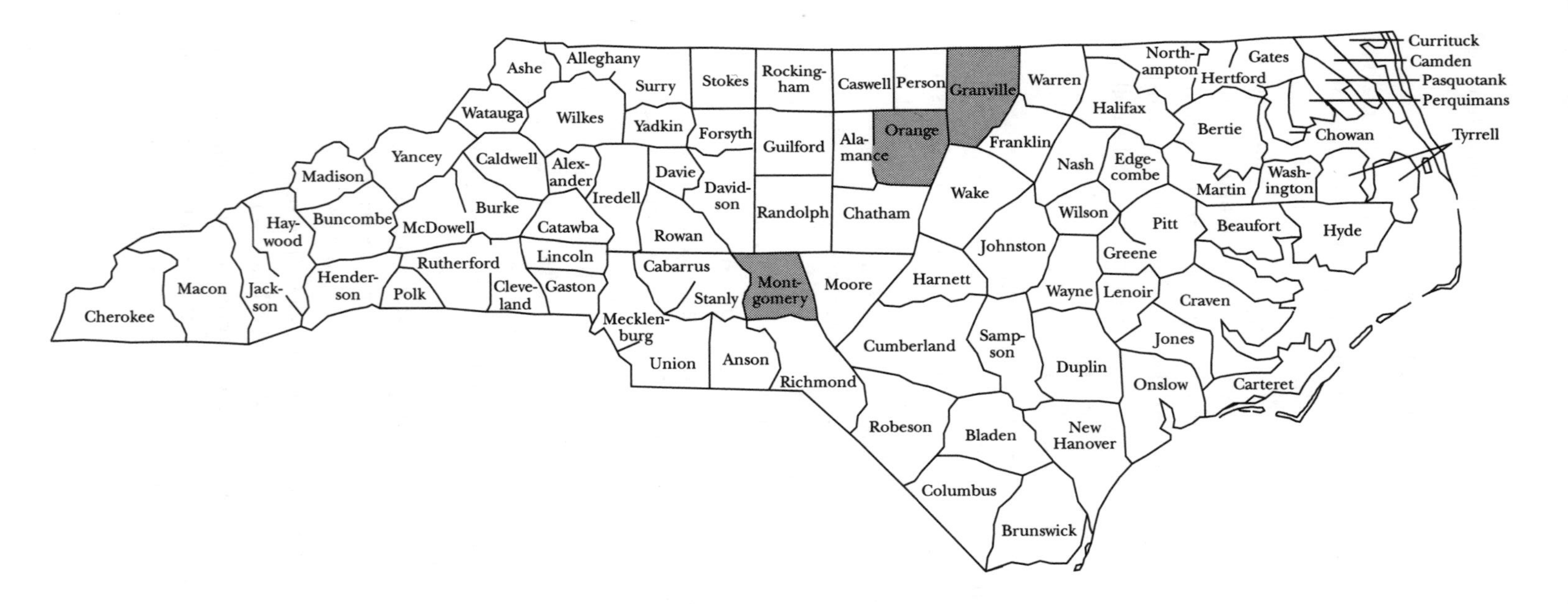

Map 1. North Carolina in 1860, Showing Principal Counties of Study

Table I.1. Population in Counties and State by Sex, 1860

	White females	Percent of white population	Free black females	Percent of free black population	Slave females	Percent of slave population
Granville	5,620	50.2	583	51.9	5,579	50.3
Orange	5,782	51.1	270	51.1	2,579	50.4
Montgomery	2,905	50.2	22	47.8	950	52.1
State	316,272	50.2	15,583	51.1	164,590	49.7

Source: U.S. Federal Manuscript Censuses, 1860, Granville, Orange, and Montgomery counties, U.S. Bureau of the Census, *Population of the United States in 1860.*

Table I.2. Female Population in Counties and State by Race, 1860

	Percent of white females	Percent of free black females	Percent of slave females	Total female population
Granville	47.7	4.9	47.4	11,782
Orange	67.0	3.1	29.9	8,631
Montgomery	74.9	0.6	24.5	3,877
State	63.7	3.1	33.2	496,445

Source: U.S. Federal Manuscript Censuses, 1860, Granville, Orange, and Montgomery counties, U.S. Bureau of the Census, *Population of the United States in 1860.*

far greater proportion of Granville's female population (over 50 percent) than in either Orange or Montgomery (see Table I.2). Free black females who owned property in Granville and Orange were fewer and poorer than their male counterparts. Their households lagged enormously in per capita wealth compared to those headed by white women, particularly in Granville County, which contained a large planter class (see Table I.3).[31]

These demographic permutations, in turn, affected the patterns of women's unruly behavior in each county, underscoring again the danger in drawing too facile conclusions about an entire state, much less

Table I.3. Wealth of Households Headed by Free Black Women, in Comparison to White, by County, 1860

	Number of black female-headed households	Percentage of all female-headed households	Percentage owning property	Per capita wealth of black females	Percentage of white female per capita wealth
Granville	42	14.9	38.0	$99.97	1.8
Orange	32	8.3	15.6	67.96	3.1

Source: U.S. Federal Manuscript Censuses, 1860, Granville, Orange, and Montgomery counties.

Note: Montgomery County reported no households headed by free black women.

the entire South. The one constant in each county was the commitment to preserving the hegemony of the slaveholding class and the stability of the slave system. In each county, unruly women challenged the sacred beliefs that underpinned the slave order. They revealed that many respected white men abused rather than protected their wives; that not all white women were repulsed by black men; that slavery was not the natural condition for blacks; and that slaveholding and nonslaveholding whites did not all share a harmony of interests in a slaveholding republic. Unruly women threatened to disrupt the underlying social structure, which depended upon the services and cooperation of all women.

One

Race, Class, and Gender in Three Piedmont Counties

Writing in 1939, historian Joseph Carlyle Sitterson commented that North Carolina "contains most of the geographic features found in the South. Consequently, its antebellum civilization was in many respects a composite of the various elements in Southern life." He further explained that the eastern portion of antebellum North Carolina contained a wealthy planter class similar to that in the Lower South but that the Piedmont region displayed a variety of self-sufficient and commercial small farmers and the beginnings of industrial manufacturing with its textile mills and tobacco factories. Finally, Sitterson pointed out, the far western mountain area of North Carolina exhibited the self-sufficient frontier economy found throughout the Appalachian region of the South.[1]

Historian Guion Griffis Johnson has described the social structure of antebellum North Carolina as a six-tiered class hierarchy that resulted from the state's regional and economic diversity. Included at the top were planters owning twenty or more slaves, prominent state officeholders, the educated clergy, and the wealthiest lawyers. Many members of this upper class originated from the middle class, which consisted of small planters and various leaders within local communities—officeholders, teachers, lawyers, doctors, parsons, and some artisans. Johnson also designated as middle class the more "solid" citizens of local communities who were educated and owned between two and three hundred acres of land and a few slaves. Below the middle class, she placed in turn: nonslaveholding yeoman farmers who possessed fewer than two hundred acres of land; poor whites, including farm tenants, day laborers, and those without visible means of support; the small number of free blacks scattered unevenly throughout the state; and, finally, slaves.[2]

In studying women whose behavior contradicted the ideals of white southern society, we get a glimpse of women from all of the above categories. For example, Mary Jenkins Chambers, the mistress of a planter household, had worked her way into the highest echelons of southern society through the time-honored fashion of "marrying up." In 1831, while still a teenager, she married Joseph Hart, only to become widowed before her twenty-first birthday. In 1834, she married Elijah Barnett, whom she also outlived, and she married her final husband, Asa Chambers, of Montgomery County, at the age of forty-one in 1856. As the owner of twenty-one slaves and eight hundred acres of land, Chambers was one of Montgomery County's wealthiest men. The new Mrs. Chambers left her native Granville County (where Asa Chambers's wealth would hardly have been unique) and joined her husband at his plantation in Montgomery County, a southwestern Piedmont county populated primarily by small farmers. After her husband died, she remained a very wealthy widow until her death in 1882.[3]

Typical of the more "middling" slaveholding class of North Carolina was Orange County's Maria Tinnen, whose father possessed land and slaves valued at $3,000 in 1850. Nancy Tinnen, Maria's mother, was even wealthier, having inherited three slaves and a share of the proceeds from the sale of her father, John Walker's, remaining slaves and land upon his death in 1844. By 1860, the widowed Nancy Tinnen possessed almost $17,000 worth of property. This wealth should have made her twenty-year-old Maria one of the most marriageable young ladies of the county, but Maria "married down." On July 26, 1863, she married William B. Murray, a nonslaveholding farmer who appears to have been a friend of the family and considerably older than Maria. Perhaps Maria married for love, since she already had wealth, or perhaps the loss of so many marriageable men to the Confederacy forced her to be less choosy. In any case, the couple began immediately to raise a family despite the disruptions of war.[4]

Rosetta Hurley of Montgomery County exemplified North Carolina's nonslaveholding yeomanry. With her two sisters, a brother, and aging parents, Hurley struggled to eke out a living by farming some one hundred acres of land near Barnes Creek in northern Montgomery County. This endeavor became increasingly difficult after the Civil War, when many of the county's small farmers, including the unmarried Hurley sisters, were pushed into the ranks of the landless and impoverished. Before the war, however, landless people were rare in Montgomery, and the Hurleys typified its many small farmers.[5]

There were many visible examples of propertyless, poor white women in Granville County. Susan Williford, an unmarried mother of several white and mulatto children, possessed neither property nor formal skills with which to earn a living. Her slide from the ranks of the yeomanry began with her illegitimate birth in 1815 and was completed when she gave birth to her first illegitimate child in 1836. She personified the label "poor white" and was thus deemed an unfit mother by county officials, who regularly apprenticed her children to propertied members of the community.[6]

Winnefred Tyler, Williford's sixty-five-year-old free black neighbor in 1860, was of even lower status, even though she owned land worth $1,500 and personal property worth $200. She had another advantage over Williford: an extensive kinship network. Before marrying Lemuel Tyler in 1811, she had been Winnefred Anderson—a member of one of Granville County's most extensive property-owning free black families. Nonetheless, Tyler's race condemned her to a legal and social status higher only than that of a slave.[7]

An Orange County slave, Harriet, personified the double burden of gender and race suffered by slave women. Dr. James Strudwick Smith of Chapel Hill purchased fifteen-year-old Harriet in 1834 as a personal servant for his daughter Mary Ruffin Smith. Although Harriet eventually married Reuben Day, Jr., a prominent free black in the county, this marriage had no legal standing because of her slave status. Harriet's husband was run off the Smith plantation by Dr. Smith's son Sidney, who raped and impregnated Harriet. Eventually, Dr. Smith's other son, Francis, also impregnated her. As a slave woman, Harriet had no rights of citizenship or rights over her own body and reproduction.[8]

Clearly, one cannot assess the place of women in antebellum southern society on the basis of gender alone. Nor is it enough simply to describe the major elements of each class or race in women's lives, for the broader meaning of gender within society as a whole would be lost. It is necessary to analyze the interlocking of gender, race, and class. One must search, then, for both the common and the unique among women such as Harriet, Mary Chambers, Maria Tinnen Murray, Rosetta Hurley, Susan Williford, and Winnefred Tyler in order to grasp the meaning of their assigned roles, behavior, and overall impact on society.

The subtleties of analyzing the significance of gender in the antebellum South become even more complex when we consider the diverse characteristics of North Carolina. Although North Carolina exhibited all the major features of the South, it was unique among southern states. The diversity of its people affected the texture of life in individual communities and complicated the task of maintaining unity within the state. North Carolina's political leaders were particularly constrained to develop an ideology, a coherent system of political symbols, that would appeal to the self-sufficient yeoman, the business-minded farmer or planter who produced cash crops and invested his profits in manufacturing ventures, and the wealthy planter of cotton, tobacco, and rice who plowed his profits back into the purchase of land and slaves.

Harry L. Watson, in his study of the political structure of Cumberland County, North Carolina, during the Age of Jackson, credited state leaders with effectively developing just such a political ethos. Public spokesmen, he wrote, addressed divergent viewpoints about "progress versus tradition" within a lively two-party system that tended "to emphasize the settled and perfect character of American institutions." Undoubtedly the most unifying maxim of the state's political ideology, one that superseded party interests, was the belief that "republicanism would not be safe unless slavery were safe as well."[9]

The expression of republican ideals that posited the need for continued white supremacy helped to defuse potential class conflicts among white citizens over slavery. But those issues not so easily buried by racial consensus—the differences of opinion over internal improvements, methods of taxation, and equal political representation (all issues derived from slavery)—were continually debated in the arena of party politics and remained potential sources of class and regional upheaval. Through domination of the state legislature, wealthy slaveholders prevented the enaction of all but the mildest reforms. As a result, social tensions were smoldering on the eve of the Civil War.[10]

The planter class of North Carolina established its hegemony primarily by political domination and secondarily by achieving a fragile consensus based on the deference of the common people. Just as the symbols of white republican manhood strengthened this consensus, so, too, did a variant of "republican womanhood" emphasize common interests and characteristics among all white women.[11] It also stressed the complementary rather than unequal nature of male and female roles in North Carolina. Particularly in the Piedmont, where middle-class planters and self-sufficient yeoman farmers predominated, an ideal of womanhood emerged between 1830 and 1850 that displayed both antiaristocratic and proslavery tenets. Like republican ideology in general, it united white people with potentially conflicting interests in a diverse region.

This unifying republican ideology could not alter the fact that a few privileged men controlled the levers of power in North Carolina. Fully 85 percent of the state's legislators in 1860 were slaveholders, although less than 30 percent of the state's free families owned slaves. Among these slaveholders the planter class was disproportionately represented. Only 3 percent of North Carolina's free families belonged to the planter class; in contrast, 36 percent of the state legislators were members of the planter class.[12]

For the women of North Carolina, a planter class powerful beyond its numbers meant two things. First, it assured the enactment of a biracial sexual code dependent upon their cooperation. Second, when rivalries between upper- and middle-class planters for control of state policy intensified over the issue of secession, leaders battled them out in the arena of "woman's sphere" as well as in party politics.

To understand the nature of planter rivalries in North Carolina, we must examine the distinctive features of the state and the structure of its political leadership. Historian Paul D. Escott finds that the diverse economic interests of North Carolina's elites created an entrepreneurial class of slaveholders. In the Piedmont, some prominent families engaged in industrial ventures, especially textile mills and railroads. Harry Watson cautions, however, against equating these entrepreneurial interests with movement toward the modern industrial capitalism then emerging in the North. Those who urged reform of North Carolina's political and economic structure (many of them planters, merchants, and lawyers) primarily sought greater commercialization of agriculture through improved transportation networks and modern financial institutions. They remained deeply wedded to the expansion of slavery in the service of a more diversified market-oriented economy.[13]

Despite their commitment to slavery, leaders in the Piedmont region did not fit the general stereotype of the southern planter; very few owned more than twenty slaves, lived on lavish estates, or made their fortunes from one-crop agriculture alone. In her study of power and politics in Guilford County, for example, Gail O'Brien shows that the leaders of that county contradicted the popular image of planters as aristocratic, precapitalist patriarchs. She argues that Guilford's slaveholding elite invested in various capitalist enterprises, including mines, railroads, and mills. Commitment to the institution of slavery did not preclude the Guilford elite from endorsing economic diversification and modernization.[14]

Piedmont editors like Edward J. Hale of Fayetteville minimized the antagonisms between Piedmont slaveholders and nonslaveholders by stressing the long-standing divisions between the eastern and western sections of the state. Hale portrayed both the Piedmont gentry and yeomanry as hardworking, altruistic, and pious in contrast to the allegedly aristocratic, materialistic, and self-indulgent eastern planter class that resembled the planters in South Carolina. Several Piedmont editors, including Hale, extended their antielitist rhetoric further by idealizing the busy farm wife as a more appropriate model of southern womanhood than the pampered, genteel lady of the aristocratic planter class.[15]

The religious, class, and ethnic diversity of North Carolina's white population encouraged leaders to cultivate an egalitarian rather than aristocratic ideal of republicanism. Even among nonslaveholding farmers there was considerable diversity. Beginning around 1750, many inhabitants of other colonies—notably, Virginia, South Carolina, and Pennsylvania—had flowed into the region. The rich soil of northeastern North Carolina attracted Virginia tobacco planters after their lands began to wear out. Wealthy rice planters from South Carolina spilled over into the Cape Fear region of North Carolina's southern coastline. By far the most numerous migrants to the state, however, were yeoman farmers seeking only enough land to supply the needs of their families. To the hardy Scots, Scotch-Irish, German, and Welsh pioneers traveling down the Yadkin River Valley from Pennsylvania, the lands of the North Carolina Piedmont proved especially inviting.[16]

The ethnic diversity of the Piedmont settlers ensured religious and cultural diversity. Scottish highlanders and Scotch-Irish introduced Presbyterianism to the state between 1735 and 1775. Scotch-Irish immigrants, who spread their settlements along the Yadkin, Catawba, and Eno rivers, constituted a major portion of the populations of Anson, Orange, and Rowan counties, while Scottish highlanders settled throughout the Upper Cape Fear region, supplying many of the settlers of the lower Piedmont, including Moore and Montgomery counties. By the mid-eighteenth century, Quakers had begun to settle in North Carolina, establishing their first community at New Garden in Guilford County. They eventually fanned out into Guilford, Alamance, Chatham, Randolph, Davidson, Forsyth, Surry, Yadkin, and Davie counties in the Piedmont. The Quaker influence in North Carolina was strong throughout the antebellum period, despite the exodus of many Quakers between 1825 and 1860 in response to the national debate over slavery. The settlements of many Quakers and Scotch-Irish overlapped with those of German settlers from the North who brought with them three Protestant sects: the Lutheran, German Reformed, and Moravian. This religious diversity expanded further when the revivals of the Second Great Awakening spawned the rapid growth of the Baptist and Methodist faiths across the state, especially in the Piedmont.[17]

As in many regions of the South, a dual society had grown up in the Piedmont. Slavery buttressed an expanding economy, but most farmers were nonslaveholders who participated only marginally in the market economy. In fact, the free family farm was the common economic unit of both the South and the North. As Gavin Wright points out, "free family farms were not governed by the same economic principles as slavery or wage labor" but operated instead through the exploitation of family members' labor by heads of households. The basic similarity of day-to-day life on the American family farm did not obliterate, but certainly diluted, the distinctive social and cultural milieus that accompanied the rise of slavery in the cotton South and the wage labor system in the industrializing North.[18]

The dual nature of Piedmont society created the potential for class conflict. During the revolutionary era and the Civil War, internal conflicts in North Carolina exploded in violence. Encroachment by the government on the relative independence and isolation of small backcountry farmers was a major cause of these explosions. "In both periods," write Paul Escott and Jeffrey Crow, "the state earned the reputation of having in its midst a large disaffected population resistant to the demands and discipline of the reigning government."[19]

As sectionalism intensified during the 1850s, social conflicts threatened to reemerge. Although state leaders suppressed the temperance and antislavery movements during this decade, neither temperance nor antislavery sentiments died in the Piedmont. Writing on the eve of the Civil War, northern journalist Frederick Law Olmsted noted that many southern yeomen and poor whites of the backcountry expressed hatred of slavery, which he attributed to the competition of slave labor rather than to a concern for human rights or objection to the oppressive class system that slavery perpetuated.[20]

Although the Piedmont was no hotbed of abolitionism, few of its people identified politically, culturally, or religiously with the wealthy planter class. Not surprisingly, three of the South's most notorious opponents of slavery—Hinton Rowan Helper, Daniel Goodloe, and Benjamin Hedrick—hailed from the North Carolina Piedmont.[21] Many of those who openly condemned slavery on political and humanitarian grounds were compelled to leave the state. Those who remained formed an important component of the opposition to secession that prevailed throughout the Piedmont up to 1861.

The egalitarian principles of Quakerism and Methodism caused some North Carolinians to oppose slavery on moral grounds. In 1851, for example, Methodist farmer William B. Hurley of Montgomery County publicly affirmed his moral and religious objections to slavery.[22] Other western Carolinians emphasized slavery's links to rich eastern planters. "There ain't no account of slaves up here in the west," explained a farmer to Olmsted, "but down in the east part of this state . . . there's as many as in S[outh] C[arolina]. That's the reason the West and East don't agree in this State; people out here hates the eastern people."[23] Religious and political resentments of slavery did not necessarily translate into antislavery activism, but they provided fertile ground for the wave of Wesleyan reformers who preached throughout the central Piedmont between 1849 and 1851 and reinvigorated the abolitionist and temperance convictions of many people.

The two men most responsible for the rise of Wesleyan Methodism in North Carolina were Jesse McBride and Adam Crooks, northern Wesleyan preachers who answered a "call" from a small group of yeomen in the central Piedmont. Within a year of their arrival, McBride and Crooks reported much success in spreading their antislavery gospel among the plain people of the Piedmont. By June 1850, Wesleyan periodicals had gained 125 new subscribers; five months later, 146 new members had reportedly joined the church. Although these numbers were small, McBride interpreted them as the beginning of a groundswell of support for the antislavery movement. He assured Wesleyan leaders in New York that fully one-half of all North Carolinians opposed slavery and withheld their opinions solely for fear of persecution.

He claimed that a variety of men and women—including black and white members of the Society of Friends (Quakers), the Baptist Church, and the Episcopal and Protestant branches of the Methodist church—attended camp meetings in Guilford and Chatham counties in 1849 and 1850. He also reported that participants, particularly free blacks, were victims of constant harassment by proslavery officials and mobs.[24]

Wesleyan Methodism had special appeal in more rural areas of the Piedmont, where camp meetings often replaced formal worship and many people had few ties to slavery.[25] In northeastern Montgomery County, several families linked to each other through generations of intermarriage and landownership prayed regularly with McBride's partner, Reverend Adam Crooks.[26] William B. Hurley and his wife, Frances Hulin Hurley, were so moved by their conversion to Wesleyanism that they named a son born in 1854 after Jesse McBride.[27] Secret prayer meetings, conducted with approximately thirty members of the Lovejoy community, began shortly after Orrin Hulin, the father of Frances Hurley, and his brother Hiram Hulin reported to Crooks that certain planters of their community had committed outrages against slaves.[28]

The reactions of the state's proslavery majority to the growth of Wesleyan Methodism attested to the movement's importance. On June 15, 1851, when Adam Crooks tried to denounce slavery publicly before the entire congregation of Lovejoy Chapel in Montgomery County, approximately one hundred proslavery citizens mobbed and jailed him and ultimately ran him out of the county. Only the protection provided by several members of the Hulin, Moore, and Hurley families prevented physical harm to Crooks when the mob forced him from the pulpit to the county jail in Troy. Slavery had divided the community along lines that transcended party allegiances, for the county's voters were overwhelmingly Whig and strongly in favor of remaining in the Union. The violence wrought by the cleavage over slavery played itself out in an arena of religious differences but nonetheless exposed a profound conflict between slaveholders and nonslaveholders of the county.[29]

Women participated widely in the Wesleyan movement in the Piedmont just as they had in earlier revivalist movements. The editors of the New York–based *True Wesleyan* struck a responsive chord among Piedmont women when they hailed the sanctity of family relations as the "basis of the order and happiness of human society" and then extended the bounds of that sanctity to include slave women. "What an outrage is American slavery upon the rights of women," wrote a *True Wesleyan* correspondent, "and upon the sanctity of home, and the family relation."[30] Like earlier evangelical leaders, the Wesleyans urged God-fearing white women to apply their "feminine" virtues of piety, charity, and love to the reform of society. To follow such a calling, especially during the tense 1850s, put Piedmont women at odds with the interests of their state's ruling class. Undoubtedly, some must have felt torn between their Christian duty and their acceptance of slavery, an institution no less entrenched in southern society than was the family.[31]

In the interest of reforming sins against humanity, and despite the dangers involved, some Piedmont women did more than simply participate in camp meetings and promote piety in the home. Delphina Mendenhall, an educated, well-to-do woman from an illustrious Quaker family, helped organize an underground movement of slaves to the North that was very active in Randolph County. Her unwavering antislavery convictions may have influenced her husband, a slaveholding lawyer who had fallen away from the Quaker faith, to defend the Reverends Crooks and McBride against the state's charges of sedition. Immediately following her husband's death in 1860, Delphina Mendenhall freed the slaves he had passed on to her.[32]

In neighboring Montgomery County, Caroline Moore, the daughter of farmer and blacksmith Valentine Moore, defected from the Methodist Episcopal church to protest the mobbing of Reverend Crooks. She soon married Jesse Hulin, another Wesleyan convert and the son of Hiram Hulin, one of Crooks's staunchest defenders. Intermarriage among the tightly knit group of farm families who had worshiped with Crooks continued throughout the 1850s and 1860s. Preserving one's culture and ideology through the institution of the family was by no means limited to those who occupied the seats of power. In this rural pocket of the Piedmont, the conflict over slavery was passed from one generation to the next.[33]

To protect themselves against possible charges that they were not "sound" on the slavery issue, editors of the *Fayetteville Observer* and the *Greensborough Patriot* denounced the "dangerous doctrines" preached by McBride and Crooks and recommended that local magistrates "adopt prompt and decided measures to silence them."[34] Nevertheless, the antislavery preachers continued to hold the support of certain elements of the Piedmont yeomanry. A citizen from Guilford County protested the persecution of Wesleyan preachers in his community and pointed out that "as to Preachers preaching seditious doctrine I have heard them a number of times; if their Doctrine is seditious, then I have always been used to hearing seditious doctrine from Methodist Preachers."[35] As Democratic and Whig leaders increasingly vied for political hegemony, repression of all dissent from political and religious orthodoxy intensified in the North Carolina Piedmont as it did throughout the South.

To analyze how ethnic and religious diversity and conflicts over slavery intertwined with relations of gender, race, and class in the North Carolina Piedmont, this study focuses on Granville, Orange, and Montgomery counties. These counties, despite their close geographic proximity, provide distinct contrasts in their religious, ethnic, and economic patterns. For example, farmers in both Granville and Orange counties produced tobacco and some cotton for market, but as Tables 1.1 and 1.2 indicate, only Granville was a major slaveholding area. By 1860, 47.4 percent of Granville's population consisted of slaves, in contrast to 30.1 and 23.8 percent in Orange and Montgomery counties, respectively, and a state average of 33.3 percent. Granville County boasted a substantial number of wealthy planters; 15.4 percent of its slaveholders owned twenty or more slaves, compared to the state's average of 11.7 percent. Men and women such as Samuel Forsyth of Cedar Creek and Sally T. Eaton of Epping Forest displayed their wealth in the traditional southern manner: the ownership of land and slaves. The more entrepreneurial Robert H. Hobgood of the Dutch District prospered by the manufacture of tobacco products; he employed both white and black labor in his tobacco factory.[36]

Despite the comparatively high proportion of planters, Granville County contained a substantial number of yeoman farmers. As Table

Table 1.1. County and State Population by Race, 1860

	Percent of whites	Percent of free blacks	Percent of slaves	Total population
Granville	47.8	4.8	47.4	23,396
Orange	66.8	3.1	30.1	16,947
Montgomery	75.6	.6	23.8	7,649
State	63.6	3.1	33.3	992,622

Source: U.S. Bureau of the Census, *Population of the United States in 1860.*

Note: 1,158 Indians are included in white population of the state.

Table 1.2. Concentration of Slaveholding by County and State, 1860

	Percent of free families owning slaves	Percent of slaveowning families owning:				Total slave-holders
		1–4 slaves	5–9 slaves	10–19 slaves	over 20 slaves	
Granville	43.0	38.7	26.3	19.6	15.4	1,006
Orange	29.1	52.3	23.9	16.7	7.1	665
Montgomery	21.8	52.6	22.0	14.4	11.0	236
State	27.8	46.4	24.4	17.5	11.7	34,658

Source: U.S. Bureau of the Census, *Agriculture of the United States in 1860* and *Population of the United States in 1860.*

1.2 shows, 57 percent of the county's free families held no slaves at all. Moreover, free blacks made up 4.8 percent of Granville's population (see Table 1.1). Of the three counties, Granville contained the largest and most cohesive free black community, although many free blacks owned no property and had few skills with which to earn a living.[37]

When considering free blacks, one must therefore recognize the disparity of wealth within the black community as well as between black and white households. Seventy-year-old Will Evans, the wealthiest free black in Granville County, owned real estate valued in 1860 at $732 and personal property valued at $3,200. His personal estate included slaves. Far more typical of the free black community in Granville County, however, were Jiles Brandon and Lucy Richardson. Brandon, a forty-year-old propertyless ditcher in 1860, lived with his wife and eight children, the oldest of whom was hired out as a farm laborer. Eighty-year-old Lucy Richardson headed a household that included twenty-five-year-old Jane Richardson (probably the mother of one-year-old Polly Richardson), forty-year-old Jane Powell, a washer (probably the mother of two-year-old Rebecca Powell), and Sam Richardson, a fifty-year-old farm laborer. Some, if not all, of the members of the Richardson household were undoubtedly related.[38] The disparities of age and gender and the order in which the census enumerators listed its members, however, indicate not a nuclear family but a household whose members pooled their individual incomes and labor in response to their impoverished conditions.

There were so many propertyless free African Americans in Granville County in 1860 that their per capita property wealth was only $26—lower than the state's average of $34 for free blacks and that of both Orange and Montgomery counties ($30 and $35, respectively). The per capita wealth of free black heads of household who owned property does not reveal much about average levels of wealth among free black families, however, because their numbers were small and the value of their property ranged from $10 to $4,400 in Orange County and from $25 to $3,932 in Granville. Thus even though few free African Americans owned property valued at more than $250, the mean per capita wealth among twenty-three propertied free blacks in Orange County was $703; among eighty propertied free blacks in Granville, it was $373.[39]

Orange County contained a more diverse population than did either Granville or Montgomery. Tables 1.1 and 1.2 show a lower proportion of slaves in the overall population than in Granville. In Orange County slaves constituted 30.1 percent of the population, while free blacks made up 3.1 percent. Only 7.1 percent of Orange County's slaveholders were of the planter class, and 70 percent of the free population owned no slaves at all.[40]

The neighborhood of Durham contained a rowdy clustering of yeoman farmers, merchants, free black and white laborers, and a few planters around the community's railroad depot, hotel, church, two barrooms, and three stores. Located just to the north of Durham, in the Flat River neighborhood, was the Orange Factory Cotton Mill, which employed fifty white workers, thirty of whom were women. Six households containing around seventeen textile workers were located in the vicinity of the cotton factory. Typical of these households, four of which were headed by women, was that of Virginetta Batchelor, a fifty-year-old spinner whose family included three female spinners between the ages of twenty and twenty-five, and an eighteen-year-old male carder.[41]

In contrast, the county seat of Hillsborough and the village of Chapel Hill, which housed the University of North Carolina, were hubs of political and intellectual activity. Student Joseph Davis wrote to his cousin in 1848 of visiting with "Miss Annie Swain," the daughter of Governor David Swain, then riding out to Dr. James S. Smith's to pick peaches with the old doctor's daughter Mary Ruffin Smith. Judge William H. Battle and Lucy Battle's son Kemp, a university student in 1850, later reminisced about the stimulation of growing up among so many eminent state leaders. One of his few complaints was of living at home, among his parents' slave women, who "had children whose wailing was not only disagreeable but seriously interfered with study."[42]

Hillsborough was also a haven for the county's professional class, including such state leaders as Chief Justice Thomas Ruffin and Justice Frederick Nash.[43] Although Orange County had its elite, its image as a commercial center and its polyglot population of farmers, laborers, and merchants caused Granville's planter families generally to snub Orange County society. Alexander Fleming expressed the low regard that many middle- and upper-class Granville citizens held for Orange County when he warned his brother and his friend, who had been socializing there, "Now for God's sake and for your own reputations just stay in Granville . . . don't go to Orange anymore." Joseph Davis expressed a similar disdain for Orange County society when he commented in regard to Annie Swain and Mary Ruffin Smith, "There is more beauty . . . in Granville and Franklin, than there is in all of Orange with Chatham to help her."[44]

The white citizens of Granville who regarded themselves as superior to their counterparts in Orange must certainly have considered Montgomery County little more than a backwater of the "poorer sort" of people. The rawness of Montgomery society both repelled and fascinated Peter Swaim, a member of a prominent North Carolina family, who lived in Montgomery County briefly in 1841 and 1842. Swaim described northern Montgomery County as a "heathenish, outlandish part of creation" that was seemingly devoid of polite society. The sight of a young woman who hoisted up the hem of her petticoat and clenched it in her teeth before mounting a horse and galloping away seemed, however, to delight him.[45]

Swaim's impressions of Montgomery County reflected his unfamiliarity with a society composed primarily of small farmers and a few miners eking out a living in the wilderness. The county did not have a single major city, and many of its villages bordered the untamed Uwharrie Mountain range. The discovery of gold at the turn of the nineteenth century had caused some inhabitants to combine mining with farming, but few got rich from their efforts.

Although Montgomery County contained a nonslaveholding majority that included almost 80 percent of free families, it had a larger proportion of planters among its slaveholders than did Orange—11 percent, almost identical to the state's average (see Table 1.2). Like Asa and Mary Chambers, however, most slaveholders lived in the county's southern half, while the northern portion of Montgomery more closely resembled neighboring Randolph County, where slaves made up only 10 percent of the total population and planters only 3 percent of the slaveholding population. Far more common than planter families were nonslaveholding farm families like the Hurleys, Moores, Cranfords, and Hulins. Because so few families in northern Montgomery County owned slaves, slaves constituted only 23.8 percent of the county's population, well below the state figure of 33.3 percent (see Table 1.1).[46]

The level and distribution of wealth in each county thus differed significantly. In 1860, the per capita wealth of Granville County's free families was almost three times that of Montgomery's and more than twice that of Orange County families (see Table 1.3). In both Montgomery and Orange counties, more than three-quarters of landed

Table 1.3. Real and Personal Wealth of Households by County and State, 1860

	Number of free families	Value of real estate	Value of personal estates	Aggregate wealth	Per capita wealth
Granville	2,340	$4,093,195	$11,400,710	$15,493,905	$6,621.32
Orange	2,287	1,785,921	5,550,375	7,336,296	3,207.82
Montgomery	1,080	743,919	1,693,037	2,436,956	2,256.44
State	125,090	179,950,134	370,372,614	550,322,748	4,399.41

Source: U.S. Bureau of the Census, *Statistics of the United States . . . in 1860.*

Table 1.4. Sizes of Farms by County and State, 1860

	Less than 50 acres	50–99 acres	100–499 acres	Over 500 acres	Totals
Granville	25.8%	25.4%	43.8%	5.0%	1,348
Orange	45.3	32.6	21.3	0.8	1,396
Montgomery	56.2	25.9	17.7	0.2	827
State	41.5	27.6	28.7	2.2	67,022

Source: U.S. Bureau of the Census, *Statistics of the United States . . . in 1860.*

families farmed fewer than one hundred acres, in contrast to Granville, where only slightly over half did (see Table 1.4). Female property holders averaged less per capita wealth than males in each county. Comparatively, female levels of wealth paralleled the broader patterns of distribution. The greatest number of wealthy women who headed households lived in Granville County; the second highest number were in Orange. In Montgomery County, female heads of household were rarely propertyless, but they owned the least amount of property overall (see Table 1.5).

The most significant gap in wealth between male- and female-headed households existed in Orange County. The per capita wealth of women there trailed men's by more than 35 percent, whereas in Granville female-headed households trailed male-headed households

Table 1.5. Real and Personal Wealth of Female-Headed Households by County, 1860

	Number of female-headed households	Percent of total house-holds	Percent owning property	Per capita wealth	Percent of males' per capita wealth
Granville	281	12.0	65.0	$5,478.59	80.1
Orange	383	16.7	44.3	2,161.72	63.2
Montgomery	125	11.5	80.8	1,980.04	94.2

Source: U.S. Federal Manuscript Censuses, 1860, Granville, Orange, and Montgomery counties.

by almost 20 percent. Consistent with the generally equal distribution of wealth among Montgomery County's households, those headed by women trailed those of men by less than 6 percent (see Table 1.5).

The disparity between Granville and Montgomery counties resulted from their different economic structures. A large slaveholding planter class in Granville engrossed much of the wealth, skewing the distribution of wealth among whites and creating a small but expanding free African American population. Less easy to explain, however, is why there were so many more poor women in Orange County than in either Granville or Montgomery. A clue is that almost 17 percent of Orange County's households were headed by women, in contrast to levels near 12 percent in both Granville and Montgomery counties. Free women, in fact, outnumbered free men by more than 2 percent in Orange (see Tables 1.5 and I.1).

These statistics suggest that men were leaving Orange County in significant numbers. This finding conflicts with Robert C. Kenzer's argument that persistence rather than out-migration was the dominant characteristic of white males in Orange County between 1850 and 1860. His tables, however, reveal that persistence was far more characteristic of older men than young men of marriageable age. Furthermore, a careful study of the manuscript census for Orange County shows that single, poor women overwhelmingly lived in the northern neighborhoods of Eno, Little River, and Flat River, where there were few economic opportunities for men, thereby encouraging their migration out. The Orange Factory Cotton Mill, located on the Flat River, provided employment for some poor women and may even have attracted some single, poor women into the county.[47]

Despite the presence of slavery and the rural character of each Piedmont county, distinctive economic and demographic features created various permutations of gender, race, and class that in turn influenced women's behavior. The varieties of unruly or defiant behavior exhibited by women and the number of women involved in such behavior reflected important differences among the counties. The proportionately greater wealth in Granville County, for example, encouraged its white women to sue more aggressively in court to protect their property and personal safety. The comparatively high number of divorce petitions filed by Granville County women reflected both concerns. In Orange County, the higher number of poor women contributed to a more visible subculture of "deviant" women than in either of the other counties and resulted in greater numbers of prosecutions for illicit sexual acts. Finally, the chief examples of unruly behavior among the women of Montgomery County—food riots and harboring of deserters during the Civil War—heralded the revolt of some Piedmont citizens against the state, particularly in those counties, like Montgomery, that were relatively homogeneous and isolated.

More than any other example of female "misbehavior," the political rebellion of Piedmont women demands that careful attention be given to the impact of regional, class, and racial variables upon an analysis of gender behavior. The story of North Carolina's Unionist men and women has only recently been told with the depth and understanding it deserves. Many citizens in central and western North Carolina eventually united in widespread opposition to the Civil War. As a result, North Carolina failed to preserve a united front in the battle to save slavery.[48]

The distinct features of each of these Piedmont counties point up the advantages of limiting a study to a single geographic region. First, such an approach makes it possible to measure the pervasiveness of the planter ideology beyond the plantation belt. The economic, demographic, and cultural profiles of Granville, Orange, and Montgomery counties remind us that ideology is shaped not only by those who lead but also by those who are to be led. Adherence to a more middle- than upper-class ideology by Piedmont leaders was a logical response to the predominantly middle- and lower-class populations of all three counties. The ideals of womanhood reveal an important aspect of the broader ideology of republicanism designed to appeal to the "ordinary" white citizens of the North Carolina Piedmont.

The relationship between race and gender is also better understood when we consider regional differences among the counties in regard to slavery. Although slavery was a crucial element of wealth and power in each county, its impact on individual communities varied significantly. For example, Granville County planters most nearly approximated a planter aristocracy, while Orange County's planters largely conformed to Paul Escott's description of an entrepreneurial class of planter-businessmen. Montgomery County planters were part of a small, powerful elite that was nevertheless forced to consider the interests of an overwhelmingly homogeneous and self-sufficient yeomanry. In each of the counties, these factors affected the status and behavior of free black and white women.

Analyzing women's experiences within the framework of a case study offers unique insights into the meaning of women's lives in a patriarchal, slaveholding society, and the behavior of women reveals much about the organization of society itself. Women embodied all the elements of diversity and conformity in the Piedmont. Concerns over order and disorder varied according to the unique features of each county, but the region shared a salient commitment: to maintain traditional relations of race, class, and power required not only racial and class subordination but also the ordering of women's social and sexual behavior.

Two

White Womanhood, Black Womanhood

Ideals and Realities in a Piedmont Slaveholding Society

Perhaps no one in the Piedmont region of antebellum North Carolina embodied true white womanhood more than Lucy Martin Battle, the wife of supreme court justice William H. Battle. She was white, from a respectable family, and had made a fortunate marriage. Furthermore, her behavior was exemplary. She demonstrated spiritual and physical strength in managing a busy household of children and slaves during her husband's frequent long absences from home. Even when wearied by the governing of twenty or more slaves, she displayed benevolence toward all her family members. Of course, she was pious, but even more noteworthy for a southern plantation mistress, she struggled to rid herself of a "most common female affliction"—a tendency toward malicious gossip. She also tried to avoid the indolence and self-indulgences often attributed to women of her class.[1]

Marriage provided the essential means by which white women fulfilled their societal role, while slavery provided the means for African American women. Whether a white wife or a black slave, the ideal woman was happily nurturing, pious, loyal, and subordinate to her husband or master. As a slave, "Aunt" Maria Slade, for example, embodied black female perfection. "She ought to have a monument erected to her when she dies," said David Schenck in 1869, rhapsodizing over the world lost by civil war and reconstruction, "by all the [white] babies she has nursed or by their mothers. She is a worthy and most excellent woman [with] a kind heart, and a maternal tenderness for her sick." Like Lucy Battle, Aunt Maria's perfection lay in her selfless attendance to the needs of the southern white family. From opposite, supposedly complementary, stations white and black women nurtured the master's children.[2]

Miscegenation especially contradicted this image of harmonious interests between white and black women. The sexual taboos that governed the behavior of white women did not apply equally to white males. Despite laws that forbade marriage between blacks and whites, many white men sexually exploited black women with little fear of censure, provided that they conducted such "affairs" discreetly. Their exploitation of slave women meant, however, that not all black women could be Mammies; there must also be Jezebels, women whose ungovernable lust made chastity impossible.[3]

White women were supposedly shielded from the sexual mixing of white men and black women. Former slave Marjorie Jones of Newton claimed that "if the Missus find out she raise a revolution. But she hardly find out. The white men not going to tell and the nigger women were always afraid to." Author Harriet Jacobs, a former slave, agreed. "No indeed," she wrote, "they knew too well the terrible consequences." Jacobs noted also the ability of many white mistresses to ignore what was before their eyes. Such was the case of Sophronia Horner, a planter's wife, who was irritated by her children's confusion over a newborn slave child nearly as white as they were. "Ah Susi you can't fool us, niggers don't be that white," her children taunted the baby's slave mother. "It is nevertheless a negroe," insisted Mrs. Horner in a letter to her husband. She refused to speculate about the race of the child's father.[4]

Some husbands flaunted their abuse of black women. Green Culbreath derived sadistic pleasure from parading his affair with a hired black woman before his wife, Nancy, who alleged in a divorce petition in 1850 that her husband regarded the black woman more as a wife than an employee. Nancy Culbreath also complained that she had been forced by her husband "to perform the humiliating drudgery of washing for the said negro and refusing to let the negro wash for her." Had Green Culbreath conducted his interracial adultery discreetly, Nancy, like Sophronia Horner, might have grudgingly pretended to ignore it. But, Culbreath had turned the biracial code of womanhood on its head. He apparently enjoyed taunting his wife with her own powerlessness.[5]

That court records usually contain only the testimonies of whites reinforces an image of white women as the primary victims of miscegenation. The Jezebel stereotype further suggests that black women and white men conspired to victimize white women, as, indeed, white women often believed. Some of them assailed and assaulted black women suspected of miscegenation; others ensured that the mixed-race children of slave women were sold away.[6]

The 1871 divorce petition of Martha Satterwhite of Granville County is unique in that the testimony of the Satterwhites' former slave Lucy Parham was included to prove Mrs. Satterwhite's charge that her husband and Parham had committed adultery while Parham was a slave in their household. Parham confirmed that William S. Satterwhite had fathered thirteen-year-old Caroline Frances, the oldest of her five children. In response to questioning, Parham told the court that she was fourteen years old when Caroline Frances was born and she remembered that it was "late in the spring" and that Mrs. Satterwhite was away on the day of conception. When asked if Mrs. Satterwhite had ever accused her of "addultry," Parham replied, "Yes Sir, she has been accusing me of it every sense I wan't but twelve years old." She noted, however, that the accusations stopped after the birth of Caroline Frances, except for once when Mrs. Satterwhite "got mad with Mr. Satterwhite."[7]

Parham's testimony reveals the twisted strands of resentment and empathy that linked African American and white women. Despite her resentment of Parham, Martha Satterwhite had begged her to return to the Satterwhite household after the Civil War. "She said she would give me twenty-five dollars a year and my vituals and teach my little daughter," recalled Parham, "and that She had rather have me than anybody else to live with her." Parham added that Martha Satterwhite even promised her a house and a lot if she would return. Free and married by 1866, Parham refused the offer. By 1871, Satterwhite sought her own escape from the household. She alleged that William Satterwhite beat her even though she was dying of consumption.[8]

Under the pseudonym of Linda Brent, Harriet Jacobs noted a similar ambiguity in the way she was treated by the wife of her master, Dr. James Norcom of Edenton, whose unsuccessful sexual advances toward fifteen-year-old Harriet provoked frequent domestic arguments. Mrs. Norcom often entered Harriet's bedroom at night and stood menacingly over her, and she often grilled Harriet about her relationship with Dr. Norcom. "Yet perhaps she had some touch of feeling for me," Jacobs later wrote, "for when the conference was ended, she spoke kindly, and promised to protect me." As Jacobs pointed out, however, mistresses seldom overcame jealousy and humiliation enough to view slave women as victims. Some clearly became torn, nevertheless, between fighting for their class privileges, on one hand, and empathizing with the sexual vulnerability of slave women, on the other.[9]

Mary Ruffin Smith, the daughter of Dr. James S. Smith, was similarly ambiguous about her brothers' ill-concealed miscegenation with her slave Harriet. As the unmarried matriarch of the Smith plantation, Mary assumed responsibility for preserving the family's illustrious reputation. To her dying day, she never publicly admitted what was obvious to her neighbors—that Harriet's four light-skinned daughters were Smith progeny. Nevertheless, she brought her slave nieces into the Smith household to be raised, churched, and educated, while Harriet remained in the slave quarters. Despite the deep chasm between Mary Ruffin Smith's privileged, opulent surroundings and Harriet's exploitation as a slave, the ungovernable behavior of their male "superiors" misshaped both of their lives.[10]

To whites, both Harriets were Jezebels. Slaves, however, recognized the coercive nature of relationships between slave women and their masters. "I know plenty of [women] slaves who went along with the old marster," recalled a former slave from Tennessee. "They had to do it or get a killing." That some slave women sought relationships with white men in hopes of gaining special favors only reinforced the stereotype of seductive, sexually insatiable black women. This stereotype made all black women vulnerable to sexual exploitation.[11]

Mattie Curtis, a former slave of Franklin County, believed that children of mixed blood helped perpetuate miscegenation. "Dem yaller wimen," she explained, "wus high falutin' too, dey thought dey was better dan de black ones. . . . Dare mammies raised dem to think 'bout de white men."[12] It is unlikely, however, that mulatto women gained much from their attachment to white men. Mary Ruffin Smith's slave Harriet did gain improved living conditions for her children, but neither her essential status nor that of her children changed in any fundamental way. In fact, her masters even destroyed her marriage to free black Reuben Day. A slave woman could expect only to be fed and clothed in return for her labor and the reproduction of additional slaves for her master.[13]

If free, an African American woman escaped the indignity of being owned by another human being, but she lived nonetheless in a white-dominated society that heralded slavery as the natural condition of her race. Because the law presumed blacks to be slaves unless otherwise proven, the movement of free black women was restricted. If she was not careful, a woman could find herself in the predicament of Sophy Jones, a twenty-two-year-old mulatto woman "of good figure, light complexion, and very likely," who was committed to the Mecklenberg County jail on suspicion of being a slave because she carried no papers declaring her free. Likewise, Fanny Mason claimed to be free, but the Orange County court jailed her because "she has nothing to show that she is free and from her appearance we think she must be a slave."[14] Before migrating to Ohio during the 1850s, several free black families of Orange County obtained from the court papers of "safe passage" that declared them both free and "respectable" members of society.[15]

Time and time again, reality intruded upon the comforting image of an organic society based on natural hierarchies of race and gender. It is not clear from the scattered references in private letters, plantation records, and testimonies of former slaves how common unruliness was among slave women because most of their "crimes" were punished within the household. Nevertheless, court records contain a few indictments of slave women for crimes.[16]

These cases reveal women who were neither Mammies nor Jezebels. In March 1836, for example, the superior court of Granville County charged Hannah, the slave of Colonel John G. Hart, with murdering her son Solomon by slashing his throat with a knife she had obtained the night before from the plantation dairy. She also slit her own throat in an unsuccessful effort to kill herself. As she lay bleeding, she called out to a black man passing by to "come there and put her away." Hannah survived to face trial and conviction on murder charges. As historian Paul Lovejoy argues, such acts of desperation and self-destruction on the part of slaves "twisted the fundamental contradiction of slavery around the necks of their masters." Slaves were both chattel and human beings; hence they possessed the ability to undermine, even destroy, their own value as property.[17]

Whites feared slave women enough on occasions to accuse them of crimes despite little or no evidence. In 1843, William Russell of Granville County accused his slave Dilcy of trying to poison his entire family, but the court found no evidence on which to indict her. Candis, an Orange County slave, languished in jail for more than two months in 1853 before being found innocent of charges that she had set fire to the home and barn of Aaron Jones, Jr., a white man. Harriet, a slave in Orange County, fled in 1845 rather than face charges that she had burned down a white man's home.[18]

Many slave women, like slave men, faced court charges simply because they behaved too much like free persons. Such was the case of Edy Black, who received compensation from the Orange County Wardens of the Poor for raising an illegitimate free mulatto girl for nearly nine years. In February 1841, the court charged her with "going at large as a free woman . . . exercising her own discretion in the enjoyment of her time." In April, the court removed the free mulatto girl from Black's custody and placed the child in the poorhouse. Slaves who demonstrated independence and the competence to handle their own personal affairs contradicted the racist rationale for slavery.

Their behavior seemed all the more threatening to slaveholders as the northern abolitionist movement grew.[19]

The court records contain many more cases of free women in antebellum North Carolina who did not measure up to the standards for sainted womanhood. Every community had its "bad" women, white and black, who traversed the town and country roads ungoverned by fathers, husbands, or masters. Some of these women were from respected families. Often despised, sometimes pitied, wayward women dishonored the values white southern society deemed sacred: the patriarchal family, the institution of slavery, and the chastity of white women.

Miscegenation, a common crime among wayward poor whites, was even more unacceptable when it occurred between white women and black men. The court trial of Candace Lucas, a white woman from Montgomery County's yeoman class, offers graphic evidence of this point. In the Montgomery County superior-court session of February 1858, Lucas, a propertied woman who resided in the home of her parents, sued her neighbor Gilbert Nichols for slander. The case eventually reached the state supreme court, which late in 1859 affirmed the lower court's decision in favor of Nichols. Lucas lost her case despite the testimony of four witnesses that Nichols had claimed, as charged, that Lucas had "a new sweet-heart, Wesley Dean's [slave] Pete; it used to be Ben Lucas and sometimes Jake Calicoat"—other slaves who lived in the neighborhood. Furthermore, Nichols had reportedly offered to pay $25 to any man who would "get the plaintiff with child." Even after Lucas filed suit against him, the irrepressible Nichols reportedly claimed that Lucas had given birth to "two or three black children" over the years.[20]

No proof was offered that Lucas had been intimate with slaves or that she had ever given birth to any illegitimate children. Rather, the decision of the supreme court hinged on whether the words of Nichols constituted slander; specifically, whether "sexual incontinence" had clearly been attributed to Lucas. The high court found Nichols's words ambiguous enough to leave doubt as to their precise meaning. "In the mildest sense," wrote Justice Matthias Manly, "it is true, they are grossly indecent and insulting, but may, nevertheless, signify something short of an actual surrender of her person to the embrace of any one of the slaves mentioned." The court reached this decision after ruling as inadmissible Nichols's remark that Lucas had parented several black children on grounds that the remark had been made after Lucas initiated her suit.[21]

The court did not always apply so literal an interpretation of words charged as slanderous. In the case of *McBrayer* v. *Hill* (1843), Chief Justice Thomas Ruffin ruled that Robert McBrayer, a married man, had indeed been slandered by Abel Hill's remark, "I kept his wife." Ruffin declared that such words clearly implied "habitual adultery" on the part of Mrs. McBrayer.[22] In hindsight, it seems just as clear that claiming a white woman had taken a succession of neighboring slaves as "sweet-hearts" suggested sexual incontinence on the part of Candace Lucas. After all, there could be no legitimate "romance" or process of courtship between a black male and a white female in the antebellum South. To claim that anyone could doubt the meaning of Nichols's remarks about Lucas was as disingenuous as it would have been for Judge Ruffin to have ruled that the phrase "I kept his wife" might be taken to mean that Abel Hill had built a fence around Mrs. McBrayer.

In reality, Lucas lost her suit because she had entered the courtroom with two distinct handicaps: her father's troubled social and financial standing in the community and that at age thirty-two, she had passed the reasonable age of marriage for women. Her case illustrates not only a sexual double standard based on the race and sex of the parties involved but also the importance of family connections in civil matters and the vulnerability of aging, unmarried white women to charges of sexual impropriety. The very fact that Nichols so boldly gossiped about Lucas and then bragged to friends that she would only harm herself if she sued him revealed the tenuous status of Lucas and her family in the Little River community of northeastern Montgomery County.[23]

Although the Lucases were an old pioneering family of the county, Candace's father, Joel Lucas, had gained several enemies among his neighbors during the five years preceding his daughter's suit. He declared himself financially bankrupt in mid-1855 after reneging on debts to several men in the community, including former sheriff Thomas C. Haltom, one of the county's wealthiest men. The anger of Lucas's debtors deepened when they discovered that he had fraudulently sold part of his land and livestock to his eldest son just before declaring bankruptcy. To make matters worse, Lucas helped his brother Willoughby in 1857 to arrange a private settlement with an eighteen-year-old woman whom Willoughby had impregnated. After arranging the settlement, Lucas bribed a court magistrate into dropping the case from the court docket.[24]

The pregnant woman, Mary Jane Nelson, was the daughter of John Nichols and the niece of defendant Gilbert Nichols.[25] Her role in Nichols's trial further illustrates the importance of a woman's behavior to her status in southern society. Although once married, Nelson had been separated from, deserted, or widowed by her husband. Her illegitimate pregnancy by Willoughby Lucas apparently estranged her from several members of her family. Nelson provided the major testimony against her uncle Gilbert Nichols, thereby deepening the rift between the Lucases and the Nicholses.

As the trial opened, members of the community chose up sides along lines of personal and family loyalties. Witnesses for both plaintiff and defendant eagerly challenged one another's credibility with stories of individual "bad" reputations or "bad blood" between families. John Nichols, Sr., attested to the "bad" character of his granddaughter, Mary Jane Nelson, and Joel Lucas's nemesis, Thomas C. Haltom (who had posted bond for Gilbert Nichols), attempted to bribe Nelson into changing her testimony to favor Nichols.[26] At stake for many witnesses was not whether Lucas had been slandered—many could not have cared—but the personal loyalties and grudges that surrounded the case.

By defaming the character of Candace Lucas, Gilbert Nichols insulted the entire Lucas family and thus fulfilled a need felt by many residents to punish Joel Lucas for playing fast and loose with the money and reputations of his neighbors. Many residents undoubtedly felt vindicated when, in 1861, as a result of the lengthy, unsuccessful suit against Nichols, Joel Lucas was again (and this time genuinely) bankrupt.[27] The resolution of Candace Lucas's suit had hinged on the damaged reputation of her family and her own status as an aging, unmarried woman. By refusing to act the pious, dependent role assigned to unmarried women, Lucas became vulnerable to the neighborhood talk that thrives in every small community. Furthermore, she undoubtedly undermined the credibility of her own testimony by calling Mary Jane Nelson as a primary witness. Nelson's willingness to testify against her own kinsman reinforced the images of both women as marginal beings whose behavior (and therefore testimony) was suspect.[28]

Marriage, of course, provided a white woman's best insurance against the slanderous whims of another. In the successful slander suit of *McBrayer* v. *Hill*, a husband sued for damages to his own reputation because of gossip about his wife. Frances McBrayer was vindicated because the remarks of one man threatened the honor of another.[29] Marriage gained a white woman entry into the mainstream of society by linking her with the central actor of society—man. Although marriage was considered the natural condition for both sexes, it was the man who married the woman, not vice versa. A woman who had passed her prime years of youth without being "chosen" for marriage had failed to fulfill her destiny. By age thirty, she was considered an old maid, a pitiable figure, who, without the proper control and guidance of a respectable family, might be tempted to commit shameful acts.[30]

The letters of Anna Bingham, Jr., of Redimon, Tennessee, to her married sister in Orange County reveal the isolation and drudgery that characterized the lives of unmarried women, who were expected by white southerners of the propertied classes to live a celibate, dependent existence in the home of married relatives. These letters, written between 1845 and 1869, catalog unending spinning and weaving, nursing of family members, and teaching in the community for little pay. "Between [caring for] old *people*, puny *children*, and clothing all, besides attending to other things," Bingham wrote, "we are busy *old maids*. I think it is well for the world that some *can't help* being old maids."[31]

An unmarried woman could do little else if she valued her reputation and that of her family. Besides marital status and family background, the final proof of a southern white woman's breeding and personal quality lay in her behavior. To misbehave was to risk the precious birthrights of social respectability and marriage, for even wealth could not prevent a woman's plunge in status if she behaved improperly. So inculcated were the values of purity and chastity among upper- and middle-class southern white women that few understood women who were forced or tempted by circumstances to defy the norms of social behavior.[32]

A white woman who willingly entered a miscegenous relationship forfeited the respect of her community and was shunned by respectable women, who feared that contact with her might also taint them.[33] When Nichols accused Lucas of having had numerous affairs with black men, he knew that he accused her of the deepest degradation possible for a white woman in the antebellum South. Whether by design or not, he had cornered the Lucas family into defending its honor.

Thus race and class divided the women of antebellum North Carolina. Although the status of white women in society was never as precarious as that of free African American women, white women without wealth or proper family connections were unlikely to gain entry into respectable social circles. In contrast to white women raised in comfortable homes overseen by authoritarian males, those who experienced poverty usually lacked the social training and status to attract a well-placed husband. Women without property and husbands often pooled their resources and lived together in the households of kinfolk and friends. Society offered them few opportunities to earn a living by their own labor. To avoid the county poorhouse, a dismal institution that did little more than warehouse the poor, some women worked long hours in the homes and fields of others and occasionally turned to prostitution, thieving, or illicit trading.

In any case, marriage did not promise poor women an escape from poverty, nor did behaving properly assure them the traditional rewards of chastity. With personal reputation less a concern than earning a living, fewer poor white women who lived outside the bonds of marriage remained celibate or tucked away in the homes of relatives. Instead, some moved within a subculture of people who did not find the rules of society to their benefit or liking. Within this subculture, poverty broke down some of the barriers between the races and between the free and the unfree, as whites and blacks mingled more than many white southerners liked to admit.

In 1846, an Orange County slave named Celia manipulated George Trice's troubled relationship with his brother to try to gain a new master. She went first to Chany Davis, a poor white woman and mother of several illegitimate children, at least one of whom was fathered by Zachariah Trice, the brother of Celia's master. Celia suggested to Davis that Zachariah collect a debt his brother owed him by stealing four of his slaves, including Celia. Zachariah set out to do Celia's bidding. Aided by his son, cousin, and a free black accomplice, he hauled away Celia and three other slaves by wagon in the middle of the night. Unfortunately for Celia, they were caught in the act, tried, and convicted of slave stealing.[34]

Racial tensions within this interracial subculture flared on occasion and spilled over into the courtrooms. For example, Sally Walker, a white woman known in Orange County for having scuffled with white and black neighbors, charged Clarissa, a slave, with having directed "vulgar chat" toward her. The court sentenced Clarissa to receive ten lashes "moderately laid on." In another case, Joel Strong, whose wife confirmed his habitual carousing and illicit trading with blacks, complained to the Granville County court in 1842 that free blacks Sally and James Fane had provided encouragement and liquor to a group of men who planned to kill him.[35]

"Uncle" Jackson of Raleigh remembered that when he was a slave child, his masters forbade him to play with "free issue" black children or "common" white children because "they was'nt fitten to 'sociate with us. You see our owners was rich folks." John Smith, a former slave from Wake County, similarly recalled that the "rich slave owners" did not allow free blacks or poor whites on their plantations "if dey could help it." He added, however, that "dey couldn't help it. Dey slipped in dere at night when de marster didn' know it."[36]

Most Piedmont slaveholders were not rich, however, and may not have found it practical to forbid poor people on their farms. Elias Thomas of Chatham County claimed that the children of both slaves and masters played with their poor white neighbors. They did so because Thomas's master, who owned only six slaves, "hired both men and women of the poor white class to work on the plantation."[37]

County court dockets reveal that the mingling of poor whites, slaves, and free blacks included the trading of goods, liquor, and sexual favors. Blacks and whites fought and gambled together, and they sometimes cohabited. With varying degrees of success, county magistrates curbed the interracial exchange of goods and favors by indicting the most flagrant offenders of both races on charges of gambling, illicit trading, prostitution, and fornication.[38]

Most free women of North Carolina were not impoverished, unmarried, or black; nor did they participate in this interracial subculture. Neither, however, did they lead the life of the delicate, pampered lady popularized in twentieth-century southern lore. Most were of the white nonslaveholding yeomanry. Fittingly, Piedmont leaders did not glorify the plantation belle; they idealized the farm wife as enthusiastically as did northern leaders. Piedmont newspaper editors, in particular, praised the practical and spiritual qualities of the busy farm wife and rejected the image of the legendary southern lady of leisure. They accused "fashionable" women of indolence, empty-headed charm, and parasitical extravagance. The ideal wife was a junior economic partner to her husband and a moral inspiration to her family. Using an article reprinted from the *Farmer's Monthly Visitor*, the editor of Orange County's *Hillsborough Recorder* harkened to the past in urging women to be busy, cheerful wives:

> The companions of men who fought in the Revolution were inured to hardships and accustomed to unceasing toil. . . . Health, contentment, happiness, and plenty smiled around the altar. The damsel who understood most thoroughly and economically the management of domestic matters, and who was not afraid to put

> her hands into a wash tub, for fear of destroying their elasticity and dimming their snowy whiteness, was sought for by the young men of those days as a fit companion for life.

He advised women, above all, to forswear the "code of modern gentility."[39]

This ideal of womanhood increased in popularity as North Carolina underwent economic change and growth. By 1850, techniques of farming, tobacco processing, and production of textiles had notably advanced. Many schools and colleges had opened, particularly in the Piedmont region, and the state had erected one of the nation's finest supreme courts. Although economic, political, and social progress fell short of the goals of many reform leaders, the state had clearly awakened from its famed "Rip Van Winkle" sleep of the 1820s and 1830s.[40] The practical needs of a farming economy and the infectious spirit of progress encouraged the view that white women should be active helpmates to their husbands rather than ornaments. The participation of women in local markets through the contribution of household and farm goods such as butter, poultry, and vegetables made the family an economic unit in which husband, wife, and children all participated.

Few North Carolina women, wealthy or not, could enjoy the leisure or afford the frailty that Piedmont editors continually warned against, although some may have affected such an image. Even among the Piedmont's elite citizens, parents generally adhered to middle-class standards of propriety in counseling their daughters about marriage and feminine duty. The eminent Dr. James Norcom of Edenton warned his daughter that being a wife "confines one to a series of low pursuits, a course of filthy drudgery, & disgusting slovenliness that leave but little time for study or quiet meditation; & very little for improving conversation or refined society." Nevertheless, for those rare women with enough virtue and grace to dignify such an occupation, he added, "They alone are destined to bless and adorn the social state."[41] In other words, a true woman transformed her lowly tasks of housekeeping into acts of love through constant devotion to others and thereby earned the honor of her society.

Norcom probably would have agreed with the writer who proclaimed in 1850 that "marrying a woman for her beauty, is like eating a bird for its singing." Another male writer warned women against abusing the "gift of liveliness." A giddy, flirtatious female might be admired while young and pretty, "but it leads to no esteem—produces no affection if carried beyond the bounds of graceful good humor." Such a woman might enliven a dull party, the writer continued, but would seldom "become the honored mistress of a respectable home." The perfect woman for marriage, advised another man who claimed to seek a wife, should have only a "small share" of beauty so as to avoid the sin of vanity; she should be of "good form"—of "middle size" rather than petite; she should be well-bred and well-informed but never coy; and inevitably, she must be domestic and homeloving, "to soften my troubles and lighten my cares."[42]

Piedmont editors urged white farm women to choose their husbands from among the sturdy yeoman class. In 1849, Edward J. Hale of the *Fayetteville Observer* reprinted a northern article that chastised mothers and daughters who worshiped "the genteel, idle gentleman" who possessed "neither means, energy, nor capacity to earn a livelihood," much less the qualities of a suitable marriage partner. Better that women set their sights on the storekeeper, artisan, manufacturer, or mechanic than the "idler" and "lounger" of so-called "better society."[43] In the commercial city of Fayetteville and the surrounding rural counties served by this newspaper, the image of the "genteel, idle gentleman" suggested the aristocratic eastern slaveholder's son, who inherited rather than earned his wealth. By the same token, the southern counterpart of the virtuous tradesman was the yeoman farmer, who also doubled as an artisan.

The idealization of white women as helpmates to white men emerged logically in a region characterized by family farms and nascent economic diversification. But the disdain expressed by Piedmont editors and orators for the pampered elite lady also reflected deep sectional divisions within the South. Although Edward J. Hale agreed that slavery must continue undisturbed, he challenged the rhetoric of fire-eating secessionists as vociferously as he condemned the northern abolitionist movement. In 1849, he accused South Carolina secessionists of "keeping them [abolitionists] alive and active, when otherwise they would die a natural death." Two years later, he declared that "if S.C. will go [out of the Union], let her go—alone."[44] Piedmont voters expressed the same sentiments in 1850 when they elected to office candidates who favored compromise with the North over slavery.[45] A decade later, North Carolina's secessionist leaders elicited support for the rebel cause only by convincing Piedmont citizens that their personal liberty—not merely the rights of slaveholders—was at stake.[46] Even then, support for the Confederacy proved to be halfhearted and short-lived among many Piedmont folk.

Pro-Union leaders in North Carolina fitted their philosophy of womanhood into the framework of their political beliefs. Just as the rhetoric of a free republic had long served both slaveholding and nonslaveholding society in America, so, too, did the "cult of domesticity" reveal remarkable suitability to varying political stances. *Fayetteville Observer* editors reacted harshly in 1850 to a "Daughter of [South] Carolina," who wrote several letters to the *Charleston Mercury* that exhorted the men of the South to compromise no more with northern leaders on the issue of slavery. The editor of the *Observer* criticized this woman as an example of the awful consequences of a lady's leaving her proper domestic sphere to join the "dirty arena of politics." Claiming that women possessed considerable powers of persuasion over men, the editor warned against the misuse of that power: "If this female is an average specimen of South Carolina, we do not wonder that nearly all the husbands in that state are fierce for the dissolution of the Union."[47]

Consistent with their image of themselves as levelheaded pragmatists opposed to both extremes of the slavery debate, Piedmont editors denounced northern women who participated in the abolitionist movement. By the early 1850s, they had extended their criticism to women's rights activists, although the editors of the *Observer* and the *Recorder* had previously reported the activities of northern feminists with little fanfare and a certain measure of respect. In 1850, for example, editor Hale had noted that at least six United States newspapers were edited by women, two of them by feminists Jane Swisshelm and Amelia Bloomer. All of these papers, commented Hale, were produced "with ability and in a manner that reflects honor upon the female sex." In a later issue, Hale praised Swisshelm for proclaiming women's intellectual and moral equality with men. He described her remarks as "advisable and well-timed," noting that they revealed a "strong sense amid unfeminine peculiarities."[48]

In the North Carolina Piedmont, where factories had yet to replace a sizable amount of women's production in the home and where the abolitionist movement was too weak to stir women toward questioning their own legal and political status, southern leaders were not unduly alarmed by the issue of women's rights per se.[49] In fact, Piedmont editors approved of women's "right" to develop their intellect through formal education for the same reason that most northern reformers did—so that women might participate in building a strong society through the teaching as well as nurture of future male leaders.[50]

Although they approved of women's education, Piedmont editors belittled the political goals of the women's rights movement. The *Observer* reported that a women's rights meeting in Providence, Rhode Island, had accomplished "nothing of consequence . . . except to call a Convention of women to meet in coming months at Worcester [Massachusetts]." The Worcester meeting, held in October 1850, proved too volatile, however, for Piedmont editors to ignore or dismiss. Speakers at the convention included abolitionist stalwarts Abby Kelley, Frederick Douglass, Lucretia Mott, and Sojourner Truth. Editor Hale accused the convention's participants of raising the "standard of rebellion against the laws of God and man" in their misguided effort to confer upon women and African Americans political equality with white men.[51] The Worcester meeting demonstrated that both abolitionist and women's rights activists challenged the foundation of southern leadership by attacking the hierarchy of race and gender. Because women's rights activists employed the same principles and tactics as abolitionists, southern editors like Hale had no choice but to condemn the goals of both groups.

The mounting sectional crisis exposed the limits of Piedmont leaders' use of northern words to define a southern ideal of womanhood. Despite the similarities between farming communities in the North Carolina Piedmont and those of the North, the importance of slavery to the economic and political structure of the Piedmont prevented the lives of white southern and northern women from being mirror images of each other. In the South, the need to maintain a clear distinction between the races required that white women be confined to white men, and the status of women was bifurcated along racial lines to enable the exploitation of black women's labor and reproduction to different ends from those of white women. But the sectional crisis revealed a division of interests among slaveholding and nonslaveholding white women of the North Carolina Piedmont that eventually transcended their common experiences as wives and mothers. During the war, these differences were played out in an inner civil war in which women were principal participants.

Although antebellum southern women failed to organize a women's rights movement, they were not inactive in the public sphere. In North Carolina, strong-minded women had long participated in reform movements. Like northern women, they had been deeply influenced by the rise of evangelicalism in the era of the Revolution, when numerous southern leaders conceded the evils of the slave system. In 1804, Sterling Ruffin confided to his son Thomas (who would later become one of the South's most noted proslavery theorists) that slavery was a "great civil, political, & moral evil." Although Sterling Ruffin opposed any "sudden end" to slavery on grounds that such action would jeopardize the "lives, property, & everything sacred and dear of the Whites," he nonetheless anticipated the day when an "Alwise, & Mercifull Creator will by a more universal revival of his blessed Religion prepare the Hearts of all men to consider each other as brothers, and put us more on an equallity [*sic*] even in temporal things." Ruffin's remarks typified those of numerous southerners, particularly those who worshiped in the Quaker, Methodist, and Baptist churches in the revolutionary era.[52]

A southern antislavery movement did not take root, but one did emerge in North Carolina in the early nineteenth century—one in which women participated from its inception. By 1825, women had formed their own auxiliaries to the North Carolina Manumission Society. Some of the women presented written addresses for male members to read aloud to the society. Gradually, the society stressed ameliorating rather than ending slavery. One group of the society's women exercised their right of petition and urged the state legislature to adopt an antimiscegenation law to protect slave women from sexual abuse by white males. They also urged that slaveholders be prohibited from selling slave children apart from their mothers.[53] Such actions did little to end slavery, and by emphasizing humanizing the institution, women may have drawn attention away from slavery as a moral issue.

Other women preferred striking at the economic base of slavery. The North Carolina Piedmont was the only region in the South where, in 1829, Quakers managed to transplant a branch of their free produce movement. Families that participated in this movement sold their goods only to buyers who refused to trade in goods produced by slave labor. In the long run, however, tactics mattered little in the movement against slavery, for the settling of the Southwest and the resulting boom in cotton production reinvigorated the institution and turned many white southerners against the antislavery movement. By 1835, the North Carolina Manumission Society had disbanded.[54]

Two landmark decisions of the state supreme court, *Newlin* v. *Freeman* (1841) and *Thompson* v. *Newlin* (1844), demonstrate the final turning away of North Carolina leaders from a philosophy of natural rights that had tentatively entertained inclusion of African Americans. Both cases involved the bequest of a slave by Sarah Freeman of Orange County to James Newlin, an antislavery Quaker. Forbidden by law to manumit the slave, Freeman sought to ensure him quasi-freedom by bequeathing him to Newlin. After Freeman's death, her husband refused to deliver the slave to Newlin, forcing Newlin to sue for possession. In 1841, under Chief Justice William Gaston, the state supreme court ruled that Freeman had the right to bequeath her slaves to whomever she chose because a deed of separate estate filed at the time of her first marriage gave her the right to acquire and dispose of personal property without the consent of her husband. Probably more important than Freeman's deed of separate estate, however, was the fact that Chief Justice Gaston represented a dying generation of southern leaders who tolerated criticism of slavery.[55]

Three years later, following Gaston's death, the widower of Sarah Freeman sued James Newlin for repossession of the slave. This time, under the leadership of Chief Justice Thomas Ruffin, the high court ruled against Sarah Freeman's right to bequeath her slave to whomever she chose. Ruffin defended the court's decision on grounds that it was the state's duty to protect its most fundamental institution. "Slaves can only be held as property," he wrote, "and deeds and wills having for their object their emancipation, or a qualified state of slavery, are against public policy, and a trust results to the next of kin."[56] After a brief and slight foundering, slavery had become more entrenched than ever.

Unlike the antislavery movement, the closely allied temperance movement enjoyed long and widespread popularity in North Carolina. Working for temperance had special appeal to white women because, like the free produce movement, it had a direct connection to their daily lives. Male drunkenness threatened the harmony of many families in North Carolina, where in 1851 more than 230 stills were reportedly operating in Guilford County alone. Yet twenty years earlier, several branches of the American Temperance Society had sprung up in the North Carolina Piedmont.[57]

Southern temperance women, unlike their antislavery predecessors, dared to speak in public. From Montgomery County, Peter Swaim reported hearing a woman speak at a May Day celebration who "*blazed* away like *fury*" at her audience. In 1848, women formed the Daughters of Temperance to complement the Sons of Temperance. That same year, Joseph Davis, a student at the university in Chapel Hill, wrote his cousin that the "Independent Order of Temperance" had held a celebration there in which all "the ladies of the village were present . . . and one of them made a beautiful speech." It was the first time that Davis had ever heard a woman address a public forum, and he was impressed with the speaker's ability and "elegant manners." He believed that the special benevolent nature of women would strengthen the moral reform of society.[58]

As the northern abolitionist movement gained strength, however, the temperance movement lost favor with southern leaders, who escalated efforts in the 1850s to suppress all antislavery activity and literature. They increasingly viewed reform movements in general as threats to state sovereignty. By late 1852, the temperance movement was on the decline, as indicated by G. W. Caldwell's remark that temperance activists had "as much right to petition this legislature against slavery" as to dictate whether his corn could be distilled into liquor. Even in the North Carolina Piedmont, the conviction that southern traditions were threatened by too much reform soon eclipsed the spirit of progress and change that had earlier characterized the region.[59]

Even editors formerly favorable to temperance pulled back from the movement. In 1857, the editors of the *Fayetteville Observer* condemned the activities of a group of "reform-minded women" in Bellville, Ohio, who broke into a liquor store and emptied the proprietor's liquor into the streets. The editors also criticized six young women of Alleghany, Pennsylvania, who were arrested for riding a tippling schoolmaster on a rail. "Nice wives these ladies will make!" wrote the editors. "Each one of them ought to be spliced to a drunkard or a rowdy."[60] A temperance woman might be fit to make miserable the life of a drunkard, but she was clearly too lacking in refinement to bring comfort to the life of a gentleman. Reform activity was no longer within the boundaries of approved behavior for white southern ladies. Those who persisted risked losing male approval, social respectability, and prospects for marriage.

During the mid-1850s, Piedmont editors began exhorting farm women to renew a supposedly weakened commitment to household duties. The editors blamed selfish materialism for women's lack of attention to the home sphere and urged them to spend more time at home and to concern themselves less with worldly activities. In 1857, the *Observer* carried two separate articles that accused farm wives of neglecting to teach the crafts of sewing and buttermaking to their daughters. The newspaper also blamed the rising price of butter on housewives who "can play the piano, but cannot churn; can dance, but cannot skim milk; can talk a little French, but don't know how to work out buttermilk."[61]

The *Greensborough Patriot* reprinted an address delivered before the Connecticut Agricultural Society in 1858 that urged mothers not to "teach your daughters French before they can weed a flower bed or cling to a side saddle." The speaker further warned daughters not to "be ashamed of the pruning-knife" and urged them to "learn to love nature, and seek a higher cultivation than the fashionable world would give you."[62] At one level, such warnings represented a continued focus on the old cult of domesticity. Yet a subtle shift in emphasis had occurred since the 1840s. Piedmont women were no longer encouraged to extend their superior moral judgment into the public realm of society. Their sphere of influence was to extend no further than the family circle.

The increased number of articles urging women to attend more rigorously to domestic duties suggests that as the nation struggled with the sectional crisis—and as freedom of speech in the South simultaneously dwindled—southern leaders feared that Piedmont white women, like northern abolitionist and southern secessionist women, had moved too far into the public sphere. In an address before the 1858 graduating class of Edgeworth Female Seminary, James A. Long warned the young women present that for them to enter the political arena was "to soil your garments with matters which do not pertain to your position in society." He emphasized that it was the duty of women to bestow their blessings on those southern men "worthy of their esteem, [for] then, and not till then, will the pure days of the Republic be restored."[63] Southern women were not to question or seek to influence public policy but only to encourage the wisdom and leadership of their men.

In North Carolina, so splintered by slavery on the eve of war, an all-encompassing "female consciousness" clearly did not exist. The salient fact that linked all women was their subordination to white males, whether as wives, slaves, or laborers. The legal and political rights of all women were inferior to those of white men, but all whites, regardless of gender, had superior rights over African Americans. So divided were antebellum southerners by stark racial boundaries that the inequities of gender and class often appeared secondary, although they, too, were tightly woven into the fabric of society. Race most clearly affected the depth of a woman's oppression, but class background and the willingness to behave in the prescribed female manner also greatly influenced a woman's status among those who wielded power in her community.

For the average white farm woman of the North Carolina Piedmont, being female meant being suited by nature for a special sphere of influence: the family circle. Piedmont leaders confirmed the worth and importance of housewifery and motherhood by regularly praising the accomplishments of busy farm wives. Unlike free women who were black or who lacked husbands and property, the wives of farmers participated meaningfully in the social and economic mainstream of their communities, perceiving themselves to be partners, if also subordinates, to their husbands. To these women, consignment to a separate sphere reflected God's ordering of society, a natural division of male and female labor consistent with the biological and mental qualities of each sex. Theirs was a vastly different world from that of the enslaved black woman, for whom the "natural" dictates of race were interlocked with those of gender. For the slave woman, the master's ability to exploit her productive and reproductive capabilities made her gender experiences distinctly different.

Thus the white farm wife and the black slave woman served the same master—the white male—from different stations in society, both of which functioned from below to uphold order and stability. Poor white and free black women, by contrast, performed no recognized function in the replenishing of the southern slaveholding order. Lacking identification with a powerful class of white males either as wives or slaves, they posed a potential threat to the social harmony of a community. The state assumed the role of patriarch in the lives of such women and, through the local courts, undermined the efforts of many of them to gain a livelihood in ways disapproved by their society.

To be a woman in antebellum North Carolina clearly was a complex and varied experience. Yet beneath the layers of class, race, and individual temperament that divided them, women shared subordination to white males, whether those males were husbands, slave masters, or court magistrates. To recognize their common oppression is not to equate the depth or form of oppression suffered by white women and black women, nor is it to suggest the existence of a conscious female bond that transcended the barriers of race and class. In fact, the various ways in which unruly women resisted or thwarted the authority of white men provide stark evidence of the barriers of race and class that divided them.

Three

The Limits of Paternalism

Property, Divorce, and Domestic Relations

Upon her death in 1855, Sally Fane left behind the usual goods of a simple, widowed farm woman: a spinning wheel, a loom, a few pigs, eight head of cattle, and a bay mare. A note attached to the estate's inventory revealed, however, that Fane had taken pains to keep her small estate out of the hands of others. "There is in my hands," wrote executor John Bullock, "some funds [that are] the remainder of the estate of Jacob Fane, dec'd[;] the amount I am unable to state as there is a long unsettled matter in connection therewith." Fane had seized $98.85 from her husband's estate following his death in 1838, and she had refused, for the next seventeen years, to surrender this amount to the estate's administrator.[1]

Sarah Ware Nuttall used more conventional means to protect her property from the claims of her husband's creditors. Before marrying Edwin J. Nuttall, the divorcee had drawn up, with his approval, a deed of "sole and separate estate" declaring her personal and real property exempt from the "controul, management, or authority of any person whatsoever." Whereas Sally Fane claimed her husband's property on grounds that he had intended it for her use only, Sarah Nuttall had learned from a disastrous first marriage that husbands, even more than creditors, had the power to impoverish and make miserable the lives of wives.[2]

Sarah's second venture into marriage proved her not a whit wiser in choosing a suitable partner. Edwin Nuttall was a violent, hard-drinking man who had been convicted of manslaughter and disinherited by his father. Chastened by experience, however, Sarah insisted on keeping her property separate from her husband's.[3] Notwithstanding her prudent planning, the combination of an ineffectual, drunken husband, an uncooperative trustee, and, finally, the Civil War made Sarah Nuttall's efforts to manage her property a lifelong struggle.[4]

Aside from gender, there was little that connected the lives of Sally Fane—a former slave—and Sarah Nuttall—a slaveholder. Fane had been purchased, then emancipated, by her husband, also a former slave.[5] As a propertied free African American couple, the Fanes belonged to a small group of black farmers and artisans who had carved out a distinctive niche among the free people of Piedmont communities. Sarah Nuttall belonged to a much larger community of white Piedmont farmers who worked their few hundred acres of land with the help of a few slaves.

Despite these differences of race, class, and marital experience, Fane and Nuttall both encountered difficulty in maintaining their own property because of the one experience they did share. They lived in a patriarchal society that merged the legal identities of wife and husband into one: the husband's. In North Carolina, as in virtually the entire United States in this period, English common law provided the basis for the system of law. Where women were concerned, common law provided a simple directive. In the words of Sir William Blackstone: "By marriage, the husband and wife are one person in law: that is, the very being or legal existence of the woman is suspended during the marriage, or at least is incorporated and consolidated into that of the husband; under whose wing, protection, and *cover*, she performs everything."[6]

The legal submersion of a woman's identity upon marriage affected more than just her right to own and control property. The law granted husbands control over the family purse strings, full custody of children, and the right and responsibility of governing wives' behavior, by physical force if necessary. Therefore, acceptance of a man's proposal of marriage constituted the most important decision most free women would likely ever make. Although many wives had far more power within the family than a mere reading of the law suggested, others found the courts of limited use in seeking relief from overbearing husbands precisely because the law so favored the authority of husbands over wives.[7] As Chief Justice Richmond Pearson stated in blunt terms after denying a divorce to a woman who had been beaten and horsewhipped by her husband, "The law gives the husband power to use such a degree of force necessary to make the wife behave and know her place."[8]

Some women never married, and others, not surprisingly, remained widows rather than remarry. In 1860, between 11 and 17 percent of all households in Granville, Orange, and Montgomery counties were headed by women. In well over half of them, women owned or managed a certain amount of property.[9] The assumptions of common law notwithstanding, if property laws were to function smoothly, such women had to be recognized by the courts. Indeed, in North Carolina as elsewhere, common law proved hopelessly narrow for the demands of a rapidly growing nation with a diverse population. The need to assure the smooth transmission and protection of private property precipitated a nationwide reform of common law. By the mid-nineteenth century, several states had revised many aspects of English law and hammered out numerous statutes designed to create coherent, working legal structures.[10]

Gender was an important factor in the formation of the nation's legal structure, and it influenced court decisions in property matters and other aspects of domestic, racial, and sexual policy. Although legal constraint and protection of wives perpetuated the paternalistic ethos of English and Anglo-American society, many innovations had occurred in the law. As Michael Grossberg points out, the courts, instead of transferring power directly to women, had assumed many aspects of traditional male authority over wives and children. Especially in the North, a "judicial patriarchy" emerged that increasingly mediated the interests of husbands and wives within the family.[11]

Gradually, a more complex definition of female status than that provided by common law emerged in American society. Individual states relied on their equity courts, which operated peripherally to superior courts of law, for reform and revision of common property law. It was through the equity courts that women such as Sarah Nuttall employed the doctrine of "sole and separate" estate to maintain a measure of control over their own property.[12]

Most wives, however, like Sally Fane, did not maintain property independently of their husbands.[13] If a woman's husband died intestate, as did Jacob Fane, a North Carolina widow had dower rights to one-third of the estate before creditors could claim their due. In an estate as small as the Fanes', dower amounted to very little. If a husband left a will, he might bequeath his wife the property she had brought to the marriage; more commonly, he left her control over part or all of the estate for the duration of her life or until she remarried. A life estate only, this endowment gave a woman no power to sell or transfer title to the property to another. The true heirs were generally the couple's children, who assumed title at the time designated in their father's will.[14]

Only by maintaining their estates separately from their husbands could wives hope for a measure of financial autonomy. Yet creation of such estates required the consent of husbands, and separate estates were usually controlled by male trustees. Sarah Nuttall eventually had to beg her trustee for some of her own money, despite her careful explanations of how the money would be used.[15]

The legal disabilities of wives partly explain Sally Fane's bold refusal to surrender her dead husband's cash assets to the estate's administrator. Her situation as a former slave may also account for her refusal. Suzanne Lebsock's observation that some free black women were reluctant to marry because "women so recently emancipated . . . did not give up their legal autonomy lightly" is probably true also of some married free black women. Although Fane had chosen to marry, she was unwilling to trade the legal bondage of slavery for that of marriage.[16]

For slave women, widowhood was legally meaningless. The experiences of Polly Delaney, a slave from Montgomery County, illustrate the limited concept of marriage among slaves, even for those allowed to marry. Dill Delaney, Polly's husband, was a free black farmer who owned seventy acres of land, farm tools, and several head of livestock when he died in 1853. Because Polly was a slave, southern law did not recognize her marriage or the patrimony of the couple's four children. Consequently, she had no claim to a widow's portion of her husband's estate, and her children could not inherit any of their father's property.[17]

Although the court denied Polly and her children access to Dill Delaney's estate, it did order them "put up for hire" to help pay his debts. Polly's legal treatment confirms the contention of Orange County former slave Thomas Hall that "getting married an' having a family was a joke in the days of slavery, as the main thing in allowing any form of matrimony among the slaves was to raise more slaves."[18]

While slave women remained civilly powerless throughout the antebellum period, free married women gradually acquired greater rights over property. The same needs that propelled nationwide reforms in property law also encouraged reforms in divorce. After the Revolution, many states, including North Carolina, had broadened the legal grounds for obtaining a divorce and streamlined divorce procedure by transferring its jurisdiction from state legislatures to state superior courts.[19] Such reform progressed unevenly, however, because the issue of divorce, even more than that of property, raised important questions about the structure of the traditional family. Northern states generally led the way. Some historians attribute the rising divorce rate in the postrevolutionary North to several interrelated factors: the growth of a more "personal outlook" that resulted in fewer arranged marriages; more emphasis on marriage as a contract between two people for the greater happiness of both; and the effect of evangelical "perfectibility" in promoting the idea that complementary partnership was attainable. Ironically, the idealization of the family that flourished during the nineteenth century contributed to a rising divorce rate as partners became less willing to tolerate miserable marriages.[20]

The widespread ownership of property undoubtedly contributed even more to the growing acceptance of divorce in American society. In contrast to informal separation, divorce protected one's title or interest in property. States that were least stratified by class and had the widest dispersal of property instituted the most liberal divorce laws.[21]

The legal climate for divorce was least favorable in southern seaboard states, where powerful interrelated families formed the core of a landed slaveholding elite that controlled much of the South's wealth and power. From this elite came many of the South's political leaders and lawmakers, who by 1830 viewed the protection of slavery as the major responsibility of the state courts and legislatures. In varying degrees, many of them perceived divorce as a threat to the South's two most fundamental institutions: the patriarchal family and slavery. Despite the "rhetoric of liberty," as Linda Kerber explains, "divorce remained nearly as difficult to obtain in the new republic as it had been in the colonies."[22]

Because the institutions of the family and slavery were interlocked, white women occupied an important place in the cultural and economic life of southern society. Wives of slaveholders served as conduits for the transmission of power and property from one generation to the next. As caretakers of the family, they also oversaw much of the daily workings of the slave system. Finally, as the repository of a southern code of honor that regarded them as symbols of racial and sexual purity, white women maintained the racial distinctions that were crucial to the continued hegemony of white men.[23]

Although a slaveholding elite dominated the highest political offices in North Carolina as thoroughly as in any other southern state, the widespread ownership of property throughout the state dictated innovations in the law similar to those adopted in nonslaveholding states.[24] The increasing use of the legal provision for sole and separate estates by North Carolina families did not signal a deliberate move toward equal property rights for women. Rather, it expressed the practical needs of propertied families. As a Granville County marriage contract drawn up in 1832 by Allen and Susanna Howard explained, "Throwing property promiscuously together among Different families when all Expect an equal Share of Such Property is a fruitful source of discontent."[25] Perhaps most important of all, deeds of separate estate provided a means of protecting family wealth from being squandered by profligate or gold-seeking husbands.[26]

North Carolina courts approved this legal mechanism, but they strictly limited its use. Whereas in England the equity courts held that a married woman might dispose of sole and separate property as though she were a *feme sole* (single woman), that is, without a joint deed of sale with her husband, in the antebellum United States only New York and Pennsylvania went this far. Though generally adhering to the doctrine of separate estate, the states applied it with varying interpretations.[27] North Carolina equity courts did not allow a husband to dispose of his wife's separate property without her consent, but the wife's right in such transactions was a defensive one. She possessed only veto power; she could not convey her property in her own name. To guard against the "force, fraud, or contrivance of her husband," judges were required to question the wife privately in their chambers to ascertain her voluntary consent to the sale of her property.[28] Although a private examination did not prove conclusively that a wife had not been coerced into selling her property, it provided at least a measure of protection against fraud. In 1856, the North Carolina Supreme Court returned a woman's lands to her heirs after her death because the county court had allowed her lands to be sold without a private examination.[29]

The North Carolina Supreme Court further limited the use of deeds of separate estate by ruling that the wording of such deeds must be "unequivocal and expressed in unambiguous terms, as such disposition is not favored by law."[30] The same principle governed bequests of property to married women. In *Bason* v. *Holt* (1855), the court held that the words "to the only proper use and behoof of my daughter Margaret" did not constitute a separate estate and thus did not deprive the husband of his marital right to it.[31]

The supreme court also guarded against deliberate efforts to deny creditors their due through a wife's separate estate. Postnuptial settlements between husbands and wives always aroused the court's suspicion of an intentional obstruction of creditors' rights. In 1840, it ruled in favor of the creditors of Edward Saunders because he and his wife had increased her private estate after its original prenuptial creation.[32] The court likewise ruled in favor of creditors in cases in which a husband had paid a portion of the purchase price of a wife's separate lands. As North Carolina Chief Justice Thomas Ruffin explained in 1851, a separate estate was for the protection of a wife against an improvident husband, but "it was not intended that he might endow her . . . and thereby defeat his creditors."[33]

Although the supreme court of North Carolina never went so far as England in regarding married women as *femes sole* in cases involving separate estates, it did debate the issue. In 1848, the state enacted legislation declaring that husbands could not sell or otherwise convey their wives' real estate regardless of whether a deed of separate estate had been filed.[34] This act seemed designed to eliminate the clumsy device of filing deeds, but the supreme court did not interpret it as increasing a wife's control over her property. The antebellum courts continued to require that a wife's conveyance of her own property contain her husband's name and signature within the body of the deed of sale.[35]

That antebellum free women had so little control over property did not result inevitably from the conservative cast of the state's supreme court. Two decisions written by Chief Justice Ruffin opened the way for a more liberal interpretation of women's property rights. In 1844, Ruffin ruled in *Frazier* v. *Brownlow* that Martha Brownlow was entitled to charge or dispose of the profits arising from her estate with "unrestricted authority" because her deed of separate estate did not specifically forbid her to do so.[36] In the past, the court had consistently denied women access to such profits unless their deeds of ownership expressly granted permission.

Ruffin's departure from tradition passed without dissent from other justices on the state's supreme court, and he cited this ruling when he issued a decision in the 1850 *Harris* v. *Harris* case. He ruled that Nancy Harris, a married woman, might convey her personal property (but not real estate) and "do all other acts in respect to it, in the same manner as if she were a *feme sole*" as long as there was no restricting clause in her deed of ownership. The court traditionally allowed such actions on the part of wives only in the event of husbands' expressed consent; it had never previously granted any *feme sole* status to married women. Ruffin, citing the precedent of the English courts, commented that it might be "against the policy of this country and the habits of our domestic relations to allow equitable property in a wife, at all. But it is too late to think of that."[37]

These "habits of domestic relations" proved too sensitive an area, however, for all the justices to agree on the issue of separate estates. Justice Richmond Pearson hotly opposed Ruffin's interpretation of the law. In his dissent to the *Harris* v. *Harris* decision, Pearson argued that allowing a wife "to act and deal independently of her husband" went far beyond the intent of North Carolina's version of the doctrine of separate estate. He further warned that the English courts' liberal interpretation of the doctrine was no recommendation, for "the English [court] reports are filled with more cases of divorce and alimony, and crim[inal] con[versation] than, I trust, will ever be found in the reports of North Carolina." He argued that the policy must remain that "a husband is disabled, but the wife is not enabled, except so far as the deed or will confers an express power."[38]

Pearson's opinion ultimately prevailed. He had become chief justice by 1859, when he ruled that the Act of 1848 left a husband's marital rights to his wife's property "unimpaired and unrestricted after [the wife's] . . . death. The sole object [of the act] is to provide a home for her, of which she could not be deprived either by the husband or his creditors." Pearson's interpretation extended to wives little more than their long-standing dower rights.[39]

A wife's right to her own property remained so restricted that in 1859, the court absolved Mary Reid, a recent widow, from paying her own debts because they were not "charged specifically upon the separate estate, with the concurrence of the trustee."[40] Although the decision was a victory for Reid's pocketbook, it symbolized the legal subordination of women. And so the situation remained until after the Civil War.[41]

The careful attention given to property laws by nineteenth-century North Carolina justices attested to the family's central position in the economic structure of the South. Social and political issues, however, prevented unity among justices on the question of women and the ownership of property. Whereas Pearson clearly feared that greater property rights for women would undermine traditional patriarchal relationships, Ruffin viewed women's control over their own property within the context of an individual family's right to protect its wealth.

Ruffin certainly did not propose that women be treated under the law as autonomous individuals. He did not hesitate to invalidate the deed of separate estate that led Sarah Freeman to believe she might bequeath her slaves to whomever she wanted, including an antislavery Quaker. Such an act, he explained, would clearly undermine public policy concerning slavery.[42] Regarding the Act of 1848, Ruffin asserted that despite the "strange anomaly" of a woman's being independent of her husband while living with him, the husband was still the legal head of the household in all respects save those concerning the wife's property. The husband had full authority over and rights to the children.[43]

The most striking evidence of Ruffin's deep commitment to preserving the traditional patriarchal family may be seen in his response to divorce suits appealed to the state supreme court. As chief justice from 1833 to 1852, he presided over most of these cases. Divorce struck more deeply at the heart of domestic relations in the South than did property. Here, Ruffin left no doubt that he regarded liberalization of divorce law as a threat to social stability. Schooled in the southern tradition of devotion to family honor and adherence to strict moral principles,[44] Ruffin treated divorce suits not as personal affairs between troubled couples but as affronts to society's most sacred bonds. "The welfare of the community," he wrote, "is to be consulted more than the wishes of the party." Divorce was "not simply a cause between the two parties to the record; the country is also a party, and its best interests are at stake."[45]

Although the state legislature had transferred jurisdiction over divorce to the superior courts in 1827, throughout the antebellum period North Carolina's high court for the most part refused either to affirm divorces decreed or overturn those denied by the state's superior courts. The high court's stance contradicted North Carolina's relatively liberal divorce laws, passed before the legislature had adopted a more conservative position on reform in response to growing sectional tensions over slavery. The state recognized two forms of marital dissolution: *a mensa et thoro* (separation of bed and board) and *a vinculo matrimonii* (absolute dissolution of marriage).[46] In the former, neither party could remarry; in the latter, only the injured party could. Despite such provision, in all but three of the fifteen suits appealed to the state supreme court between 1830 and 1861, justices denied divorce petitions despite litanies of abuse ranging from adultery to beatings and whippings.[47]

Even interracial sexual relations, which many white southerners regarded as the greatest moral outrage against their society, were in several cases subordinated to the apparently greater threat that divorce presented. For example, the superior court of Buncombe County had denied Marville Scroggins a divorce on grounds that his wife, who was white, had given birth to a mulatto baby. Mr. Scroggins's attorney, shocked by Lucretia Scroggins's affair with a black man, argued that the offense of adultery presented "a picture of comparative innocence and harmlessness" compared to that of miscegenation.[48]

Although Ruffin concurred in the enormity of Lucretia Scroggins's crime, he preferred to strike at what he considered the roots of such "degradation." Noting that the plaintiff had been aware of his bride's pregnancy when he married her, Ruffin declared Scroggins "criminally accessory to his own dishonor in marrying a woman he knew to be lewd." It was, he wrote, the duty of honorable men to resist wanton women although "the fascinations and total depravation of an unchaste woman have been proverbial."[49] The state had laws designed specifically to control and punish these "unchaste" women; Ruffin refused to allow their behavior to disrupt the bonds of marriage simply to alleviate the embarrassment of a man's deserved shame.

Ruffin believed it a man's duty to honor only chaste women with his company and a husband's duty to protect his wife from moral degeneracy. In an 1836 appeal, Ruffin quoted Scripture to justify the lower court's denial of divorce to Andrew Whittington, who had abandoned his wife, Lucy Whittington, and then sued her for divorce on grounds of her subsequent adultery. "Whosoever shall put away his wife, save for the cause of fornication," wrote Ruffin, "causeth her to commit adultery."[50] He similarly declared in an 1841 suit that since the sued wife had been "seduced, traduced, degraded, [left] destitute, and abandoned" by her husband, the latter was accountable for her seeking shelter in an adulterous union. Ruffin's pronouncements expressed the essence of paternalism applied to the subordinate status of wives.[51]

A white woman's purity was a delicate prize entrusted to the protection of her husband. More practically, Ruffin surely recognized that a woman divorced on grounds of immoral behavior had few resources with which to make her way in the world. Even if he believed Lucy Whittington guilty of her husband's charges of adultery, he may have reasoned that granting divorce in such cases left little or no control over errant wives. In the interest of maintaining order, Ruffin insisted that husbands be held to their custodial responsibilities over wives.

The Ruffin-dominated court not only refused to treat adultery as grounds for divorce, but it also denied divorce to women subjected to brutal violence and general abuse by husbands. As guardians of social stability who cherished the ideal of paternalistic harmony within husband-wife relationships, high court justices rationalized the violence complained of by wives in numerous divorce suits. Their reasoning in such cases resembled that of Ruffin, who, in the landmark decision of *State* v. *Mann* (1829), upheld the right of a master to beat his slave because "the power of the master must be absolute to render the submission of the slave perfect."[52] The court ruled in 1852 that husbands had the right to strike wives as long as they did not do so from "mere wantonness & wickedness." By ruling that wives could testify against husbands in cases of assault and battery only if they had sustained "lasting injuries," Chief Justice Frederick Nash further legitimized the physical dominance of husbands over wives.[53]

Justices of the high court did not intentionally sanction abuse of wives and slaves. They merely expressed the ideals of a planter class disposed to believe in the weight of moral principles as a barrier to abuse of the powerless by the powerful. Ruffin believed that in an ideal master-slave relationship, "the frowns and deep execrations of the community upon the barbarian who is guilty of excessive and brutal cruelty to his unprotected slaves . . . will produce a mildness of treatment and attention to the comforts of the unfortunate class of slaves."[54] He also wrote that "in a civilized society it was universally considered dishonorable and disgraceful for persons in elevated situations to lift their hands against their wives."[55]

The records of North Carolina courts reveal, however, that many husbands and slave masters controlled their dependents through physical force. Although wives, unlike slaves, had the right to sue in court when they believed the limits of a husband's power had been exceeded, the supreme court's decisions in cases involving domestic violence did little to encourage women to seek its protection.

As overlords of a legal system that sanctioned white men's physical chastisement of wives and slaves, North Carolina justices struggled to define the limits of that right. The very different statuses of slaves and wives only complicated the task. For example, no one would publicly have dismissed the murder of a white wife as callously as G. W. Caldwell of Charlotte dismissed the murder of a slave. In advocating that the guilty master's fine and imprisonment for manslaughter be reduced, Caldwell referred to the slave's death as "one of those casualties which may happen to any person in the severe punishment of a slave."[56] Although murders of white wives shocked communities, many people, including lawmakers, defended the husband's right to strike a misbehaving wife and left it to the courts to decide the limits of marital discipline.[57]

Balancing the tension between the repression and protection inherent in paternalistic relationships taxed the skills of even the most able and articulate southern lawmakers. Although Chief Justice Ruffin insisted that husbands fulfill their paternalistic duty to provide a home for their wives, he was unwilling to consider whether that duty in some cases endangered a wife's physical safety and mental stability more than did her abandonment. In an 1849 divorce suit, Ruthy Ann Hansley testified that on several drunken binges, her husband had beaten her, locked her out of doors for entire nights, and continually committed adultery with a slave, once in her forced presence. The lower court granted Hansley a divorce *a vinculo matrimonii*, but Ruffin overturned the decision on grounds that her petition did not detail sufficiently her husband's adultery *after* her departure from their home. Ruffin ruled that without evidence of continued adultery on the part of the husband, there was reasonable hope for the couple's reconciliation.[58]

Other justices used similar reasoning to illustrate that they were determined to preserve the ideal of a harmonious, organic society held together by the bonds of family. In 1849, Justice Nash refused to sanction a privately written deed of separation because it would be "loosening another screw in the machinery of married life."[59] In 1851, the state supreme court overturned a divorce decree despite the defendant's crime of forgery and subsequent adultery after his wife's departure from the home. "She agreed to take him for better or worse," Justice Pearson rationalized.[60] And in 1857, the court overturned a divorce granted on grounds of the husband's physical abuse of his wife, stepchildren, and slaves. Justice Battle ruled that plaintiff Matilda Everton had failed to include in her petition the "specification of time, place, and circumstances" necessary to prove that her husband's behavior had been of "malicious intent."[61]

Despite consensus among the justices on the undesirability of divorce, the court granted two divorce decrees in the decade following Chief Justice Ruffin's retirement from the bench. In 1854, Chief Justice Nash declared adultery the "greatest indignity" a husband could inflict on a wife, and he approved a separation of bed and board (*a mensa et thoro*). "Personal injuries she might endure, blows and brutality from drunkenness she might suffer," added Nash, "but woman's nature must and will rebel against this last indignity; or mind itself give way."[62]

Justice Battle commented similarly in a divorce case heard two years later. A sensitive, virtuous woman, he argued, reacted to accusations of infidelity by her husband "with a far keener anguish than would be inflicted by a blow."[63] Although Nash and Battle rewarded feminine frailty with divorce, their belief that a white woman's personal honor depended more on mutual sexual fidelity within a marriage than on freedom from a husband's physical abuse only reinforced the passive, dependent marital role assigned to women.[64]

Local judges and juries granted divorces far more readily than did justices of the high court (see Tables 3.1 and 3.2). Undoubtedly influenced by greater personal knowledge of the litigants, superior court

Table 3.1. Judgments Delivered in Divorces Petitioned by Females in Superior Court, 1830–1860

Petitions	Granville	Orange	Montgomery	Total
Granted	14	2	1	17
Denied	0	3	1	4
Uncertain	11	4	3	18
Total	25	9	5	39

Source: Divorce Records, Granville, Orange, and Montgomery counties, NCDAH.

Table 3.2. Judgments Delivered in Divorces Petitioned by Males in Superior Court, 1830–1860

Petitions	Granville	Orange	Montgomery	Total
Granted	4	6	1	11
Denied	0	1	0	1
Uncertain	2	4	0	6
Total	6	11	1	18

Source: Divorce Records, Granville, Orange, and Montgomery counties, NCDAH.

judges also were concerned with somewhat different issues than supreme court justices. Whereas state leaders feared the erosion of the traditional family structure if divorce were too easily obtainable, local leaders judged divorce suits more on the basis of the parties' standing in the community and the threat to property that continuing in a marriage entailed for the plaintiff. For example, when Sarah Ware Nuttall sued her first husband, Henry Ware, for divorce on grounds that he had abandoned her and committed adultery, jurors considered Ware's status in his previous community as well as his treatment of Sarah. That Henry Ware had been convicted of trading with slaves, was reputed to be a habitual liar, and had once been run out of town by his neighbors helped his wife to secure the divorce.[65]

By the same token, a defendant's position of power in the community could hinder a plaintiff's chances of winning a divorce. In 1839, former widow Martha Trice sued her second husband, Zach-

Table 3.3. Complaints Filed by Female Plaintiffs in Divorce Cases Heard in Superior Court, 1830–1860

Complaints	Granville	Orange	Montgomery	Total
Wasting property	5	1	1	7
Adultery	7	6	1	14
Physical cruelty	5	5	1	11
Desertion	5	4	1	10
Drunkenness	2	4	1	7
Total	24	20	5	49

Source: Divorce Records, Granville, Orange, and Montgomery counties, NCDAH.

Note: The complaints here add up to more than the total 39 cases filed by females because some plaintiffs filed more than one complaint.

ariah Trice, for divorce in Orange County's superior court, charging that his penchant for slave trading had led him to squander the fortune she brought him from her first marriage. She also complained that her husband had denied her money for basic necessities, beaten her on several occasions, and committed adultery. Although Zachariah Trice was a controversial figure who had been involved in numerous disputes with neighbors, he was a justice of the peace at the time of his wife's suit. In September 1842, the drawn-out court case was dismissed in favor of the defendant, with all court costs assigned to the plaintiff.[66]

Martha Trice returned to her father's home, where she contributed to the family economy by housekeeping and sewing. As a well-to-do widow without a provision of separate estate, she had entered a second marriage with her property at risk. Her failure to win a divorce left her penniless and as dependent on her family as a child.[67]

Unlike Martha Trice, most plaintiffs won their suits in superior court. The combined extant records of Granville, Orange, and Montgomery counties between 1830 and 1861 contain fifty-seven petitions of divorce, thirty-nine by women, eighteen by men. In the thirty-three cases in which a final judgment was recorded, the court granted twenty-eight divorce decrees (see Tables 3.1 and 3.2). The most common charge against spouses in these suits was adultery (see Tables 3.3

Table 3.4. Complaints Filed by Male Plaintiffs in Divorce Cases Heard in Superior Court, 1830–1860

Complaints	Granville	Orange	Montgomery	Total
Wasting property	0	1	0	1
Adultery	3	12	1	16
Physical cruelty	0	0	0	0
Desertion	0	1	0	1
Drunkenness	0	0	0	0
Total	3	14	1	18

Source: Divorce Records, Granville, Orange, and Montgomery counties, NCDAH.

and 3.4). Among male plaintiffs (whom female plaintiffs outnumbered by more than two to one), it was virtually the only charge. Female plaintiffs cited a wider variety of grievances—adultery, drunkenness, physical and mental cruelty, wasting of property, and abandonment.

Of the three counties, Granville courts adjudicated the largest number of divorce suits, and there is no record of dismissal of a single divorce petition (see Tables 3.1 and 3.2). Four-fifths of the county's plaintiffs were women, nearly one-half of whom charged their husbands with desertion or wasting their property. A typical example was Hannah Russell Mitchell, a widow who had brought a "handsome estate" to her marriage to Robert Mitchell in 1817. After her husband wasted her property and abandoned her and their three children, leaving them dependent on the charity of family and friends, she sued him for divorce in 1831.[68] The exceptional wealth of many Granville County women undoubtedly gave them greater resources with which to seek divorce. The superior court was sensitive to their efforts to protect what was after all not merely their own wealth but that of some of the leading families of the county.

Nevertheless, Granville County wives possessed little legal power. Divorce plaintiff Susan Phillips negotiated to maintain her property through the intermediation of her brother John Lemay. Phillips sued her husband for divorce after he moved her to Alabama and then sent her back to North Carolina alone, destitute, and in poor health. To prevent her husband from appropriating six slaves valued at $2,400 that she had inherited from her mother, Phillips obtained a court judgment that released her brother, the administrator of their mother's estate, from his legal obligation to deliver Phillips's slaves to her estranged husband in accordance with the husband's legal marital rights.[69]

The Phillips case illustrates the important role of the family patriarch in protecting white women against abuse and destitution. Since married women did not enjoy full legal rights, the court transferred patriarchal authority to the brother of Susan Phillips to prevent the loss of her property to an abusive husband.

The extremely harsh nature of abuses cited by divorce petitioners makes it clear that women viewed the dissolution of marriage as a last resort and recognized that a divorce was unlikely to be granted unless their suits spelled out very serious grievances. Divorce plaintiffs needed the financial resources to live outside marriage and the emotional fortitude to withstand the public airing of private miseries. Martha Cape survived insults and whippings from her husband only to spend her final years in the Orange County poorhouse. Martha Trice received sustenance from her father (but no divorce from the court) at the cost of enduring witnesses' telling personal details of her life that supported attorneys' claims that she had provoked her husband's physical violence. Cornelius Cook testified that he would have "knocked down" a wife who contradicted a husband as often as did Martha Trice.[70]

It is no wonder that some spouses endured decades of marital discord before seeking a divorce. Eliza Cooke claimed that her husband of over thirty years, Methodist preacher Thomas Y. Cooke, had beaten and whipped her numerous times before she finally sought a divorce because she had been so "sensitively alive to the character and standing of her family and particularly her children" in the community.[71] Dr. Barnabas O'Fairhill's personal shame was already the talk of his neighborhood when after twenty-three years of marriage, he sued his adulterous wife for divorce. When it became obvious that he would not live long enough to obtain the decree, O'Fairhill wrote a will that recognized his wife's claim to dower but disinherited their children because he was convinced that he was not their father.[72]

Although women suffered greater physical vulnerability than men, not a single woman received a divorce solely on the grounds of having been beaten by her husband. The courts offered other means, however, through which a woman might seek protection from physical abuse. If threatened with physical violence, she could initiate a peace warrant requiring the accused to post a bond assuring twelve months' peaceful behavior toward her. If beaten again, she could charge her assailant with assault and battery.

How effective it was to petition the court for protection against an abusive husband is debatable. Some women repeatedly charged their husbands with physical cruelty before either fleeing their homes or suing for divorce.[73] Before turning to the courts, women probably appealed to male kin and friends for help. In true patriarchal fashion, a white woman's safety from one male depended largely on her protection by another.

Considering the extreme conditions that preceded the decision to pursue a divorce, it is not surprising that free blacks—with their limited financial resources and the added burden of exposing grievances before white-dominated courts—seldom sought legal divorce. Granville County's Beverly Richardson, who sued and won a divorce on grounds that his wife had committed adultery with a slave, was the sole exception in the three counties in this study.[74] Free African American couples probably preferred to work out their marital arrangements among themselves rather than allow the legal arm of white authority additional power over their lives.

Considerations of time, money, and personal pride probably caused many unhappy couples to endure their misery or to separate informally. Enduring an unhappy marriage could erupt in violence. In 1834, the Granville County superior court indicted free black John Allen for beating his wife, Priscilla, to death. In Orange County, free black Anderson Mayo was charged in May 1841 with murdering his wife, Jessie, after accusing her of adultery.[75]

Despite the reluctance of free blacks to seek divorces in the superior courts, they were very visible, particularly in Granville, in court proceedings involving marriage, property, and civil or criminal misbehavior. By 1860, the Anderson, Evans, Chavis, Bass, Mitchell, and

Pettiford families had been intermarrying for over seventy years, passing their artisanal skills and property from one generation to the next. Compared to this network of free African Americans, Jacob and Sally Fane were newcomers to free black society. As early as 1771, George Anderson, a free black of Granville, had left a small estate to be divided among several descendants bearing the surnames Anderson, Bass, and Pettiford.[76] In 1814, Lewis Anderson similarly named as heirs members of the free black families of Anderson, Bass, and Mitchell. County marriage records from the period 1780 to 1820 confirm extensive intermarriage among all six families. As the county's free black population increased, intermarriage expanded to include families surnamed Tyler, Kearsey, Curtis, Taborn, and others. Frequent marriage between members of these founding families continued right up to the Civil War.[77]

By the eve of the Civil War, members of the Anderson, Evans, Tyler, and Kearsey families were the most prosperous free African Americans in Granville County. The three wealthiest were seventy-year-old Will Evans, whose property was valued at $3,932, Archibald "Baldy" Kearsey, a forty-year-old farmer, who claimed $2,400 worth of property, and sixty-five-year-old Winnefred Tyler (whose maiden name was Anderson), who owned property valued at $1,700. They lived on the outskirts of Oxford, the county seat. Evans and Tyler were neighbors, and Kearsey was married to Frances Tyler, most likely related to Winnefred Tyler. Of the eighty heads of free black households in Granville who claimed property, at least fifty bore the county's oldest free black surnames: Anderson, Evans, Bass, Chavis, and Pettiford.[78]

A smaller network of relatively prosperous free blacks existed in Orange County. Many of them had the same surnames as their Granville County neighbors. A comparable free black community did not emerge in Montgomery County, where only forty-six free blacks lived on the eve of the war. Even in Orange County, only twenty-three heads of black households owned property. The richest was David Moore, a barber with an estate worth $4,400. With the exception of Adeline Bowles, whose estate was valued at $1,450, no other free blacks in Orange County had property valued at more than $750.[79]

Among the most visible, if not the wealthiest, free black families in Orange County were the Days, described by a former slave as "hard-working, thrifty, and proud as tom turkeys."[80] Like the propertied free blacks of Granville, they struggled for autonomy in white society. The most infamous of their family was Reuben Day, Jr., whose sexual liaisons with white women led to legal prosecution on charges of fornication. Later, his refusal to accept the economic and racial imperatives of Reconstruction prompted Sally Walker, on whose land he worked as a tenant farmer, to complain to Governor William W. Holden that Day was "a mighty headstrong, violent, passionate man [who] . . . thinks he can and will have the whole sole control of everything on the plantation."[81]

In Granville County, free black women of propertied families were a social anomaly. They lived in a society that deemed them fit for hard labor and unfit for the deferential courtesy extended to white women, but they belonged to an exceptional group of free blacks who had unusual economic and social resources. Many retained long-standing, if tenuous, ties to the white community. The Fanes, for example, maintained close ties to the white Bullock family, which had supported Jacob Fane's petition for freedom in 1805 and had owned James Fane and possibly Jacob at one time. In 1842, Sally and James Fane were accused of supplying liquor and arms to one of the Bullocks.[82]

Most free black women, even when propertied, had to become more self-sufficient than their white counterparts and were generally more visible in the public sphere because of their need to earn a living. They often worked as domestics, washers, or weavers, and a few operated unlicensed taverns that offered whites and blacks the opportunity to gamble, trade, and drink hard liquor together. For example, Nancy Anderson, who was indicted in May 1856 for maintaining a "disorderly house," operated a tavern that authorities believed was a center for interracial socializing.[83]

Underground taverns were often suspected of trafficking in prostitution and other illicit goods and services. The courts rarely accused free black women of prostitution, however; most prostitutes were poor white women. White men's sexual access to slave women no doubt lessened the market for black prostitutes, but some free blacks further deterred prostitution by energetically discouraging it in their neighborhoods. In Orange County, Silvia Chavis, a free black mother, became so outraged by a slave's attempt to entice her teenage daughter into prostitution that she successfully sued the slave and his master in the county court.[84]

The direct participation of Granville County's free black women in the commerce of their communities caused them to become more involved than white women in the street life of their respective neighborhoods. Especially in Oxford, the county seat, free black women participated in intrafamily feuding that often brought them into the county court. Nancy Anderson, for example, was in frequent scrapes with white and black neighbors. In 1837, the court charged her and Elizabeth Pettiford with beating up Hezekiah Hobgood, a white man. In 1840, Nancy's relative Jerry Anderson initiated a peace warrant against her. She and nine members of the Anderson and Taborn families broke into the home of Franky (Frances) Anderson in 1854 and beat up Franky and two other free black women.[85]

Between 1851 and 1856, the county court charged women from the Anderson, Taborn, and Chavis families at least a dozen times with fighting in public. Whether white authorities used harassment or unusual diligence in policing Oxford's free black community is impossible to determine. Whatever the case, Oxford's free black women bore a striking resemblance to New York's unruly working-class women in the nineteenth century. As historian Christine Stansell shows, the boundaries between households and streets among the urban ethnic poor were fluid, easily drawing women from their own households into the homes (and lives) of others. The streets were a "woman's theater of discord replete with the rhetorical flourish of insult and revenge."[86]

Despite the frequent presence of free black women in Granville County court, far fewer initiated peace warrants against husbands than did white women (see Tables 3.5 and 3.6). Isabella and Harriet Chavis, both of whom were washers, and Peggy Anderson, who owned property in her own name, held their own well enough in battles with their husbands to cause neighbors on different occasions

Table 3.5. Crimes of Violence Committed against Women Charged in the Lower Courts, 1850–1860

	Granville		Orange		Montgomery		Total	
	Black	White	Black	White	Black	White	Black	White
Assault and battery	17	19	1	24	0	6	18	49
Peace warrants	3	20	2	12	0	2	5	34
Rape	1	1	0	2	0	0	1	3
Total	21	40	3	38	0	8	24	86

Source: Criminal Action Papers, Granville, Orange, and Montgomery counties, Criminal Actions Concerning Slaves and Free Persons of Color, Granville County, NCDAH.

Table 3.6. Crimes of Violence Committed by Women Charged in the Lower Courts, 1850–1860

	Granville		Orange		Montgomery		Total	
	Black	White	Black	White	Black	White	Black	White
Assault and battery	16	7	0	11	0	2	16	20
Peace warrants	2	2	2	1	0	0	4	3
Affrays	12	2	1	1	0	0	13	3
Total	30	11	3	13	0	2	33	26

Source: Criminal Action Papers, Granville, Orange, and Montgomery counties, Criminal Actions Concerning Slaves and Free Persons of Color, Granville County, NCDAH.

to charge the couples with disturbing the peace. In assault cases, Granville's free black women, unlike their white counterparts, were more often reported as participants in than as victims of violence.[87] Still, proportionate to their numbers, free black women in Granville were victims of violence far more often than white women.

As in the case of rape, black women's greater vulnerability to violence reflected the convergence of sexual and racial systems of domination. Aggressive behavior perhaps enabled some to escape the victimization common among slave and many free black women. On one hand, they may have been more reluctant than white women to report abusive husbands to white-dominated courts. On the other, some probably concluded that meek or docile behavior was of little use in the daily struggle to raise families and make a living. Black women had to decide whether to protect the privacy of the black community or seek legal protection for themselves. Since white male lawmakers were hardly symbols of justice to them, most black women chose to work out personal conflicts within the black community.[88]

In spite of the deference expressed toward white women by paternalistic southern leaders, some women felt compelled to seek court protection against abusive males. Orange and Granville counties, with their more economically diverse populations of whites and blacks, reported many more violent crimes committed against or by women than did less-stratified Montgomery County (see Tables 3.5 and 3.6). The levels of violence, in general, were higher in Granville and Orange, where the incidence of murder was much higher in proportion to the total population than in Montgomery. Between 1830 and 1860, there were twenty-three murder indictments in Granville and twenty in Orange, compared to only one in Montgomery. Ten of the total forty-four murders were interracial; thirteen occurred between males and females,[89] with men committing seven and women six of those homicides. White men who murdered black men were generally convicted of manslaughter if convicted at all. Conversely, a black man who killed a white man faced an almost certain death sentence.[90]

White wives, like slaves, were subordinate to white men, but unlike slaves, they shared society's most intimate bonds and ties of family and race with their masters. The reverence that southern society held for the "gentler sex" caused many people to consider wife-beating a shameful act and to recoil in horror at the thought of a man's murdering his wife.[91] Nevertheless, citizens and lawmakers looked very closely at the factors surrounding individual cases in which husbands were charged with murdering wives. The question arose, at what point did abuse so far beyond the bounds of legitimate chastisement as to result in a wife's death constitute first-degree murder?

The 1856 murder trial of Alvin Preslar is instructive. While drunk on a night in November, Preslar struck, choked, and kicked his wife so brutally that she fled with two of her children but died before reaching her father's house. Although the jurors of the Union County superior court convicted Preslar of murder and the judge sentenced him to hang, a petition and three accompanying letters reached Governor Thomas Bragg asking him to commute the death sentence.[92]

More than three hundred petitioners pleaded that Preslar should not have been convicted of first-degree murder for two reasons. First, they argued, he had not intended to kill his wife but had beaten her as "the result of a drunken frolic." Second, the petitioners reasoned, since Mrs. Preslar, despite having suffered chills for two days previously, had voluntarily left the house on a rainy night after her husband had fallen asleep, she bore some blame for her own death.[93] Although another citizen countered the petition by informing the governor that Alvin Preslar had shown "more cruelty and barbarity toward a wife than [in any] other case I ever witnessed," Governor Bragg granted Preslar a reprieve until the following February.[94]

That so many members of a community—many of whom were described as "ladies"—would defend Preslar on grounds of his drunken state illustrates a central theme in the conflict over the legitimacy of violence in relationships between unequal partners.[95] White males were expected to punish their wives (and occasionally to drink too much), just as they were expected to punish slaves. Although excessive or unwarranted punishment might bring tragic results, as in the death of Mrs. Preslar, some people believed that allowances should be made for the husband's rights of authority over his household. By contrast, to have defended on grounds of drunkenness a wife or slave who murdered a husband or master would have defied social norms.[96]

Richmond County slaveholder Walter L. Steele believed that physical abuse of wives and daughters, especially in lower-class families, must be expected and tolerated. For example, he defended Steven Cole's brutal beating of his wife on grounds of *her* drunkenness and evil temperament. In his defense of Cole, he advised Governor Bragg that "some allowance should be made, in the gradation of punishments, for walks of life in which parties move," because among the upper classes, "a harsh word or an unkind look on the part of the husband is far more injury to a refined and sensitive woman, than a blow, to one who is groveling and debased."[97]

Thomas Ruffin, Jr., son of the eminent jurist, argued similarly for African Americans in recommending that Governor Bragg grant clemency to a slave who had murdered another slave for sleeping with his free black wife. "If his were the case of a white man—I should say, let the law take its course," said Ruffin. "We know, however, the defects in the moral and mental training of those who belong to this prisoner's class, and it may be proper that they should be judged by a rule less strict."[98]

Finally, some ninety petitioners asked Governor Bragg to be lenient with Alderman Merritt, a white man who had beaten his fifteen-year-old daughter. Although the petitioners acknowledged that the beating was the "severest castigation ever inflicted in a civilized community," they argued that Merritt should be pardoned because of his low breeding and degraded morals.[99]

Despite a high tolerance for physical violence, some North Carolina citizens deplored abuse of the powerless by the powerful, arguing that tolerance of wanton abuse undermined the paternalistic basis of social relationships in the South. In Chowan County, J. C. Badham of Edenton pleaded clemency for a slave sentenced to die for breaking into a smokehouse and stealing a small amount of meat. If slavery, as defenders claimed, was a humane system that served the needs of blacks as well as whites, then how, asked Badham, could the courts justify executing a slave for stealing only enough food to satisfy his hunger?[100]

Two other cases are also illustrative. In Orange County, the superior court convicted and sentenced Obediah Christmas to hang for the brutal, unprovoked murder of Nathan, a slave belonging to Thomas Taylor of Granville County.[101] And in 1855, Chief Justice Nash refused to allow a defense of drunkenness in a case involving the murder of a free black woman by a white male.[102]

Significant as these examples are, they all addressed abuses that occurred *outside* the formal boundaries of patriarchal authority over slaves and wives. Granville citizens knew that Christmas was a violent man who held a grudge against Nathan's owner, and they abhorred his cold-blooded murder of a slave. Court decisions that punished such crimes reinforced the belief of many white southerners that their society protected the rights of inferiors. At the same time, however, because Nathan was not the slave—and the unnamed black woman not the wife or the slave—of the men who murdered them, these cases did not challenge the true domain of white patriarchal power: the plantation and the home.

Although black men who attacked white men received swift justice from white-dominated courts (if not first from vigilante mobs), it is more difficult to assess lawmakers' reactions to white women who attacked white men. According to Kemp Plummer Battle, the son of Lucy and Judge William Battle, only one white woman ("Mrs. Silver") was ever hanged in antebellum North Carolina. Mrs. Silver murdered her husband after he came home drunk and beat her with a stick. She then allegedly tried to hide his body by cutting it into pieces and burying it.[103]

Few women publicly assaulted white males, and even fewer committed murder. Some women, however, were indicted for murdering their husbands. For example, Mary Meadows, a Granville County farm wife who, apparently tired of abuse by her husband, James Meadows, allegedly hired a slave named George to kill him in 1846. The Granville superior court indicted Mrs. Meadows and the slave for premeditated murder, but it convicted and hanged only the slave.[104]

Mary Meadows was acquitted despite the fact that several neighbors, including a relative, supplied evidence that she had arranged the murder of her husband. John B. Duncan testified that Meadows had offered to indenture herself to him almost a year before the murder if he would kill her husband. Samuel Jackson testified that he had seen James Meadows abusing Mary at a public gathering. According to Jackson, Mrs. Meadows called out to him to knock her husband's brains out and yelled that she would do it herself if she were a man. Another witness testified that Meadows had declared shortly before the murder that her husband would soon be through "scandalizing" her, for in a short time he would be "the worst whipped man" ever seen.[105]

No one offered a motive as to why George would have wanted to kill James Meadows, except for the possible promise of a reward.[106] The Granville court perhaps used George's involvement to avoid the question of how to punish a wife who had retaliated against her husband after years of abuse and humiliation. Convicting a slave instead of a wife enabled the court and the community to focus on the outrage of a black man's killing a white man rather than confront the thorny issue of violence within a marriage. The conviction of George and the acquittal of Mary Meadows sidestepped the question of whether the courts would have hanged a white woman who had deep roots in the community.

Mary Meadows's alleged complicity in murder and the depth of spousal abuse suggested by her desperation challenged societal beliefs about white female meekness and the protective instincts of husbands. In contrast, the notion that a male slave had killed a white man contradicted paternalistic ideals far less because of the greater capacity for violence attributed to males and the alleged barbarian nature of African Americans. Thus conventional wisdom demanded the conviction and swift execution of George to protect the inviolability of the master class. George's execution buried disturbing questions about marital relationships among whites and the proper response of women to abusive husbands. The court's decision resolved the dilemma and preserved justice—in appearance if not in fact—without challenging the underlying assumptions about white women and black men.

These trials illustrate the limits of paternalism in protecting southern wives, not to mention slaves. The paternalistic ethos of southern leaders crippled efforts to extend greater legal rights to married women. For example, antebellum lawmakers moved only haltingly toward granting wives control over their own property. Moreover, legislators and judges who considered divorce laws and domestic relations failed to resolve the conflict between male authority and a woman's right to safety. Instead, the laws that governed the family and slavery protected masters' domination of both institutions. Courts protected dependents only if such protection did not threaten the superior rights of husbands, fathers, and masters. Ideally, state leaders reasoned, masters provided authority and protection to other household members.

Thus, how wisely a free woman married determined to a large extent the quality of her life. After all, North Carolina lawmakers expected the male-headed household, not the courts, to be the primary instrument of social control over women. Despite the regional biases of local courts and differences of intellect and temperament among individual justices, the law recognized the privacy of the male-headed household and seldom intruded. In cases in which the white male head of household was absent, the courts enforced the norms of female behavior. As we will see, in the case of women who violated the norms of southern womanhood, the courts were less concerned with upholding paternalistic ideals and more concerned with protecting society from the contaminating effects of "deviant" women.

Four

Punishing Deviant Women

The State as Patriarch

On April 8, 1861, Susan Williford pleaded with the magistrates of the Granville County court to allow her to maintain custody of her two youngest children—Nancy, aged eight, and Louisa, aged six. Williford charged two planters of the county with forcibly removing the girls from her home despite her objections. In defending the right to raise her own daughters, Williford declared in an affidavit that although she was poor, through "industry and frugality" she had always supported Nancy and Louisa comfortably and, further, that she was an "honest and hardworking woman . . . much distressed at being separated from her children of such tender years." The court ordered an investigation but apparently did not rescind the apprenticeships.[1]

Susan Williford's predicament was not unique. Courts in the antebellum South often apprenticed children judged to be indigent, ill-raised, illegitimate, orphaned, or of free black parentage. The apprenticeship of illegitimate or free black children removed them from the homes of their parents (usually single women) to those of court-appointed masters (usually white men) for whom they were bound by contract to labor in return for their livelihood. Rarely did the contracts specify that a skill be taught the children other than farming for boys and spinning for girls.[2] Though Williford, a white woman, might truthfully argue that she loved and took good care of her children, the fact that they were the illegitimate offspring of a racially mixed union branded her a social deviant incapable of raising them properly. Committing the crime of miscegenation condemned her to a legal rung just above slavery—a rung usually reserved for free black women.

Williford's life from childhood to middle age demonstrated how courts punished women who defied the sexual and racial constructs of southern society. How and why did she become an outcast, even an outlaw? Although she suffered from poverty and the stigma of deviancy throughout most of her adult life, her family roots probably originated among the yeomanry of Granville County. The economic and sexual vulnerability of women, however, had reduced her mother, Elizabeth Williford, to the ranks of poor whites. Elizabeth never married, and the illegitimate birth of her daughter Susan ensured poverty and degraded status for both.[3]

At age six, Susan Williford was apprenticed to a farmer, William Gordon. Growing up could not have been easy for children like her who were separated at very young ages—sometimes as young as one year—from their mothers. In Susan's case, separation was made worse by an abusive master. In November 1822, her mother charged Gordon with mistreating Susan, but not until February 1823 did the court remove the child from Gordon's home. Perhaps Susan's childhood apprenticeship experiences influenced her impassioned plea for custody of her children forty years later.[4]

The court's treatment of women like Williford demonstrated that, despite southern leaders' idealistic vision of women's absorption within the family circle, state and local judges recognized that some women were neither the wives nor the slaves of white men. Such women had no place or function in southern society. Unmarried, propertyless women were not the vessels through which white male property and progeny passed. Instead, many were mothers of a troublesome white and black laboring class.[5]

By contradicting society's cherished beliefs about women's natural delicacy, servility, and virtue, the behavior of some poor women compounded their inferior status. Besides violating prescribed norms of female behavior, poor women broke taboos against interracial social and sexual intercourse more often than did economically privileged women. Respected white southerners regarded deviant white women as "vile," "lewd," and "vicious" products of an inferior strain of humanity. They considered unmarried free black women naturally lascivious and amoral by virtue of their race. These attitudes, in turn, legitimized the power of the courts to punish such behavior and limit the freedom of poor women.[6]

Enforcement of laws governing bastardy, prostitution, fornication, and apprenticeship provided the chief means through which courts punished sexually active women and appropriated the labor of their children. Class, race, and marital status dictated which women were most likely to be summoned before county magistrates. An unmarried woman who did not remain celibate might frequently find herself in court throughout her childbearing years.

Despite the tremendous social and legal costs, some unmarried women led sexually active lives, entering into a subculture of mostly poor people who did not abide by the rules of polite society. This behavior allowed them a measure of personal choice in a world that otherwise restricted poor or unmarried women to lives spent serving others. Chart 4.1 reveals the connections that two deviant women—Susan Williford and Parthenia Melton—forged among yeoman, poor white, and free black members of the neighborhoods surrounding the township of Tally Ho in Granville County. The Hobgoods, Adcocks, Willifords, and Curtises had frequent contact with each other throughout the antebellum era. The Hobgoods and Adcocks intermarried, and many of the free black Curtises were apprenticed to, or worked for, their white neighbors. In addition, illicit liaisons created cross-class and interracial relationships.[7]

Williford and Melton were pivotal to these kinships. So was John R. Hobgood, who fathered children by both women in 1836 and 1837, respectively.[8] He probably concluded from Williford's déclassé status that no harm was done by impregnating her, but he clearly "ruined" Melton, who probably was his sixteen-year-old niece (see Chart 4.1). Hobgood seemed particularly addicted to dissolute living. Like Williford and Melton, whose legal problems began with their pregnancies by him, he was in and out of court all his adult life, eventually entering the county poorhouse. His immediate family was plagued by violence. Two men beat to death his brother Shelton in 1828, and Mary Meadows, his

Chart 4.1. The Creation of a Subculture

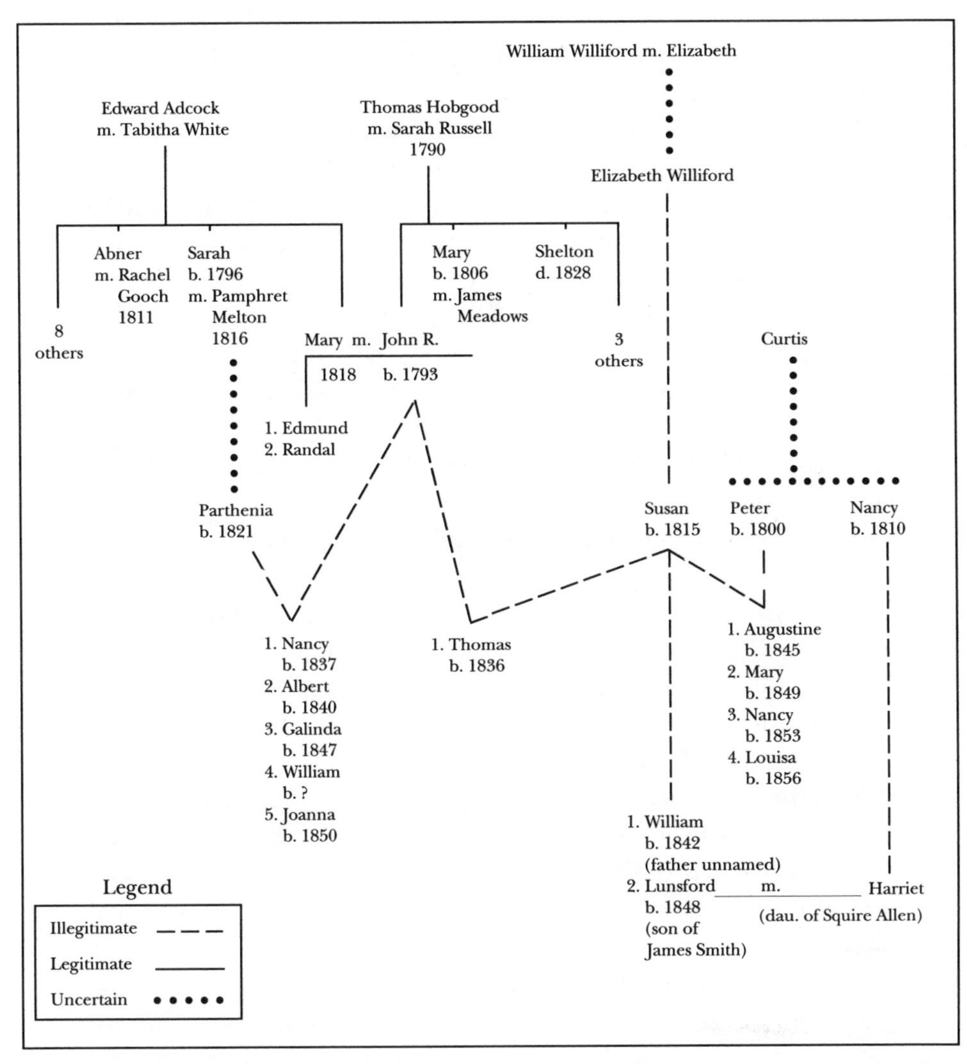

Sources: U.S. Federal Manuscript Censuses, 1850, 1860; Estate Records; Apprenticeship Bonds; Bastardy Bonds; Marriage Bonds; Granville County, NCDAH.

notorious sister, was accused in 1847 of arranging the murder of her husband. Despite the solid yeoman background of the Hobgoods, the behavior of John, Shelton, and Mary mired them in Granville's impoverished subculture.[9]

The relationship between John R. Hobgood and Parthenia Melton was long-lasting, despite its illicit nature. By 1850, the couple had five children, although they never married and apparently never shared a home. Melton, like Susan Williford, lived in a world of poverty and violence, and her control over her children was precarious. She was charged with bastardy once and, along with John Hobgood, for fornication twice. In 1851, the court took custody of all of her children and apprenticed two of them. It placed the remaining three children in the county poorhouse to await further action regarding their custody. In 1860, thirty-nine-year-old Melton lived alone with her youngest child, Joanna, whose custody she regained, while sixty-seven-year-old Hobgood languished in the county poorhouse.[10]

Williford's social status dropped even lower than Melton's and Hobgood's in the 1840s, when she entered into a permanent relationship with Peter Curtis, a free black man of her community. Denied by law the right to marry the partner of her choice, although she lived with him for at least fifteen years, Williford lost all her children by Curtis when the court ruled that they were subject to apprenticeship because they were illegitimate. In addition, the court regularly charged Williford and Curtis with fornication.[11] Whereas free black couples found it extremely difficult to prosper in a white slaveholding society, interracial couples found it almost impossible to maintain a traditional family life.

Living with Curtis instead of alone probably enhanced the personal safety and economic security of Williford, despite increased harassment by the courts. In 1840, before taking up with Curtis, she was beaten up and her house was torn apart by a white man—an experience all too common for poor white women of outcast status. Joining the Curtis family, which had numerous relatives among Granville County's vital community of free black farmers and artisans, lessened her vulnerability. Living among the Curtises also provided a community in which her mulatto children were accepted. Three of her

Table 4.1. Charges of Sexual Misconduct and Larceny Brought against Women in the Lower Courts, 1850–1860

	Granville	Orange	Montgomery	Total
Prostitution	8	11	0	19
Fornication	21	43	5	69
Bastardy	33	94	42	169
Larceny	5	2	1	8

Source: Criminal Action Papers and Bastardy Bonds, Granville, Orange, and Montgomery counties, Criminal Actions Concerning Slaves and Free Persons of Color, Granville County, NCDAH.

children married into black families of their neighborhood in the 1860s.[12] Thus at the price of utter condemnation by white society, Williford gained greater physical protection—something outcast poor white women generally lacked—by crossing the color line.

Crossing the color line also reveals the larger connection of female sexuality and reproduction to issues of race and poverty. Because of the counties' significant free black populations, the Orange and Granville courts enforced laws against prostitution and fornication as often to punish miscegenation and limit sexual contact between free blacks and slaves as to punish white couples guilty of adultery (see Table 4.1). Indictments for prostitution particularly targeted women who engaged in interracial social activity or who operated taverns at which blacks and whites were suspected of gambling, drinking, and exchanging illegal goods. Prostitution was usually included within the general charge of operating a "disorderly house," rather than being the sole issue of an indictment.[13]

That court magistrates sought to control rather than eliminate prostitution is indicated by their general indifference toward white prostitutes who confined their services to white males. These women appear to have quietly plied their trade without legal challenge,[14] perhaps because many white citizens believed that the availability of lower-class white prostitutes (as well as slave women) protected respectable women from defilement by lustful males. Few citizens seem to have thought much about the prostitute herself except to label her "vile," "dissolute," and the like.[15] Respectable townspeople for the most part ignored prostitutes unless, if white, they crossed the color line or, as in the case of Nancy Glasgow who was caught milking the cow of Thomas Pleasants without his permission, they imposed upon more prosperous members of the community.[16]

Their marginality in society makes it difficult to reconstruct the lives of prostitutes or women who ran underground taverns. Most of those accused of prostitution or of operating "disorderly houses" were poor women who lived in female-headed households and lacked extensive kinship networks in their communities. Some, like Orange County's Emily King, Lucinda Woodrow, and free black Patsy Huckabee and Granville's Nancy Glasgow and Sally Short, had illegitimate children in their younger years. Others, such as Catherine Mincey (Minzey) and Mary Perry of Orange County, were probably of illegitimate birth themselves.[17] In virtually every case, ostracism from respectable society preceded involvement in prostitution.

Few owned any property of substance, and many were omitted by census takers in their enumeration of households.[18] Consequently, most of the evidence that survives in the public records is negative, identifying such women as witnesses or victims of crimes. Criminal records, for example, record Nancy Glasgow's beating by well-to-do hotel keeper Simon G. Hayes—an incident suggesting that Glasgow perhaps tried to conduct business in Hayes's hotel.[19] In Orange County, Emily King was subpoenaed as a witness to a murder that occurred during a drunken brawl at her place of business.[20] Prostitutes and female tavern keepers clearly were visible figures in the shadowy social world denied to ladies of the community, a world in which violence and illicit sexual activity were commonplace. This and the fact that prostitutes were forced to cater to men who despised them even while they exploited their services left women of this underground subculture highly vulnerable.

In contrast to prostitution, indictments for fornication focused on women who gave rather than sold sexual favors. Targeted were those who cohabited with slaves (primarily free black women), participated in interracial sexual activity (mostly poor white women), or engaged in adulterous relationships with married men.[21] The first two categories included some couples who considered themselves married but were legally forbidden to marry.[22]

Although marriages between slaves and free blacks were not legal, slave masters sometimes allowed informal arrangements. The slave-owner might disrupt these informal marriages at any time, as in the case of Reuben Day and the slave Harriet, but such marriages were plagued by more than the master's interference. It was difficult to build intimate, stable unions when marriages lacked legal sanction, privacy, and complete freedom of movement.

The case of Sarah Boon is illustrative. Sarah, a Wake County slave, was married to James Boon, a free black carpenter. She remained tethered to her master's plantation while James traveled the country-side in search of work. For almost a year, she beseeched him in letters to return to the plantation, where the couple had a cabin, garden, and livestock. "Your hogs are running wild," Sarah warned, "and I fear they will all be destroyed." She told James that she felt very "loane-some," and she experienced the anguish of jealousy when she learned that he was seeing another woman. "My Dear Husband," she wrote, "I frealy forgive. . . . I wish it to be banished from our memories and never to be thought of again and let us take a new start."[23]

It must have been particularly frustrating that James's new lover was a free black woman who could travel with him and legally marry him. James Boon later married Mahala Buffalo without having to make even a gesture to Sarah, who, according to the law, had never been married.[24]

It is not entirely surprising that James Boon opted not to sacrifice his mobility to live permanently on the plantation with his slave wife. Their situation typified the dilemma of slaves and free blacks who were allowed to cohabit. Emma Stone recalled that her free black mother, Polly Mitchell, chose to live and raise her children on the Chatham County plantation of her slave husband. This decision, as Stone pointed out, led to quasi-slavery for the Mitchells: "We chilluns, long wid her, wuz [treated] lak de udder slaves."[25]

Polly Mitchell's gender may have played a key role in her decision. As a free black woman, she was less likely than James Boon to have a marketable artisanal skill. Furthermore, her children were free even though their father was a slave. Thus getting the permission to live as the wife of her slave partner from his master may have been contingent on her staying on the plantation. The decision apparently allowed her husband's master to appropriate the labor of her children.

Laws against fornication discouraged free blacks from seeking mates who were slaves. The illegality of marriage among slaves greatly reduced the pool of marriageable partners available to free black women, many of whom found partners among cousins, uncles, and other relatives. In the process, they built kin lines every bit as interwoven as those of the planter elite.[26] A small pool of potential marital partners meant, however, that many free black women never married and instead probably carried on clandestine affairs with slaves, married free black men, or white men.

Free black women strained the boundaries of the southern racial code in efforts to meet their own personal needs. Adeline Bowles, an unusually wealthy free black woman of Orange County, purchased her mate, a slave, from his master after the two were charged with fornication.[27] Most free black women, however, did not have the means to buy their mates or find masters willing to sell them. Some, like Kate and Mary Durham, carried on liaisons with male slaves for years before finally being charged with fornication. To these women, such unions often constituted marriages even though court officials treated them as adulterers and apprenticed their children in the manner accorded to bastards. Only after the war were Kate and Mary Durham able to legalize their respective marriages and regain custody of the children born to them before the war.[28]

In those indictments of fornication aimed at punishing miscegenation, magistrates prosecuted primarily white women and black men rather than white men and black women.[29] This uneven application of the law reflected the structure of gender and racial relationships. White males claimed the right to govern all women, regardless of race.[30] The sole sexual possession of white women by white men assured perpetuation of the dominant "pure" white race. Possession of a black woman by a white man, whether of her person, labor, or body, demonstrated the powerlessness of the black man, who could not claim sole rights of possession even to women of his own race. Black women were especially vulnerable. Subjected to sexual exploitation because of their gender, they were denied protection against sexual harassment on account of their race.

A white man might seek sexual activity with a black woman with little fear of censure from society provided he did not treat her in a manner that suggested the respect reserved for white women.[31] Certainly, a white man should not appear at social gatherings with his black mistress. Just such behavior resulted in a rare case in which a white male was charged with fornication with a black female. By socializing publicly with Tabby Chavous (Chavis), a free mulatto woman, Thomas Peace so angered his brother Dickerson Peace that in 1844 the latter initiated charges of fornication against the couple. Undaunted by the charges, however, Thomas continued to escort Chavous to public gatherings well into the 1850s until Dickerson, unable to contain his rage, attacked and accidentally killed him at a neighborhood barbecue.[32]

This violent end to a decade-long relationship illustrates the profound connections between sexual behavior and ordering of racial boundaries. The sexual possession of both white and black women symbolized men's power, but in very different ways. At a basic level, such possession signified the dominance of men over women. White women, however, were prizes; the higher a particular woman's family status, the better it spoke of the man who "won" her. Possession of black women, by contrast, symbolized a man's virility more than his honor, a virility manifested in racial domination.[33] Thus a white man must never, as in the case of Thomas Peace, elevate a black woman to the status of a white woman.

Most white men treated their affairs with black women with the discretion required in antebellum society. Indictments of racially mixed couples for fornication usually targeted white women and black men. In a society steeped in the mythology of white female purity and black inferiority, such couplings, though rare, were disturbing. Most nineteenth-century Americans viewed sexual intercourse as an act done *to* women rather than one in which women participated. Thus a black man's sexual "conquest" of a white woman potentially empowered him and humiliated white men. A white woman who chose a black mate had to be lowered in status to prevent the elevation of the black male who possessed her and, of course, to confirm white males' cherished notion of themselves as the preferred sexual choice of any decent white woman.[34]

White couples whose sexual behavior offended the community might also find themselves indicted for fornication. Many such cases involved poor white women and propertied (usually married) white men. An indictment for fornication could also serve as a prelude to a suit for divorce,[35] or it might simply reflect feuding among members of a community. Many people routinely used the courts to punish and embarrass each other.

Efforts to embarrass a man by linking his name with a disreputable woman sometimes extended beyond neighborhood feuds. Susan Mason, an unmarried white woman who had several illegitimate children, demonstrated the power (if it may be called such) of an unchaste woman to challenge the credentials of a southern gentleman. When Mason named wealthy, upper-class William Stanford Moore as the father of one of her bastards in 1848, Moore won a reversal of the lower court's decision in favor of Mason in superior court.[36] Eight years later, when two editors of the *Raleigh Register* again linked Moore's name with Mason's, Moore sued the men for slander, labeling Susan Mason "a woman of a base and infamous character . . . [who is] in all respects unchaste in the highest degree, [as well as] low & degraded."[37] Mason's flagrant sexual behavior had rendered her an "untouchable" in white society, the sort of woman who could send a gentleman scurrying into court to protect his good name.

Using the courts to harass one's enemies was particularly popular in Montgomery County, although magistrates rarely indicted anyone for fornication and never charged any women with prostitution. The county simply lacked enough free black, kinless, or landless people to develop the underground of dramshops, gambling, and illicit sexual activity that leading citizens in Granville and Orange counties feared would bring social chaos if left unchecked. Indictments for fornication did occasionally provide a convenient weapon against one's enemies, however. When Gilbert Nichols gossiped to neighbors that Candace Lucas had taken as "sweet-hearts" several slaves of the community,

Lucas's uncle and brother promptly charged Nichols's uncle, who lived with a mulatto woman, with fornication.[38] The timing of the Lucases' suit suggests not so much indignation over miscegenation as an effort to even the score in the ongoing battles between the families.

That seven interracial marriages went uncontested in Montgomery County before the war further indicates that personal animosity rather than racial concerns animated the charges and countercharges of miscegenation between the Nichols and Lucas families. Six members of the Hussey family, all of whom passed in appearance as white despite having a mulatto grandmother, married white partners and raised large families without legal challenge until the Civil War brought the issue of race to the fore.[39] Wilson Williams, a mulatto, and Disey McQuean, a white woman, also lived as husband and wife in Montgomery County without apparent challenge.[40] The greater homogeneity of Montgomery County's population made its white citizens more willing to tolerate a few cases of interracial cohabitation than their counterparts in communities with higher numbers of free blacks and slaves.

The racial concerns that influenced the enforcement of civil and criminal laws also influenced the use of the apprenticeship system, which functioned as an instrument of racial control as well as an early attempt to institute a system of social welfare for the poor. Several categories of children were subject to apprenticeship: fatherless children "who have not sufficient estate to be educated on the profits"; children deserted without support for at least one year by their fathers; children not living with a father and living with a mother deemed by the court an improper parent; all free illegitimate children; and all children of "free negroes or mulattoes, where the parents do not employ their time in some industrious, honest occupation."[41] The courts used the system most consistently to apprentice the children of free blacks.

County court officials removed poor children from their mothers through the apprenticeship system because women had no legal rights of guardianship over their children unless specifically endowed with them by courts. Fathers were by law the "natural" guardians of children. The courts defined as an orphan any child without a living or

Table 4.2. Number and Race of Children Apprenticed between 1850 and 1860

	Granville	Orange	Montgomery	Total
Black	60	71	13	144
White	34	40	17	91
Total	94	111	30	235

Source: Apprenticeship Bonds and Minutes of the county courts, Granville, Orange, and Montgomery counties, NCDAH.

legitimate father. All minor orphans were legal wards of the court regardless of whether they had living mothers. In strict legal terms, the courts "allowed" a mother to raise her children by virtue of her marriage to the children's legal "owner," their father. Hence the law required that widowed mothers apply in court for legal guardianship over their "orphaned" children, though in cases involving propertied families, the court usually granted such guardianships routinely.[42] The likelihood that the children of propertyless widows and unmarried mothers would be apprenticed was much greater.

As Table 4.2 shows, more free black than white women lost custody of their children through the apprenticeship system. An unmarried mother of a black or mulatto child could certainly expect her child to be apprenticed. Between 1850 and 1860, black and mulatto children accounted for 61 percent of the children apprenticed in Orange, Granville, and Montgomery counties even though free black women made up only 9 percent of female-headed households.[43]

Stripped of political and legal rights by virtue of both gender and race, most unmarried free African American mothers had little choice but to endure separation from their children. A few resisted apprenticeship, however, or challenged in court masters who abused apprenticeship laws. In 1848, for example, Cassandra Pollard, a "poor" but "respectable" free black woman of Wake County, obtained a lawyer and sought freedom for her daughter Elizabeth, whose master had illegally removed her from the county of apprenticeship and had retained custody of her beyond the age of twenty-one.[44] In Orange

County, Sarah Jackson sued to rescind her son's apprenticeship to Solomon Fuller on unspecified grounds after four years of service.[45]

Because of their race, black women were less able to resist apprenticeship of their children. Court officials did not apprentice all illegitimate white children; instead, they focused on those who manifested obvious signs of poverty and neglect.[46] White women had greater rights in court than black women and, not being part of so small and visible a minority as free blacks, probably found it easier to hide their children from court officials. Yet the stigmatization of poverty and deviant behavior, grounds in the first place for the removal of a woman's child, severely undercut the white woman's advantage of race.

Giving birth to a black man's child eliminated the racial advantage for white women. In an 1855 suit similar to Susan Williford's, Nancy Midgett, a white mother of two mulatto children, appealed to the state supreme court to rescind her children's apprenticeships on grounds that she was living an industrious life and able to support them. Judge Pearson denied the request and reminded her that the county court "has power to bind out *all* free base-born children of color, without reference to the occupation or condition of the mother."[47]

The circle of control over the sexual and reproductive activity of poor women technically was complete. Midgett, like Williford, could not legally marry her children's black father. Thus she had no legal right to the custody of her children. By denying the labor of their own children to parents who did not conform to the ideal of a (preferably white) male-headed, propertied household, North Carolina courts sometimes crippled the tenuous economic base of a fatherless or free black family. They also shattered many poor people's potential for forming affective family bonds.

In some cases involving single or widowed women who were unable to provide decent homes for their children, the interests of the children would probably have been better served had the apprenticeship system removed them from the custody of their mothers. In 1860, Mary Ann Inscore, a twenty-three-year-old white woman, apparently still had not named her three- and two-year-old illegitimate children. She lived with William Ferrill, who had been charged in November

1857 with operating a "disorderly house" that included prostitution.[48] It is no surprise that in a society that socialized women to be dependent on others and decreed marriage women's only viable vocation, those who failed to marry wisely or at all might lack the financial or emotional resources to raise their children. In such cases, the apprenticeship system provided an alternative to the poorhouse and, in theory at least, an opportunity for an indigent child to learn a skill. Most orders of apprenticeship, however, did not address a woman's ability to raise a child but merely cited the fatherlessness of a child as a priori evidence of that fact.

Recognizing the inevitability of losing their children, some free black women initiated apprenticeship so they could have some say in their children's placement. In 1828, Lusey Morgan, a pregnant free black woman, pleaded with county magistrates to bind her children to William Chamblee, an Orange County slaveholder. She had been bound to Chamblee as a young girl and lived with him as an adult with two children. She feared that her children might be apprenticed to someone else in the community and thus separated from her. In separate cases, Milly Richerson and Leaney Mitchell, free black women of Granville County, likewise initiated their children's apprenticeships to white planters on whose plantations they lived and worked. These planters may also have been the fathers of their children. Requesting that her children be bound to John C. Connell, Richerson explained, "I am now living on his land, and am unable to support myself only bi [*sic*] the hire of said children."[49] Had the women waited for the court to order the apprenticeships, they would have risked having their children bound to masters not of their choosing. Unable to broaden their opportunities for employment and avoid the apprenticeship system, women like Morgan, Richerson, and Mitchell negotiated to maintain at least the company of their children.

Because of its small free black population, Montgomery County courts apprenticed far fewer children than those in either Orange or Granville. But despite a free black population half the size of Granville's, Orange County had the highest apprenticeship numbers, reflecting the higher level of poverty among all women of that county. The differences between the Granville and Orange County courts' apprenticeship numbers demonstrate also that, despite racial barriers, free blacks, like whites, benefited under the law according to their socioeconomic status and family connections.

More prosperous free black families resisted the apprenticeship of black children to whites. In 1824, Elizabeth Gooch, a white woman of Granville County, accused free blacks Reuben Day, Sr., and his wife, Nancy, of "stealing" her two black apprentices. Other free blacks prevented whites from gaining custody of black children by having the children apprenticed to themselves. Jeremiah Day of Orange County gained custody of his orphaned nephews in this manner.[50]

Free black men and women who became the masters of apprentices bore the surnames of the most prosperous and extensive free black families. In Granville, William Evans (August 1830), Anderson Pettiford (May 1852), Joseph Curtis (August 1854), and Lucy Richerson (August 1852) took in black apprentices. In Orange, Jeremiah Day (August 1854), Sophia Mitchell (September 1855), and Elizabeth Mayho (February 1836) did so. In the cases of Richerson and Mayho, the apprentices were their own children.[51] These families used the apprenticeship system as a form of foster parentage for orphaned or illegitimate children subject to being bound out.[52]

These exceptions notwithstanding, the apprenticeship of one's child measured one's powerlessness in North Carolina society. Those against whom the apprenticeship system was most consistently applied were those who ranked lowest in the social hierarchy. This group included deviant white women and especially unmarried free African American women.

Although racial biases shaped the application of the apprenticeship system and the prosecution of women guilty of fornication and prostitution, lawmakers claimed that they were interested only in the economic ramifications of the directly related issue of bastardy. The state justified prosecuting parents of illegitimate infants as a means of preventing such children from becoming public charges. Given the greater economic resources of most men, it made sense to assign financial responsibility for bastards to fathers rather than mothers, and so the courts did. As early as 1714, the colony of North Carolina had required that fathers support their bastard children.[53]

Judges cultivated an image of moral neutrality in their handling of bastardy suits, claiming that their sole interest was to prevent bastards from becoming public charges. Chief Justice Nash explained in 1854 the practical goals of bastardy statutes: "The community says to the marauder, you have no right to amuse yourself at the public expense; if we can catch you we will not punish you, but will compel you to do that which every principle of honor, justice, and humanity binds you to do."[54] An unwed mother or pregnant woman was legally required to reveal the name of her bastard's father. Those who refused were fined $5 and expected to post bond for the support of their child.[55]

The burden of proving innocence was upon the accused father, who until 1851 was legally barred from citing the "bad reputation" of the bastard's mother. Chief Justice Nash explained in 1844 that allowing such allegations as proof of a man's innocence would leave bastardy almost impossible to prosecute. He added that most mothers of illegitimate children were of inferior character.[56]

Nash's assumption that a pregnant single woman automatically exhibited a weak character flowed logically from nineteenth-century beliefs about the purity and innocence of respectable white women. A woman's true character would reveal itself in her behavior, and nothing provided more irrevocable proof of an inner moral weakness than sexual misbehavior. The poverty that engulfed so many women charged with bastardy only confirmed the widely held belief that poverty signified an innate inferiority passed from one generation to the next. Although some lawmakers recognized that a lack of opportunity led poor women to act in a deviant manner, most viewed economic poverty as the outward manifestation of an inner poverty of spirit and intellect.[57] Like upper-class citizens in general, lawmakers expected poor women to misbehave in greater numbers than middle- and upper-class women. Such behavior seemed consistent with the natural order of society rather than an indication of the structural barriers of class, race, and gender that poor women faced.

Most women charged with bastardy in Granville, Montgomery, and Orange counties were, indeed, poor. Almost half of sixty-seven women so charged between 1850 and 1860 whose profiles I have constructed lived in propertyless households on the eve of the war. Most

Table 4.3. Household Composition in 1860 of Women Charged with Bastardy, 1850–1860

	Granville	Orange	Montgomery	Total
Head of household	5	12	4	21
Living in female-headed household	3	7	6	16
Living in male-headed household	5	14	8	27
Living in poorhouse	0	3	0	3
Total	13	36	18	67

Source: Bastardy Bonds, Minutes of the Wardens of the Poor, U.S. Federal Manuscript Censuses, 1860, Granville, Orange, and Montgomery counties, NCDAH.

of these households were headed by the mother or another female. Just over half of the remaining thirty-five women who lived in propertied households lived in homes headed by males. All but one of the women who lived in households with property valued at more than $500 lived in male-headed households, usually those of their father. Usually unskilled and unlikely to marry, most mothers of illegitimate children lived in or on the edge of poverty. Fully half of them lived in households containing no apparent kin other than their illegitimate children (see Tables 4.3 and 4.4).

Despite their modest resources, relatively few unwed mothers became wards of county poorhouses during the antebellum era. The courts' policy of assigning financial responsibility to the fathers of bastards perhaps kept most unwed mothers off the county charity rolls. So, too, perhaps, did the lack of personal freedom, dreary surroundings, and general degradation associated with public charity. Officials closely monitored the work habits and behavior of poorhouse inmates.

The buildings that housed paupers were at best functional, and the food and clothing supplied were predictably monotonous and plain. In 1857, inspectors of the Orange County poorhouse found the building's walls almost entirely rotted behind its brick facade. Inside,

Table 4.4. Combined Real and Personal Property Values of Households of Women Charged with Bastardy between 1850 and 1860

	0	$1–$200	$201–$500	$501 and over
Head of household	15	6	0	0
Living in female-headed household	6	5	4	1
Living in male-headed household	8	6	6	7
Living in poorhouse	3	0	0	0
Total	32	17	10	8

Source: Bastardy Bonds, Minutes of the Wardens of the Poor, U.S. Federal Manuscript Censuses, 1860, Granville, Orange, and Montgomery counties, NCDAH.

they discovered that the portion of the floor where the paupers slept had "generally mouldered into [the] earth." The diet consisted primarily of chicken or pork, corn, oats, milk, and coffee, while clothing was made from "good, substantial linsey." To enter the poorhouse represented a final loss of individual autonomy, and only those women on the brink of starvation chose the security of food and shelter over remaining in their communities.[58]

Although most women charged with bastardy were poor, this does not mean that only poor women gave birth outside of marriage. In their zeal to prevent illegitimate children from becoming charges upon county funds, court magistrates tried to force poor unmarried women to name the fathers of their children in court. The illegitimate children of wealthy women did not present the same economic burden to society. Yet, despite the courts' efforts to prosecute the fathers of poor women's bastards, many men nevertheless found ways to protect their identity or evade full financial responsibility for their illegitimate children. A common practice was to post the woman's bond and pay her fine in return for her silence. In 1857, Joel Lucas wrote a letter to Montgomery County justice of the peace John McLennan that suggested a political reward for McLennan's cooperation in keeping Mary Jane Nelson's bastardy suit out of court: "We dont want hit in cort [and] The Thing is [settled] with the woman. . . . I now want you to [do] this for me and you Shall Lose nothing By hit[.] I will Bee at Cort to morrow and expect to [hear of] you Beeing . . . Candat for Cleark."[59]

The court subsequently approved the $30 cash settlement provided for Nelson by the Lucases and ordered no further child support payments. Lucas's out-of-court settlement with Nelson prevented her from dragging his married brother through a public trial. It also considerably lowered the amount of support Willoughby Lucas had to pay for his illegitimate child. Out-of-court settlements of similarly small amounts were common in homogeneous Montgomery County.[60] That most of the women and men charged with bastardy were of the same race and class and probably came from families who had known each other for generations perhaps encouraged informal negotiations of child support.

Either out of fear or affection, many women like Mary Jane Nelson did not prosecute the fathers of their children. The married father of the child of Martha Day, a Granville County widow, promised Day a home in return for not naming him in court. He threatened her with violence when she did so anyway.[61] Mary McQuean, who kept house for Kindred and Nancy Stewart of Montgomery County, refused to name the father of her two illegitimate children, despite town gossip that the father was Kindred Stewart and the fact that Stewart posted her bond during each pregnancy.[62]

Finally, Susan Clements of Orange County protected the identity of Dr. Bartlett Durham, for whom the town of Durham was named, probably in return for financial support. Faced with entering the poorhouse upon Durham's death in 1857, Clements unsuccessfully sued his estate for support of their two illegitimate children.[63] A woman's protection of a man's identity, often in return for his private support of an illegitimate child and perhaps in hopes of continuing the relationship, was risky business. As Clements discovered, such financial support could end at any time unless it had been mandated by law.

While some white men evaded financial responsibility for illegitimate children, those who fathered black or mulatto children were rarely charged with bastardy.[64] For this reason, bastardy numbers in the records of Montgomery and Orange counties are far higher than in Granville, where many fathers of bastards may have been slaves, free blacks, or whites who wished to remain anonymous.[65] Besides, court officials could show less interest in prosecuting the parents of free black bastards because the practice of apprenticing all such children from the age of five until twenty-one considerably lessened the need for county aid.[66]

The inability of blacks to testify against whites in court further relieved the courts of prosecuting white fathers of mulatto children. Only a single bastardy case involving a free black mother and a white father reached the state supreme court in this period, and it was decided in favor of the father. In 1848, the high court ruled that free black mother Lucinda Simpson was by law "incompetent to give testimony against a white man," which the imputed father of her child happened to be. Two years after denying Simpson's suit, the state supreme court ordered William Haithcock, a free black of Orange County, to support his illegitimate child by a white woman.[67] Consistent with social custom, the courts punished blacks and women, but seldom white men, who violated the taboo against interracial sexual relations.

White men profited from their ability to bribe court officials and coerce women into silence. For a woman, the extensiveness of her family roots was the most decisive factor in how she fared in court. Montgomery County's most notorious unmarried mothers—Hannah, Rosetta, and Ann Hurley—were from an extensive and long-standing yeoman family of the community.[68] Hannah and Rosetta Hurley successfully sued their children's fathers for support when court-ordered payments were not forthcoming.[69] Although the Hurley sisters' sexual conduct may have cost them their reputations, their strong roots in the community gave them the confidence and resources to demand their legal due.

Auley McAulay, a respected small slaveholding farmer of Montgomery County, sued John Birckhead, his daughter's lover, for support of their bastard child, and he sued him for seducing his daughter. McAulay took his suit all the way to the state supreme court. At one point Birckhead demanded a trial outside of Montgomery County because of McAulay's extensive family connections. McAulay won his suit, despite proof that Mary Ann, his daughter, had consented to the affair with Birckhead. "[The] Consent of party seduced," wrote Justice Pearson, "does not bar the right of the parent in bringing damages for seduction by loss of service, nor will it serve to mitigate the offense of the seducer."[70]

In cases of seduction, the courts applied a master-servant definition to the relationship of fathers and daughters. This legal fiction allowed a father to obtain financial compensation for the loss of his daughter's "purity and innocence" and, of course, for injury to the name of a respected family like the McAulays.[71]

Poor kinless women, in contrast, received little protection against sexual exploitation. Men considered lower class women, particularly African Americans, a sexual proving ground for those too "gentlemanly" to disturb the "finer" sensibilities of higher-class women.[72] Women of loose reputation also risked blame for provoking the violence of men repulsed by their behavior. In 1851, thirty-six citizens of Halifax County petitioned Governor David Reid to pardon Lemuel Nevill and Davis Shearin, who had brutally beaten Polly Gaffin because she had committed adultery with the husband of Nevill's sister and had given birth to a mulatto baby.[73] The legal right of husbands to "chastise" wives physically encouraged a general consensus that men at large could discipline women at large—much like the attitude of white men toward African American men.[74]

Similarly, prosecutions for rape focused on the reputation of the victim as well as the evidence against the accused. Conventional nineteenth-century thought regarded rape as the theft of a woman's most prized possession—a body reserved exclusively for her future or present husband. Under these terms, protection of sexually active single women would have degraded the pure white women whom the law was designed to protect. Given the attitudes of most white southerners, it hardly occurred to them that a black woman could be raped.[75]

Neither, apparently, could an unchaste white woman. In several cases involving charges of rape of white women by slaves, women of low, debased reputation—specifically, those guilty of miscegenation—were considered unworthy of the execution of a valuable slave. In such cases, white men admitted that some white women willingly had sexual intercourse with black men—and they were of course correct—but labeled such women "base prostitutes" whether they sold their services or not.[76]

The existence of unmarried sexually active women, many of whom lived in female-headed households, provided a striking contradiction to the ideal of a woman's place as either wife, daughter, or slave within the patriarchal structure of southern society. Women who lived outside the family structure and lacked economic independence were a familiar sight in local courts, where they were summoned by judges empowered to regulate their sexual and reproductive behavior. Although apparently unburdened by paternalistic responsibilities, the state assumed the role of patriarch in governing the lives of women who lacked proper male figures of authority to control them.

Throughout the antebellum period, social leaders and lawmakers treated single, sexually active women as outlaws and outsiders. The frequent presence of deviant women in the local courts reminded all women of the price of misbehaving, and prosecution of such women probably did curb antisocial behavior to a certain extent. Thus on the eve of the Civil War, North Carolina had a well-developed, if unevenly applied, system of laws that, despite the persistent misbehavior of a small, distinct subculture of free black and white women, reinforced the structure of the white family and preserved at least the appearance of sexual separation of the races.

Five

The Struggle to Survive

The Lives of Slave, Free Black, and Poor White Women during the Civil War

The eruption of the Civil War in the spring of 1861 upset the boundaries of gender and race long sanctioned by custom and law in the South. In North Carolina, families were separated, control over slaves threatened, and local courts crippled by the sudden absence of white men whose domain of power included heading households, overseeing slaves, and serving as judges and jurors. Although it has long been an axiom among historians that the women left behind faced food shortages, increased crime, and a mounting death toll with courage and fortitude, only recently have we learned about the behavior of southern women during the war, except for those who volunteered their services to soldiers' aid societies and hospitals. Indeed, we know very little about women from the enslaved and nonslaveholding classes, although they suffered the greatest deprivation during the war.[1]

The difficulty of tracing the behavior of enslaved and poor women, who often waged a desperate struggle to survive, lies in the dangerous world that war always creates. War encourages women to "take cover" to escape victimization by warring males. During the Civil War, there was no single enemy, which increased women's traditional vulnerability to the "enemy" male. Southern women, both black and white, feared Yankees, runaway slaves, and roving bands of deserters and evaders of the Confederacy whose numbers increased steadily as the war dragged on. Since women tended to avoid the dangerous world outside their homes, evidence about poor women's struggle to survive the war is more impressionistic than quantifiable. Nevertheless, the scattered records of their wartime behavior provide snapshots of how poor women coped with the exigencies of war.

The statuses of enslaved and poor women in antebellum North Carolina left them simultaneously enemies and victims of the Confederacy—slave women because they were members of the institution that ignited the war, poor women because the war turned poverty into a desperate struggle for survival. The Confederate government served the interests of neither group of women; consequently, its efforts focused on controlling rather than eliciting popular support from them. The inability of Confederate officials to gain adequate control over its lower orders of people foreshadowed the ultimate failure of southern nationalism during the Civil War.[2]

Women, especially poor women, had long appeared in the civil and criminal courts of North Carolina, but the nature of their court appearances changed significantly during the war. Economic desperation accounted for the changing behavior of poor women. Property matters and sexual misconduct were the subjects in most summonses of women to court during the 1850s; charges of larceny were rare. From late 1861 to early 1866, however, prosecutions for the traditional female "crimes" of fornication, bastardy, and prostitution decreased, and charges of larceny, forcible entry, and rioting increased substantially (see Tables 5.1 and 5.2).

Heightened tensions between masters and slaves increased even before the Civil War as rising hopes for freedom among slaves collided with fears of the same among slaveholders. Knowledge of the northern antislavery movement was passed among slaves by the more literate or well-traveled of them. Former slave Sarah Gudger recalled that she heard rumors of coming freedom from an old slave woman

Table 5.1. Number of Women Charged with Civil and Criminal Misconduct in the Lower Courts, 1850–1860

Charges	Granville	Orange	Montgomery	Total
Prostitution	8	11	0	19
Fornication	21	43	5	69
Bastardy	33	94	42	169
Larceny	5	2	1	8

Source: Criminal Action Papers and Bastardy Bonds, Granville, Orange, and Montgomery counties, Criminal Actions Concerning Slaves and Free Persons of Color, Granville County, NCDAH.

Table 5.2. Number of Women Charged with Civil and Criminal Misconduct in the Lower Courts, 1861–1866

Charges	Granville	Orange	Montgomery	Total
Prostitution	1	4	0	5
Fornication	7	8	15	30
Bastardy	8	47	17	72
Larceny, forcible entry, rioting	20	12	11	43

Source: Criminal Action Papers and Bastardy Bonds, Granville, Orange, and Montgomery counties, Criminal Actions Concerning Slaves and Free Persons of Color, Granville County, NCDAH.

bought by her master from a Virginia slave driver. Gudger remembered that she and the other North Carolina slaves laughed at the old woman's predictions of black freedom. After freedom came, the Virginia slave had the last laugh, explained Gudger: "She say 'I tole yo' all, now yo' got no larnin', yo' got no nothin', got no home; Whut yo' gwine do? Didn't I tell yo'?' "[3]

Other former slaves recalled masters' increased abuse as the sectional crisis mounted. Fearful that slavery would someday be abolished, some masters became even more coercive and abusive in efforts to control slaves; others simply became more neglectful of "property" likely to be lost soon. Roberta Manson named three members of a slave family who she alleged froze to death because of their master's neglect. Manson further claimed that "de ole men an women dat was unable to work was neglected till dey died or wus killed by beatin' or burnin'."[4]

Another former slave similarly believed that the approaching war accounted for the behavior of the cruelest master he had ever known: "After thinking about him I have come to believe he was so mean because he felt that the war was coming; [consequently] he got harder and harder." The same former slave made special reference to the master's cruelty to slave women. "Some of the things I saw him do to women," he said, "is too low to tell." Even a master whom he described as "good" would "go to the shack and make the woman's husband sit outside while he went in to his wife." The former slave added that this master "wasn't no worse than none of the rest."[5]

The abuse of slaves was certainly not unique to this era of southern history, but the sectional crisis may well have increased its severity. In response, some slaves became more aggressive and insolent. For example, in a letter written during the Civil War to her brother in Orange County, Mag Bingham complained about the misbehavior of her slaves, especially the females. "The boys are not so insolent," she wrote, "the women are inclined to be so." She added, however, that she was better off than her neighbors, many of whose slaves had run away by late 1862.[6]

The surest way for slaves to leave behind a public record of their unruliness was to murder their masters. During the four years preceding the Civil War, two shocking murders of slave masters by their slaves occurred in Granville and Montgomery counties. A third potential murder was aborted in Orange County on Christmas Eve 1856 by five justices of the peace who learned of a planned slave insurrection on the plantation of Thomas Lynch.[7]

Slave women were principal participants in both the Granville and Montgomery murders. In Granville County, two slaves, Joe and Massey, were sentenced to hang in 1857 for the bizarre murder of wealthy planter Lewis B. Norwood. Slaves held Norwood down, then forced boiling water down his throat while holding a cloth over his mouth and nose.[8]

Granville County's superior court records offered no motives for so heinous a murder, but the memory of former slave Dave Lawson some eighty years later did. Although Lawson was a baby in 1857, the story of a murder strikingly similar to that contained in Granville's court records was passed down to him by his father. Slave legend named Lawson's own grandparents as the murderers and further claimed that the slave couple was hanged without a trial. There are discrepancies between Lawson's description of the murder and that of the court, but there are striking similarities that leave little doubt that both accounts describe the same murder. Lawson referred to the murdered master as "Drew" Norwood rather than Lewis Norwood, and his grandparents were named Cleve and 'Lissa, rather than Joe and Massey. The latter could indicate the involvement of four different slaves in the murder, two of whom made it to trial, two who didn't. Lawson correctly identified Granville County as the location of the murder, placed the time of the murder shortly before the Civil War, and described perfectly, and in more detail, the manner in which the slaves murdered Lewis Norwood.[9]

Unlike the court record, Lawson's version supplied a motive for the Norwood murder. According to his account, Lewis Norwood, "de meanes' white man de Lawd ever let breath the breaf of life," administered cruel beatings to his slaves (and wife). Lawson claimed that Norwood sold the baby of Cleve and 'Lissa and then sold 'Lissa in 1857. The murder took place on the night before 'Lissa was to depart. Lawson said that a screech owl—the "death bird" in folk beliefs—had perched on Cleve and 'Lissa's cabin before the murder and signaled that God had ordained the death of Norwood. The slaves then kidnapped Norwood, shoved a funnel into his mouth, and, soon, "water scalded its way down his throat, burnin' up his insides." Lawson claimed that Norwood approached his fate "cussin' all niggers an' Abraham Lincoln."[10]

Three years later, Clara, a Montgomery County slave woman who was a cook for the wealthy family of John E. Chambers, concluded that the persistent crowing of a hen each morning similarly ordained the death of her master. She reportedly told Sarah, another Chambers family slave, "I feel sorry for Master, he's going to die soon, didn't you hear the Hen crowing in the Black Jack every morning when he comes out?" Soon after, on May 23, 1860, neighbors found the beaten and bullet-ridden body of John E. Chambers partially hidden in a creek on his own land.[11]

To draw attention away from themselves, Chambers's slaves apparently concocted an elaborate story and description of a runaway slave from Virginia who was allegedly lurking on the premises just before the murder. Eventually, however, the slave Sarah provided evidence that led to murder indictments against five of Chambers's slaves. Clara's son Jim was convicted of the actual shooting, and she was convicted for having used her position as a house slave to obtain the bullets for him. The court sentenced both to hang.[12]

Sarah's testimony about the murder provided a clue to the slaves' motives. According to Sarah, Clara defended Jim's murder of Chambers on grounds that Jim had done "no harm, for it was life for life and she had often heard that when it was life for life it was no harm."[13] Perhaps emboldened by growing uncertainty over slavery's future, Clara and Jim, like Cleve and 'Lissa, employed religious beliefs to hasten God's retribution for the cruelty of their masters. The religious folk culture of slaves enabled endurance and resistance to slavery, but in times of stress, it may also have provided sanction for the violent overthrow of their masters. That slave women played so prominent a role in these murders underscores their vital participation in the definition and defense of their world.[14]

Although conspiratorial murders of masters by slaves remained rare in North Carolina throughout the Civil War, hearing of only one would escalate whites' fears and mistrust of slaves in their midst. Granville County slaveholder Willis Royster, an acquaintance of Lewis Norwood at the time of Norwood's murder, reportedly lived the remainder of his life gripped by fear that his slaves might likewise murder him. These fears probably increased when, shortly before Royster's death in 1863, two murders of masters by their slaves occurred during the same month in neighboring Orange County. So heightened were whites' fears and hysteria over the murders that Paul C. Cameron and Henry K. Nash—leading citizens of Orange County—and Hugh Guthrie, the county sheriff, urged Governor Zebulon Vance to authorize an early trial in order to calm white citizens and prevent a lynching of the suspected slaves.[15]

Not surprisingly, white women occasionally expressed fears of slave uprisings when they sought exemptions from the Confederate army for their sons and husbands. "Why Gov. Clark," wrote Emily Jenkins on November 11, 1861, "the negroes wile Kile ale we women and children if they take ale the men away." Yet beyond the murders recounted above, massive violence by blacks against whites did not materialize in Orange, Granville, and Montgomery counties. Sarah A. Elliot of Oxford in Granville County complained to Governor Vance on January 6, 1864, that all her household goods were destroyed during the "Negro Raid" on South Mills, but hers was the only suggestion of an organized mob of blacks raiding the homes of whites. Overall, blacks operated clandestinely when they stole from whites and as individuals or in small groups rather than in mobs.[16]

The image of black males as rapists of white women, so assiduously cultivated by white supremacists directly after the war, is also not borne out by evidence.[17] Only two cases of rape were prosecuted during the war in Orange, Montgomery, and Granville counties, and in both cases, attempted rather than actual rape was charged. Fifteen-year-old Wesley McDaniel, a free black from Montgomery County, faced being hanged in 1864 for burgling the home of Mary Boyd, an unmarried thirty-three-year-old white woman, as well as threatening and throwing rocks at her and attempting to rape her. A petition signed by many leading citizens of the county, however, won McDaniel a reprieve from the governor. The citizens, many of whom were slaveholders, claimed that Boyd had been convinced by her friends to make false charges of attempted rape.[18]

Elias, an Orange County slave convicted of trying to rape Martha Burton, a white woman, may not have been so fortunate as McDaniel. Burton testified that Elias "threw me down and held me a good while and said he intended to jump me" but was interrupted by Victoria Toler, who testified that she heard Burton hollering and came to her aid. Elias's master, Christopher Stevens, sought a reprieve from the court on condition that Elias enlist in the army. It is uncertain whether the reprieve was granted.[19]

The context in which the dominant white society viewed rape made it impossible to identify rapists and determine the number and victims of rape during the Civil War. During wartime, rapes, like prostitution and fornication, must have increased. But these crimes were viewed as the result of sexual passion or immorality and thus not directly threatening to the state, except, of course, when committed by slaves against "respectable" white women and therefore against the white men who "possessed" them as wives and daughters. The traditional view of rape as an assault on a family's and a woman's honor, rather than a violation of a woman's right to control her body, meant that prosecutions of rape cases centered around the class, race, and reputation of the female victim. The women most vulnerable to rape during the war—those unprotected by wealth or family—were those considered virtually unrapeable in the sexual lore of the Old South. A slave sentenced to hang for raping a free black woman, for example, received clemency from Governor Vance in July 1864 with no discernible public outcry, on condition that his master sell him out of the state.[20]

An extreme expression of the entrenched belief that sexually active single women invited sexual assault appeared in a Guilford County petition to Governor Henry Clark dated August 23, 1861. Petitioners requested that the governor reduce a ten-year prison sentence for rape to four months, on condition that Wesley Gray, the white assailant, join the army. Attorney John A. Gilmer and 128 other citizens pointed out not only that Gray was only fifteen years old at the time of the rape but also that the mother of the victimized young girl was "of *very bad* character and her daughter . . . [was] completely under her domination." In other words, although a small child could hardly be characterized as a lewd woman who encouraged unseemly sexual advances by men, simply being the female child of a lewd woman might incite a man to rape because no one's honor was at stake. Gray received a pardon from Governor Clark.[21]

Even when female and family honor were at stake, however, rape charges were unlikely to reach a courtroom. Deeply embedded notions of shame and honor, as well as plantation justice, encouraged private vengeance rather than public justice. Instead, the courts focused on crimes against property, such as larceny and trespass, which southern leaders regarded as more serious threats to the Confederate government.

In one form or another, attachment to a male—preferably a white one—presented the surest means of safety and survival for women during the war. Loneliness and material deprivation led some soldiers' wives to commit adultery during their husbands' absence and drove some to prostitution. Among the nine men who filed for divorce between 1866 and 1869, four sued on grounds that their wives had taken lovers while they were away in the army. Granville County's Wyatt Belvin claimed that his wife, Agnes, committed adultery soon after his departure in 1864. James M. Wells of Orange County registered a similar complaint in his petition for divorce from Nancy Jane Wells. Although Mrs. Wells had moved into her father's home after her husband left for the army, rumors of her unfaithfulness reached her husband by February 1863. By 1864, Mrs. Wells reportedly had given birth to another man's child.[22]

Another plaintiff, Willie G. Couch, returned home after a two-year absence to find that his wife was the mother of a weeks-old infant. Finally, John Bowling named four different men with whom he believed his wife, Elizabeth, had sexual intercourse. In less than a year's time, he complained to the court, "His house had been converted into a brothel."[23]

For these women, there was no return route to respectable society. Even allowing for exaggeration on the part of angry husbands determined to win their divorce suits, similar fates probably awaited some women found guilty of betraying the cardinal principle of female chastity. After committing adultery, Agnes Belvin reportedly moved to Petersburg, Virginia, where she lived with Maria Banks, a "common and notorious strumpet and owner and keeper of a house of ill-fame." She then moved to Richmond, where she took lodging in a "common whorehouse." Nancy Wells and Emma Couch were described separately by their respective husbands as having earned reputations as "common prostitutes" in their neighborhoods. Like Agnes Belvin, Elizabeth Bowling left town. John Bowling reported that she was living "an adulterous, dissolute life" in Person County.[24]

If these fates seem extreme, consider that the only truly honorable alternative for fallen women in Victorian society was suicide. Although so extreme an act may have been more the province of the upper than lower classes, an adulterous woman could expect the scorn of her neighbors. In Randolph County, the father of a young soldier whose wife had been unfaithful sent Governor Jonathan Worth a petition in 1867 containing one hundred signatures in an attempt to convince him to "repreave him [his son] of the woman he married" because the family had no money to pay for a divorce.[25]

The errant young Randolph County wife prudently fled to Missouri with her lover, opting, as did the others, to live a life of shame. The condemnation that greeted them likely convinced these women that they deserved no better. And yet one wonders if the same women would have committed adultery had the war not disrupted their recent marriages. These were young women who were probably tempted by loneliness, fear, and boredom to submit to the attentions of equally bored or unscrupulous men. Shattered personal lives were another by-product of the war.

The siphoning off of North Carolina's lifeblood—its manpower, foodstuffs, and textiles—into campaigns elsewhere also left the state's women, children, and aged vulnerable to hunger, shortages, and the predatory activities of speculators and renegades. Many women especially suffered at the hands of speculators. Distillers often turned precious grain into liquor, and unscrupulous merchants speculated in staples, driving the prices of goods to exorbitant levels. E. T. Graham of Burke County reported to Governor Clark on November 20, 1861, that "extortionists . . . in every locality" preyed upon desperately poor men and women by hiring them to "produce [goods] for the exchange of artickles, & paying them a *little sort* of no kind of a price for the produce by puting disgracefully high prices on their artickles of exchange & making the Poor believe things cannot be had *possibly* for a lower price." Complaining that "capitalists" were "defrauding the helpless" people of his county, Graham predicted that mobs would form in protest unless the Confederate government ended such speculation and extortion.[26]

In contrast to these "capitalists," so-called renegades such as deserters and runaway slaves provided some poor women a crucial lifeline of stolen food and household goods. Although Confederate leaders of North Carolina tried to curb the behavior of speculators and thieves, their inability to halt speculators contributed to an increase in the number of thieves. Poor women, unable to obtain reasonably priced goods through legitimate channels of trade, sometimes turned to illegal sources for those goods.[27]

A typical wartime thief was Mary Canaday, a white woman, who lived with her two illegitimate children in a propertyless household with eight relatives. Canaday helped her parents to rob neighbor Fanney Ivey (herself a poor woman) of a yearling, which the Canaday household butchered and ate before being brought to trial. Also typical was Sophia Day, a free African American woman who lived with her husband, Anderson Day, and Nancy Day, her mother-in-law. Sophia Day and her husband were charged in separate cases with stealing corn from wealthier members of the community.[28]

The actions of women like Mary Canaday and Sophia Day must be viewed within the context of the grim alternatives many poor women faced during the war. Like many other wartime thieves in Granville, Orange, and Montgomery counties, these women apparently had never been charged with theft before the war. Wartime scarcities, however, pushed many marginal people over the edge of poverty. Not all poor women survived. For example, a white woman and her child starved to death in Wilmington late in 1863 in the outhouse they had moved to after the woman's husband was imprisoned for criticizing the Confederacy. Stealing perhaps saved Canaday and Day from similar fates.[29]

To be free, female, and poor was to be vulnerable; to be black as well intensified the struggle to survive. The difficulties faced by free black women during the war were poignantly illustrated by Sally Scott of Wake County, who in 1863 requested enslavement of herself and her infant son to a white man of the community because, the petition read, "she is tired of being free and she finds it difficult to support herself and is desirous of having a master."[30]

Many wives of free black men had to shift for themselves after an act passed in April 1863 mandated the conscription of free black men.[31] Most free black males subsequently mustered into Confederate service served without protest or tried (usually without success) to obtain exemptions. Wilson Williams, a free black Montgomery County farmer and shoemaker, who owned one acre of land and hired himself out to support his wife and six children, applied for detail duty on grounds of family necessity. Enrolling Officer T. H. Haughton of the Seventh Congressional District supported Williams's request. "I think his family could not support itself in his absence," Haughton wrote to Chief Enrolling Officer D. C. Pearson. That Williams was married to Disey McQuean, a white woman, did not prejudice Haughton, who added, "I do not think her large family of little children should suffer on that account." Although Pearson agreed with Haughton, his superior officer vetoed both men's recommendations and ordered Williams to camp.[32]

Most applications of free blacks for exemption from Confederate service, even when sponsored by white members of the community, failed to gain the sympathy of enrolling officers at any stage of the process. Enrolling Officer Lieutenant E. R. Holt took an especially cynical view of such requests. "The principal feature in white persons making applications for free negroes," he wrote to Captain Pearson, "is that they can rent their lands [to free blacks], and get one-third of the produce."[33]

Impoverished black and white women sometimes participated in the illicit commerce in goods and services that flourished during the war. Such commerce was not new but an extension of the underground network of trade and services that had long existed among slaves, free blacks, and poor whites.[34] Many former slaves recalled vividly their integral role in this trade, which expanded during the war to include white deserters of the Confederacy. Charity Austin remembered that as a child she and other slaves stole eggs from their masters' henhouses and sold them to poor Irishmen, whom they knew "would not tell on them." In the deserter-infested lower Piedmont, the black Reverend Squire Dowd of Moore County recalled stealing for deserters during the war because "they paid us for it." Some slaves, however, feared the deserters and runaways who hid in nearby woods. "De woods wus full of runaway slaves an' Rebs who deserted de army," remembered Jane Lee of Selma, North Carolina, "so hit wus dangerous to walk out."[35]

Deserters often robbed plantations directly instead of bargaining first with slaves. Their raids provided poor women a direct source of desperately needed goods. Jane Deaton, a free black woman of Montgomery County, joined a band of deserters who robbed a wealthy planter family. Deaton was arrested in spring 1865 and charged with aiding "certain deserters in robbing the house of Archibald Campbell of a set of cups and saucers and other articles." In the same county, four white women—Elizabeth Wright, a widow with a small farm, her daughters Sarah Wright and Milly Floyd, and her daughter-in-law Nancy Wright—were indicted for receiving goods stolen from planter William Burney. A band of deserters, who included the sons and son-in-law of Elizabeth Wright, had supplied the goods to the women. Similarly, Margaret Church, a white woman, joined a band of robbers in Mitchell County and was reported wearing and selling clothes stolen from a family in the area. The war's creation of a new class of outlaws—deserters—had transformed the long-standing traffic in stolen goods into a far more volatile underground industry.[36]

One of the trade's most notorious participants was Archibald Kearsey, who embodied the type of free black most resented by white leaders. White resentment turned to fear as desperate poverty and mounting opposition to the Confederacy encouraged ever greater interaction between poor whites, free blacks, and slaves. Kearsey, a propertied member of Granville County's oldest and most stable free black community, had more resources and confidence with which to defy white authorities than did most free blacks. Sheriff William Philpott described him to Governor Vance as "the worst rogue and seducer of slaves I have ever known. He has a range from here to the extremity of the state east, as he has been trading that way for years." Furthermore, Philpott reported, Kearsey had recently broken out of jail with the aid of two white men.[37]

Slaves and deserters funneled plantation goods to whites and free blacks, who then passed the goods on to others. White authorities sought in vain to halt illegal trafficking by arresting suspected whites or harassing free blacks who seemed too independent and "high-minded" for members of their race. For example, the white leaders of Goldsboro suspected that Elizabeth Burnett's home, a popular meeting place for blacks of that city, was a center of trade in stolen goods. At the behest of city authorities, policeman Blount King went to her home to investigate. Burnett, however, did not politely defer to King's entrance into her home or appreciate his allegations. A melee broke out that ended with the officer's beating up Burnett.[38]

After the war, when Burnett pressed charges against King, more than 120 whites of the city signed a petition expressing outrage that a white policeman who had done a fine job of keeping blacks in their "proper place" would be punished by the law. The citizens called for dismissal of all charges against King, pointing out that Burnett was well-known for "rude and insulting" behavior toward whites and that in the past she had even "threatened to whip respectable people."[39] Like Archibald Kearsey, Burnett was an assertive (petitioners called it "high-tempered") free black who refused to extend the deference demanded by whites. She perhaps escalated fears among whites of what possibly lay ahead in a free society that did not explicitly subordinate blacks to whites.

The added threat of black-white cooperation among the poorer classes prompted indictments of fornication against a number of stable, previously tolerated, interracial marriages. For example, after years of marriage and six children, Matilda Leonard, a white woman, and N. J. Steward, her mulatto husband, were charged by the Orange County court in the fall of 1861 with fornication.[40]

Even more malicious were the charges of fornication against six legally and long-married couples in Montgomery County, whose marriages probably had not been considered interracial by most citizens of their community before the war. Six sons and daughters of John and Eleanor Hussey—Milly, Nelly, Sarah, Mary, Samuel, and Lindsay—although indistinguishable in appearance from whites, were descended through their father from Milly Turner, a free woman of one-eighth African ancestry. Turner had been accepted as white in her native South Carolina, where she married a white man, Samuel Hussey, and raised her son John as a white. John Hussey married

Eleanor, a white woman, and they migrated to North Carolina, where they and their children were accepted as white until the Civil War. First initiated in the fall of 1861, the fornication charges were not dropped until late 1864. Further harassment of the family is indicated by the arrest of John Hussey in 1863 for illegal possession of firearms, a charge traditionally reserved in the antebellum South for free black males.[41]

Efforts by local authorities to control potentially unruly and subversive members of their communities ultimately proved futile. Poverty, the most compelling catalyst for unruly behavior during the Civil War, increased dramatically as the war dragged on, contributing to the erosion of support for the Confederate government among usually law-abiding white farming folks.[42] In response, North Carolina editors implored white women to believe that the Civil War was being fought to preserve their safety and honor. The *Greensborough Patriot* published a poem on March 12, 1863, that included the following lines:

> Dear Woman! 'tis for you we fight—
> For you we bravely dare
> The piercing cold—the scorching heat
> The deadly shafts of war.

But the farm women of North Carolina had become increasingly inured to such rhapsodical tributes. By the time these lines appeared, food riots led by white farm women had occurred throughout the Confederacy.[43]

That most women rioters were the wives and mothers of Confederate soldiers at first brought measured sympathy from the same editors. The *Greensborough Patriot* lauded "Another Female Raid" in Johnston County as a strong message to those who speculated in staple goods. But when a mob of women soon after raided stores on the outskirts of Greensboro, *Patriot* editors declared that rioting had gone far enough. "We would fondly hope that this will be the last frolic of the kind that will be attempted," they wrote, warning that the civil courts of North Carolina would not tolerate further lawlessness.[44]

Governor Vance issued his own warning to women on April 9,

1863: "Broken laws will give you no bread, but much sorrow; and when forcible seizures have to be made to avert starvation, let it be done by your county or state agents."[45] Many white farm women took the governor's advice. Before resorting to illegal or illicit behavior, they complained to local and state authorities about their increasingly desperate plight. Primarily nonslaveholding, rural, and semiliterate, these women displayed a striking sense of themselves as "the people" and had a corresponding faith in the government as an instrument of their will. They informed their leaders of the wrongs being done to them expecting that the government would right those wrongs.

In a letter to Governor Vance in January 1863, a group of women from Forsyth County named ten men from Forsyth, Yadkin, Davidson, and Davie counties who were distilling corn into liquor. Orange County's Lydia Brassfield complained to the governor in March 1863 that she had borrowed money and walked for five days to buy corn, only to find that merchants would not accept her Confederate money. After informing Governor Vance that she had to feed three children while her husband was serving in the Confederate army, Brassfield lamented that "pore soldiers [are] . . . wading thue mud and water for our beeloved cuntry while urthers at home [are] specerlating."[46]

Similar letters from Harriet Dickey and Mary Clayton, also the wives of landless Orange County soldiers, followed in June and July,[47] but disappointment too often awaited such requests for government action. We do not know if Governor Vance responded to these women, but he did order an investigation into Martha A. Allen's complaints against the food commissioners of Orange County. A soldier's wife and the mother of three children, Allen learned from the local food commissioners in May 1863 that she could not obtain any more rations before July 13, 1863, because of the three-month waiting period between dispersals. She had already exhausted the rations that she received in April. Commissioner Jehial Atwater responded to Governor Vance's investigation by dismissing Allen's complaints: "She has herd of some women writing to you and getting help and no doubt that's the main cause of her letter." Despite Atwater's mistaken conclusion that "very little if any suffering" from extreme material deprivation existed in Orange County, almost 20 percent of white women and

35 percent of white children under the age of eight received county aid in January 1865. Clearly, overburdened county commissioners could not meet the needs of the common people as long as the Confederacy waged war.[48]

Amid increased suffering, several local women criticized the Orange County cotton mill known as Orange Factory. In separate letters written in 1863, Louena Cates and Lucinda Glenn of Durham complained to the governor that the factory's owner refused to accept Confederate money in exchange for desperately needed cotton yarn. Cates, who had six children to feed and clothe while her husband was away in the army, claimed the owner would accept only wool and cotton cloth, which she did not have, in exchange for yarn. Glenn, a spinner by trade whose husband was also in the army, asked Governor Vance to assist her in obtaining "a few bunches of cotton yarn to clothe myself and little children" because the nearby factories would not sell to her.[49]

Lackluster, sometimes hostile, responses from local and state officials shook white farm women's faith in the government. In the face of growing complaints about speculators, the *Fayetteville Observer* printed an article sympathetic to the proprietors of the Cumberland County textile factory. The article's author claimed that women sometimes lied to obtain precious yarn. He cited the case of a woman who presented herself to the factory superintendent as a soldier's wife and a mother but was recognized by the superintendent as "a single woman, with no husband or children . . . [who] *borrowed* the children to enable her to get the yarn to sell again at nearly 3 times as much as she paid for it."[50] Women, the author suggested, abused a system designed for their benefit. No doubt some women did attempt such deceptions to obtain yarn at a reasonable price, but the suggestion that ordinary women were speculating at the expense of hardworking mill owners must have enraged women like Brassfield, Glenn, and Cates.

Complaints about Orange Factory continued throughout 1863. In August, Margaret Guess and Bettie Horner informed Governor Vance that ordinary people would probably be "naked and freezing" by winter, yet the proprietors of Orange Factory sent their cotton to Hillsborough, where wealthy residents paid $18 to $20 per bunch.

Martha A. Veazey of the Knapp of Reeds community in Granville County reported in December that Orange Factory continued to demand bacon, lard, and tallow in exchange for cotton.[51]

Material hardships increasingly drove a wedge between white farm women and Confederate officials in the North Carolina Piedmont. By 1863, the impoverishment of the yeomanry had emboldened white farm women to criticize their local leaders and officials—in other words, the Confederacy itself. Although Margaret Guess and Bettie Horner had warned Governor Vance that if the army began conscripting men over the age of fifty, the "nigers will Kill all the rest," white farm women now devoted less time to expressing their fears of slaves and Yankees and more to criticizing government leaders. Indicative of the growing discontent with Confederate officials was C. W. Walker's complaint that the militia sent to her Orange County community to keep order and protect women and children were instead "ruining the poor at home." "I her you cry out to these men to stop this extortion," Walker told the governor, "when they are the men that is doing the buisness."[52]

Other poor white women took to the streets. During 1864 and 1865, mobs of women rioted in Granville, Orange, and Montgomery counties, as they did throughout the Confederacy. They directed their attacks on the two groups most obnoxious to poor people by 1864: merchants and Confederate agents. Rebecca Davis, Nancy Bowers, and Nancy Carroll—white women from propertyless households in Orange County—raided William McCown's mill in early 1864 and stole flour reserved for the government. Davis and Carroll were married and the mothers of four and six children, respectively.[53]

That same spring, Lucy and Sally Fuller, the daughters of a propertyless gardener, attacked James O. Coghill, a prosperous landowner, while he was "discharging [his] official duties." The attack was probably the same "battle of Whites Mill" that Coghill's son described in a letter to his sister Mit on March 28, 1864. The image of "two women on papa" outraged the younger Coghill, who wrote, "I would have given anything almost to have seen the frollick . . . for I am certain that fer would have flew and before I let them loose they would have known which side of thare bread was buttered . . . by the time I throwed my paws on the side of her head a time or two."[54]

Lawlessness spread, despite the younger Coghill's threats of counterforce, newspaper warnings against food riots, and numerous arrests. Poor people feared starvation more than they feared the law or, apparently, their wealthier, more powerful neighbors. In the final months of the war, a mob of ten women and three men, most of them related by kinship or marriage, descended upon the Granville County plantation of Stephen E. Dement, where they "unlawfully, violently, forcibly, and injuriously" stole one hundred pounds of picked cotton in the presence of the Dement family.[55]

Throughout the war, organized raids on grain warehouses, merchants' stores, and mills remained the province primarily of white women. African American women—and poor white women of outcast status—dared not commit acts of theft and destruction too openly in a society that already held them in the lowest esteem. The social legitimacy, if not status, enjoyed by married white farm women enabled them to direct their unruly behavior toward more openly political ends. Indeed, white farm women were central figures in the yeomanry's resistance to Confederate authority in the western Piedmont.[56] By late 1863, that resistance had erupted into an inner civil war. Included within the orbit of this inner war was Montgomery County, where women participated in such a fierce battle between the family and the Confederate state that their story must be told separately to be understood fully in terms of region, class, religion, and gender.

The free black and unmarried poor white women of North Carolina, however, were among the earliest enemies of the Confederacy, despite the mostly unorganized and clandestine nature of their lawlessness. Already impoverished, scorned, and marginalized, poor women never entertained the illusion of being "the people" or the "fair sex" for whom the Civil War was fought. Along with deserters and profiteers, they exposed the ideal of a "solid South" as a myth, and they contributed to the internal chaos that by 1863 had sapped the strength of the Confederacy.

Six

"The Women Is as Bad as the Men"

Women's Participation in the Inner Civil War

Writing on December 28, 1864, to her brother, newspaper editor Marmaduke S. Robins, Easter Robins mentioned in passing that a neighbor, Nathan York, having been denied an exemption from Confederate service, had declared that "he [would] not go [into the army] untill they come after him."[1] Such news would hardly have surprised editor Robins. By late 1864 fully two-thirds of North Carolina's enlisted soldiers were reported absent without leave. By the war's end, the state had contributed one-fourth of the Confederacy's total 103,400 deserters and one-sixth to one-seventh of the total number of men who served.[2] North Carolina had the highest number of deserters of any southern state, and the greatest concentration of these disloyal men hailed from Easter Robins's own county of Randolph. There, desertion rates over the course of the Civil War averaged 22.8 percent, compared to a state average of 12.2 percent.[3]

The ambivalence of the state's citizens and political leaders toward disunion—manifested by North Carolina's late entry into the Confederacy—has long been recognized by historians, although most have dismissed Unionist sentiment within the state as temporary and quickly dissipated by President Lincoln's call for troops to put down the insurrection at Fort Sumter, South Carolina.[4] More recent work, however, emphasizes that opposition and, later, outright disloyalty to the Confederacy were rooted in long-standing political, economic, regional, and cultural divisions among the people of North Carolina that remained strong during and after the war.[5] The inner civil war that erupted between 1863 and 1865 in the North Carolina Piedmont reflected a tension between yeoman and planter society that had long existed throughout the South. The large number of nonslaveholding farmers in North Carolina's western half, coupled with its unusual degree of ethnic and religious diversity, heightened the explosive potential of this division.[6]

The participation of women in North Carolina's inner civil war has received only scattered attention, although women altered the balance of power between Confederate and Unionist men and their behavior sharply contradicted traditional notions about the "natural" timidity and deference of their sex. Indeed, in their struggle to protect the traditional order of their communities, many North Carolina women displayed a striking level of untraditional disorderliness. They clearly preferred to join the struggle that divided community and state rather than become its victims. The intensity of the confrontation left men little choice but to welcome aggressive behavior from female kinfolk and friends. This was particularly true of disloyal men, who depended on the willingness of women to act in a manner commonly thought unrefined, even "degraded," for their sex.

An anonymous North Carolinian heralded the contribution of "bold" women to southern Unionism in the following lines of a poem sent to Governor Zebulon Vance:

> Then chiear up you Union ladies bold
> For you[r] courige must be told
> How youv withstood abuses
> When your property they'd take
> The witty ansers you would make
> That would vanish their rude forces.[7]

Women, this writer recognized, had held their own very well on the "front lines" against encroaching militia officers sent to disloyal regions of the state to arrest deserters and evaders of the Confederate army.

The necessity for many men and women to redefine gender roles temporarily during the war may have prompted a peculiar night of reveling described by Easter Robins: "You ought to have been at home last saterday nigh. . . . There came a crowd of . . . girls dressed in boys cloathes and boys dressed in girls cloathes. Linsey Leonard conducted the crowd with his bonet and rideing dress on. . . . You could have had some fun."[8] In her studies of culture and crowd behavior in early modern France, Natalie Zemon Davis has found that the ritual of sex role reversal, like that of status reversal, has long served to restore stability and order in a "world-turned-upside-down"—that is, in communities where outside forces threaten the traditional structure.[9] Viewed in this light, the "celebration" by the people of Randolph County, with its comic and festive reversal of sex roles, authorized a temporary deconstruction of rules governing gender behavior. It provided symbolic recognition—and sanction—of the extraordinary behavior required of both sexes to preserve the integrity of the community.

At least for a brief moment in history, the men and women of the North Carolina Piedmont shared a rough equality that lent power and sustenance to their endurance of the war and, for many, their resistance to the Confederacy. Although most members of either sex did not intend that equality to be anything more than a temporary expedient, women's participation in North Carolina's inner civil war proved just how far their true capabilities transcended "woman's sphere."

Ironically, the very duties ascribed to nineteenth-century women—nurturance of family and maintenance of hearth and home—lent the greatest force to women's exhibition of "manly" behavior. With anti-Confederate men forced to hide in surrounding woods, women were often the first to face the threats and demands of Confederate authorities. Their deep loyalties to husbands and sons, as well as their determination to prevent damage to and confiscation of property, prompted many women to ignore the boundaries of prescribed female behavior. A militia officer stationed in northwestern Moore

County, describing how a woman had delivered a "very hearty blow" to another officer who had shot and wounded her son, complained that "the women is [as] bad as the men down here."[10]

Such aggressive behavior was not evident among farm women during the first two years of the war, although southern women had expressed an ambivalence about the war from its inception. This ambivalence reflected the special concerns of their gender. Before early 1863, however, women typically expressed their misgivings in an imploring and deferential manner suitable to the "softer" sex. Typical of the response of the propertied classes was a letter written to the governor in 1861 by Elizabeth Flowers of Fayetteville. Defying her husband's decision to force their fifteen-year-old son into the Confederate army, Flowers pleaded with Governor John Ellis to release her son from service, explaining, "He is hardly able to shoulder a muskit. . . . Sir if you was to see him I think that you would discharge him."[11] Other women, as we have seen, played upon masculine sympathies for white women who faced starvation and potential slave revolts.

A growing conviction that conscript laws were unjust and that exemptions were unfairly granted inflamed the Piedmont and Appalachian yeomanry. Martha Coletrane of Randolph County appealed to Governor Vance to "look to the white cultivators as strictly as congress has to the slaveholders." In Montgomery County, John Beaman expressed the outrage of many farmers in the region. He warned Vance that farmers and mechanics would be forced to "revolutionize" if exemption laws were not changed and speculation curbed. "I have mad moor corn and mor wheat and more bacon than any slav holder . . . I have dun more smithin than any [black] smith in hour county," he complained, "yet I must go to fight for the see ceceders." Like scores of others, Beaman eventually deserted the army.[12]

As the war dragged on, letters from women to the governor became more numerous, less imploring, and increasingly strident. In February 1863, a self-styled group of female "regulators" from Bladen County objected to giving up sons, brothers, and husbands to a war being fought for the "big man's negros." These women complained that the war had been started without "the voice of the people." Pointing out that many people were starving, they warned Governor Vance that if he did not set limits on the price of bread, they would make "examples of all who refused to open there barn doors."[13]

Their threats were not idle. Five women convicted soon after of raiding the Bladenboro grain depot of six sacks of corn and one sack of rice were apparently from this group.[14] Farther west, exactly one month after their warning to Vance, a group of women wielding axes and hatchets demanded grain from the government depot in Salisbury. When warned by an agent that it would be useless to raid the depot, the women rushed him and left him "sitting on a log blowing like a March wind." They then rolled away ten barrels of flour.[15]

What was the source of this growing militancy on the part of white women? Some women, like those of Bladen County, expressed resentment toward the planter class. Others expressed religious doubts about a war fought to advance slavery: "Slavery is doomed to dy out; god is agoing to liberate neggars and fighting any longer is against God."[16]

By far, however, most women complained about the economic deprivation the war had caused. Most were members of the nonslaveholding yeomanry—a class traditionally dependent upon the labor of all household members for its self-sufficiency. Many of them were on the brink of starvation by 1863. A letter from three women of Wayne County demanded that Governor Vance explain how a woman could maintain a household on a soldier's pay of $11 per month. These women wrote that because of speculating merchants, they had to pay two dollars a bushel for grain and fifty cents a pound for bacon—prices well over the normal market prices of one dollar per bushel and fifteen cents per pound, respectively. In other areas, during the same year, grain was reported to be as high as six dollars, and bacon as high as seventy cents.[17] Since feeding a family of four required a minimum of three to four bushels of corn per month (substantially more if one raised one's own hogs for bacon), many farm women faced a real crisis by 1863, particularly with the additional loss of husbands' and sons' labor.[18]

The longer Confederate leaders failed to quell the mounting anguish and anger on the home front, the more desperate people became. The most notorious clash between citizens and Confederate forces occurred not in the Piedmont but in the Laurel Valley of far western Madison County. In early January 1863, a band of some fifty people from the valley raided the meager salt supply being hoarded by rebels in the county seat of Marshall. Local Confederate authorities immediately launched a hunt for the raiders and eventually executed fifteen men and boys ranging in age from thirteen to fifty-seven—without trial and without solid evidence that they had participated in the raid. During the foray, Confederate soldiers surrounded the house of Nancy Franklin, a Unionist farm wife, and slaughtered her three sons in her presence. The same soldiers reportedly whipped and tortured several women and girls of the Laurel Valley.[19]

On May 23, 1863, twelve women of the Laurel Valley petitioned Governor Vance to grant them money "on account of troops eating up all our provisions & killing our men and property and destroying the country." But despite widespread outcry against this outrage both within and outside the state, no aid was forthcoming for the women of the Laurel Valley.[20]

The tragedy that became known as the Shelton Laurel Massacre foreshadowed numerous less spectacular clashes between Confederate soldiers and Piedmont citizens during the final two years of the war. The war threatened the survival of farming families and exacerbated the deep political divisions in the region. Both in words and behavior, women vividly expressed the yeomanry's mounting opposition to North Carolina's participation in the war.

Unionism existed in varying degrees throughout the state, but by late 1862, the heart of disaffection with the Confederacy was the state's "Quaker Belt," an area encompassing much of the Piedmont but centered principally in Randolph County and surrounding portions of Davidson, Guilford, Alamance, Chatham, Moore, and Montgomery counties (see Map 2). Many factors, including partisan politics, contributed to the antisecessionist bias of this region. They included the beginnings of textile and tobacco industries dependent on free labor and tied to northern markets; a substantial class of artisans and farmers who resented competing with slave labor; and the presence of several religious groups—Quakers, Wesleyan Meth-

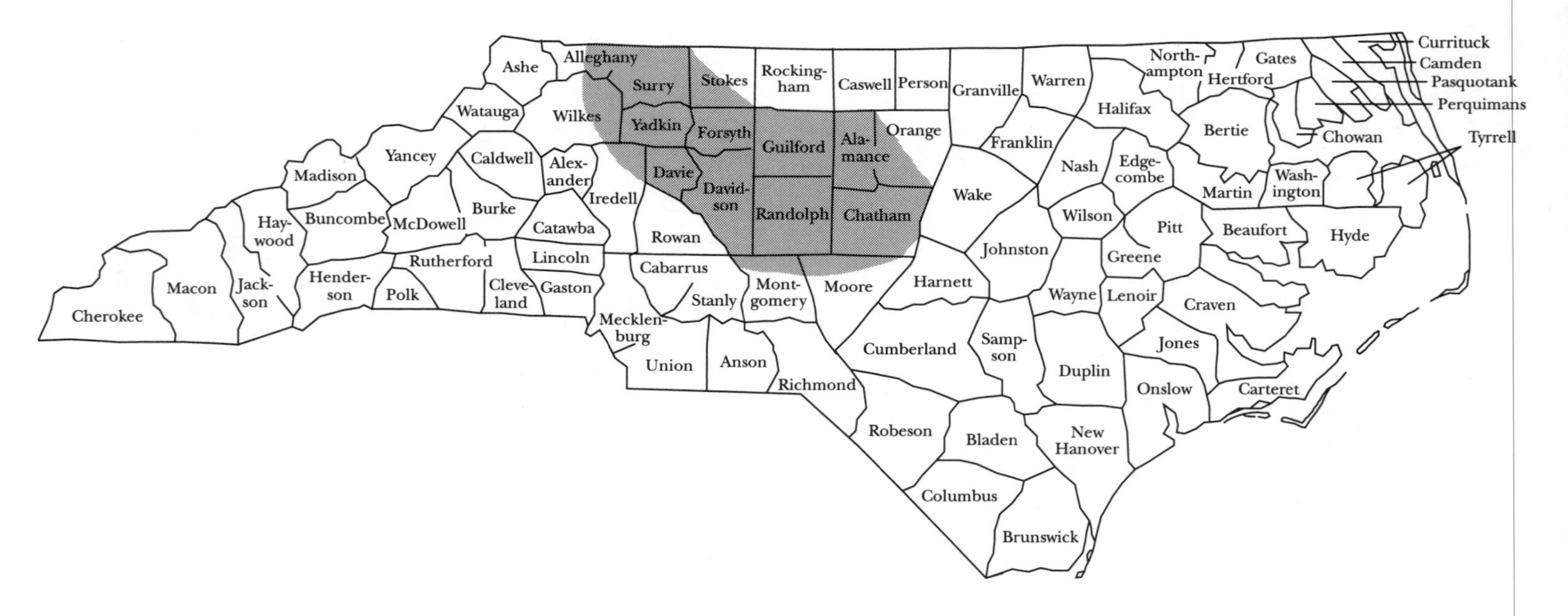

Map 2. North Carolina in 1860, Showing Principal Areas of Unionism during the Civil War

odists, and Moravians—hostile toward slavery.[21] In the lower and middle portion of the Piedmont, the relative wilderness and the absence of railroads and telegraph lines allowed residents eventually to mount the state's boldest challenge to Confederate forces. Unionist activity in this region of the Piedmont had commenced well before the war began.[22]

Northeastern Montgomery County, northwestern Moore County, and southern Randolph County constituted a hotbed of desertion, disloyalty, and persistent Unionism.[23] Like much of the Piedmont, the area was a stronghold of Whiggish Unionism and contained large numbers of Quakers and Wesleyan Methodists. In northeastern Montgomery County, a small network of families, connected through intermarriage, land, and Wesleyan beliefs (see Chart 6.1), opposed the Confederacy from the outset, as did the Quakers to the north. Most prominent among these families were the Hulins, Moores, Beamans, Hurleys, and, to a lesser extent, the Cranfords, Reynoldses, and Crooks. Not all branches of these families were equally Unionist; some were staunch defenders of the Confederacy. It was intermarriage and participation in the Wesleyan antislavery movement during the 1850s that most characterized those branches that opposed secession and war from the outset.[24]

Only a month after secession, complaints from Randolph County reached Governor Ellis about the "Abolitionist and Lincolnite among us." Likewise, Marinda Moore wrote to her mother that "there are many abolitionist in Randolph, some of which have had to leave for their large talking in favor of Lincoln. Othars keep quiet and are let alone."[25] Meanwhile, Governor Ellis received reports that approximately five hundred men in Guilford and Davidson counties had organized a secret association that opposed the forming of the Confederacy on constitutional grounds. This group was probably the Heroes of America, a pro-Union organization whose statewide membership was estimated at ten thousand at the peak of its strength. Its members were described as nonslaveholders of considerable property.[26] By late 1862, many other families in the area had joined the Wesleyans and Quakers in neighboring Randolph County in their

Chart 6.1. Wesleyan Unionist Families of Montgomery County, Showing Intermarriage of Hulins, Moores, Hurleys, and Beamans

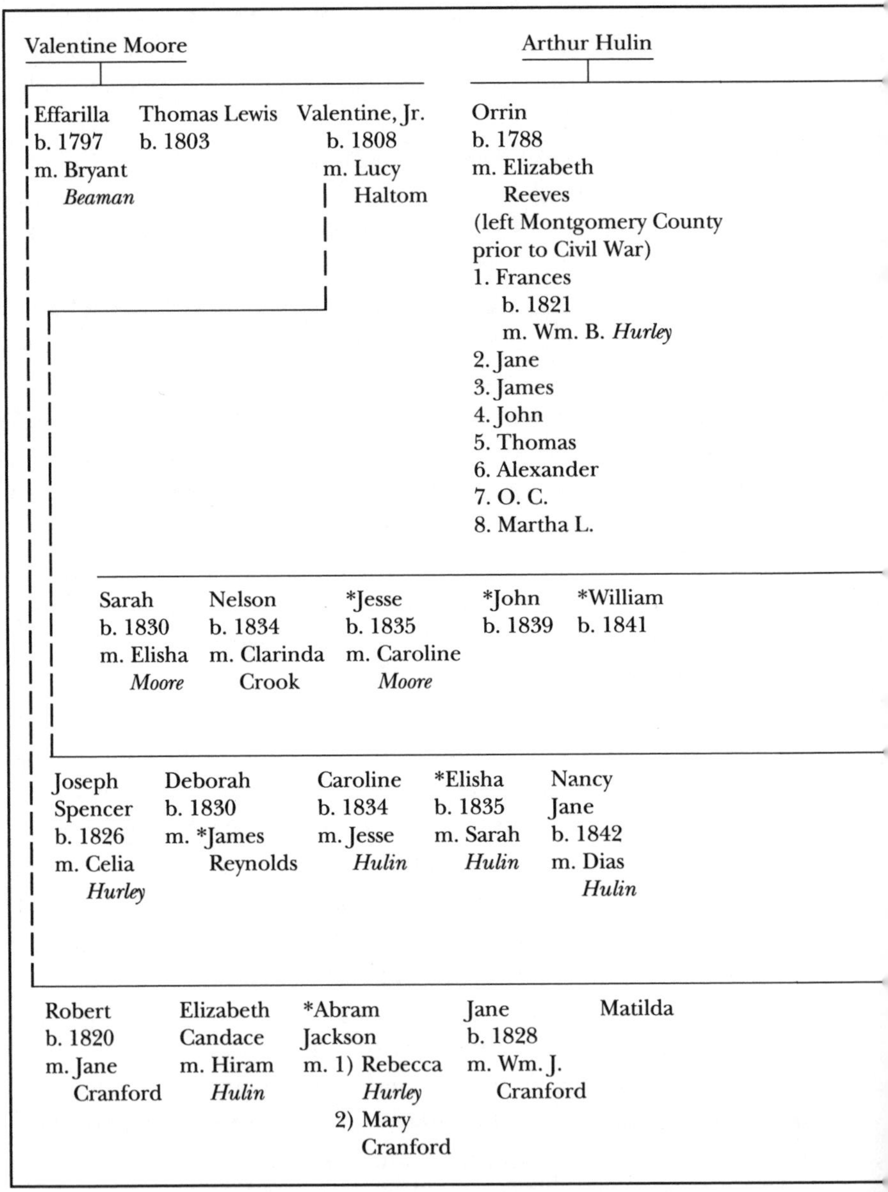

Valentine Moore

Effarilla
b. 1797
m. Bryant
Beaman

Thomas Lewis
b. 1803

Valentine, Jr.
b. 1808
m. Lucy
Haltom

Arthur Hulin

Orrin
b. 1788
m. Elizabeth
Reeves
(left Montgomery County
prior to Civil War)
1. Frances
b. 1821
m. Wm. B. *Hurley*
2. Jane
3. James
4. John
5. Thomas
6. Alexander
7. O. C.
8. Martha L.

Sarah
b. 1830
m. Elisha
Moore

Nelson
b. 1834
m. Clarinda
Crook

*Jesse
b. 1835
m. Caroline
Moore

*John
b. 1839

*William
b. 1841

Joseph
Spencer
b. 1826
m. Celia
Hurley

Deborah
b. 1830
m. *James
Reynolds

Caroline
b. 1834
m. Jesse
Hulin

*Elisha
b. 1835
m. Sarah
Hulin

Nancy
Jane
b. 1842
m. Dias
Hulin

Robert
b. 1820
m. Jane
Cranford

Elizabeth
Candace
m. Hiram
Hulin

*Abram
Jackson
m. 1) Rebecca
Hurley
2) Mary
Cranford

Jane
b. 1828
m. Wm. J.
Cranford

Matilda

Sources: U.S. Federal Manuscript Censuses, 1850, 1860; Estate Records; Marriage Bonds; Desertion Records; Adjutant General's Roll of Honor, all

Hiram
b. 1806
m. 1) Nancy
2) Elizabeth
Candace *Beaman*

Cornelius Hurley
b. 1795
m. Elizabeth Bean

William B.	*Cornelius	*Armistead	Celia	Mary
b. 1821	b. 1824	b. 1825	b. 1826	b. 1830
m. Francis *Hulin*	m. Jane Deberry	m. Mary Ann *Beaman*	m. Jos. Spencer *Moore*	

Eliza	Dias	Chana	James
b. 1844	b. 1848	b. 1852	b. 1854
m. Caswell Epps	m. Nancy *Moore*	m. Valentine *Moore*	

Lucinda	Valentine Lindsay
b. 1844	b. 1846
m. *William J. Reynolds	m. Chana *Hulin*

*John A.	Adaline
b. 1834	b. 1835
m. Malinda Cranford	

Note: Asterisks denote men who deserted or evaded the Confederate army.

for Montgomery County, NCDAH; Confederate Conscript Papers, Papers of Alexander Carey McAlister, SHC, UNC-CH.

Table 6.1. Combined Real and Personal Property of Household Heads of Fifty Deserters or Draft Evaders of Montgomery County, 1860

	Value of property			
Type of household	Under $100	$100–500	Over $500	Total
Female-headed	5	2	6	13
Headed by male other than deserter/evader	2	8	9	19
Headed by deserter/evader	5	10	3	18
Totals	12	20	18	50

Source: U.S. Federal Manuscript Census, 1860, Montgomery County.

dissent, filling the surrounding woods with deserters and evaders of the Confederate army.[27]

Of fifty Montgomery County deserters or evaders, most were between twenty-one and thirty-five years old, owned modest farmsteads, were married, and had one to three children (see Tables 6.1 and 6.2). Still, almost one-quarter of the men from this sample came from households headed by women[28]—in a county in which, on the eve of the war, women had headed little more than one-eighth of all families. Many of these men were teenagers or in their early twenties.

Obviously, these young men shouldered much of the burden of labor required on the farms or plantations of widowed and single women, although not all female-headed households were poor. In fact, almost half of the thirteen deserters and evaders from female-headed households were from families reporting substantial holdings. Still, of the twelve deserters who came from poor households—those reporting property valued at less than $100—in which the loss of able-bodied men and boys threatened the very survival of all family members, almost half were from families headed by women[29] (see Table 6.1).

Factors associated with gender, as well as class, region, and religion, affected a man's decision to desert. The traditional dependence of

Table 6.2. Number of Dependents under the Age of Eighteen in Households of Fifty Deserters or Draft Evaders in Montgomery County, 1860

	Number of dependents			
Type of household	None	One to three	Four or more	Totals
Female-headed	3	8	2	13
Headed by male other than deserter/evader	1	8	10	19
Headed by deserter/evader	5	9	4	18
Totals	9	25	16	50

Source: U.S. Federal Manuscript Census, 1860, Montgomery County.

women on male labor, the likelier poverty of unmarried or widowed women, and the greater apparent willingness among women than men to countenance desertion combined to increase desertions among female-headed families. By mid-1863, spiraling desertion rates throughout western North Carolina compelled Governor Vance to send the state militia into the most disloyal regions to assist local Home Guard units in keeping order. His action instead fueled an inner civil war that threatened the lives of women and children as well as men.[30]

Caught between his loyalties to the Confederacy and his sympathy for the plain farmers of the west, Vance, who was from the far western county of Buncombe, ultimately remained true to the former. He expressed his exasperation over the inner war in a famous statement to Confederate Secretary of War James A. Seddon on December 21, 1863: "If God Almighty had yet in store another plague—worse than all others, which he intended to have let loose on the Egyptians . . . I am sure it must have been a regiment or so of half-armed, half-disciplined Confederate cavalry!" In August 1864, however, Vance told Lieutenant Colonel Jesse Hargrave of Randolph County that "the business of your command is to arrest deserters. . . . All obstacles thrown in the way by Sympathizers & others must be removed."[31] Vance authorized the taking of all citizens, male or female, suspected of aiding or harboring deserters into military camps until their trial could be arranged or the hunt for deserters was completed.

Despite the risk of arrest, women hid and cared for deserters and draft evaders with whom they shared kinship and anti-Confederate convictions. Many of them camouflaged their aid to these men under the everyday duties of cooking, washing, and caring for other family members. Thus, while unmarried deserters often raided Confederate neighbors for food, weapons, and clothing, married deserters usually banded together in the surrounding woods and mountains and either returned home at night or relied on their wives to supply them with food and blankets and to keep their whereabouts secret.[32]

The support of wives and mothers undoubtedly made desertion more feasible for men, but it also demanded from women behavior well beyond the traditional duties of their sphere. In Montgomery County, devout Wesleyans Elisha Moore and Jesse Hulin lived in the woods surrounding their community after refusing to enlist in the Confederate army. The men were married to each other's sisters, Sarah Moore and Caroline Hulin, who traveled different routes each time they visited their husbands, taking care not to leave trails of broken twigs or overturned stones. When Elisha Moore contracted pneumonia, his wife and sister nursed him back to health by fashioning him a bed from leaves and blankets and by carrying to him special teas kept hot in iron kettles, along with the usual food.[33] Throughout the Piedmont, wives of deserters devised various methods to warn husbands not to come out of the woods: ringing cowbells, blowing whistles, or hanging out quilts that signified by color or pattern whether a deserter might safely visit his home.[34]

Some women retaliated against authorities who arrested male kinfolk. In Randolph County, Tabitha Brown and Adeline Bolin threatened to burn the premises of Captain W. R. McMasters if he did not release James and Joseph Brown. The captain ignored their threats and, that very night, unknown persons torched his barn.[35]

It was not long before state militia and Home Guard officers recognized that supportive family networks presented a formidable obstacle to arresting deserters. The widespread Unionism among families related by blood and marriage soon became an excuse among Confederate officers and soldiers for ransacking homes, knocking people about, and confiscating private property. To complaints that his men flagrantly abused citizens in lower Randolph County, Home Guard Lieutenant William A. Pugh responded: "I do not wonder at [local citizens] preferring these conscripts and deserters [to the presence of Confederate troops] as the whole section are relations."[36]

The harassment of local citizens by Home Guard and militia soldiers included efforts to coerce them into revealing the whereabouts of deserters. Gender did not protect women; rather, the duties of wife and motherhood that kept most women close to home made them easy targets for abuse. Phebe Crook, a young Montgomery County woman related by marriage to the Wesleyan Unionist Hulin family, explained to Governor Vance that militia soldiers preyed on women who were "in no fix to leav [their] homes and [on] others [who] have little suckling infants not More than 2 months old." Officers and county magistrates, reported Crook, were gathering up women suspected of harboring deserters and "Boxing their jaws and nocking them about as if they ware Bruts," in efforts to force them to confess where their menfolk were hidden.[37]

Crook probably had in mind the torture of her own kinswomen. Militia soldiers tried to extort information about the husbands of Caroline Hulin and Sarah Moore by placing the women's hands under a fence rail and then having another soldier sit on the rail.[38] A similar torture committed on the wife of William Owens, the notorious leader of a band of deserters that terrorized the lower central Piedmont, is well documented. Colonel Alfred Pike slapped Owens's wife when she cursed his men and refused to reveal her husband's whereabouts. According to Pike, his men then "tied her thumbs together behind her back & suspended her with a cord tied to her two thumbs thus fastened behind her to a limb so that her toes could just touch the ground. . . . I think [then] she told some truth, but after a while, I thought she commenced lying again & I . . . put her thumbs under a corner of the fence, [and] she soon became quiet and behaved very respectfully." To the charge that the torture of deserters' wives was inexcusable, Pike replied that he would leave the South "before I will live in a country in which I cannot treat such people in this manner."[39] The importance of a woman to her husband's (or any male's) success in evading the militia was the source of her greatest vulnerability. She was the visible partner and the guardian of children who might be abused and property that might be stolen or damaged. She also was the likeliest person to know the whereabouts of her husband or son.

Not all of the soldiers who abused Unionist women were from outside the region. Alfred Pike, for example, was a deputy sheriff from Randolph County. Many local men who had made their peace with the Confederate government served in the Home Guard to avoid military duty elsewhere and to harass personal or political enemies. Phebe Crook claimed that the men guilty of the worst abuses were "leading men of this county" who served in Home Guard units and bragged openly that they themselves would hide in the woods if ever transferred from the Home Guard into national battle.[40]

Thus, while men chose sides and went to war—either against the North or against their neighbors in nearby forests—women, children, and aged parents suffered the retaliatory assaults on property and life that accompanied both the internal and national civil wars. Women who remained loyal to the Confederacy, especially those who had lost sons or husbands to the war, often deeply resented the men who deserted and hid in the surrounding woods. Martha Jane Hogan exemplified the vulnerable position of many pro- as well as anti-Confederate women caught in the battles between local rebel and Unionist men. A soldier's wife left to tend the couple's baby and small farmstead, she shared her home with a sister widowed by the war and with the sister's two children. Angered by Governor Vance's eventual proclamation of amnesty for repentant deserters, Hogan informed the governor that the depredations of "outliers" (deserters and draft evaders who hid in the surrounding woods) made it "not worthwhile for us women to work and make corn an wheat if times don git better." As for granting amnesty to deserters, Hogan declared that if Yankees could "punish my husband [with death] you can lay the Same punish[ment] on them [deserters]."[41]

Other Confederate women expressed hatred for deserters in similar terms. For example, Miss M. M. McMasters of southeastern Randolph County recommended to editor Robins that the governor send troops to her neighborhood "that will take no prisner" and that deserters and those who harbored them should be "swung up and let hang [by their] Toenails." Jane Sugg of the same county declared that she "could nock them [deserters] in the head with a ax just as fast as they would bring them tow me and never flinch at it."[42] Though the Piedmont counties had all been overwhelmingly Unionist in their sympathies right up to North Carolina's secession, the war had torn through the communities, producing deep divisions between those who proclaimed loyalty to the Confederacy and those who did not.

Caught in the crossfire, women suffered threats of violence from deserters who turned to pillaging and looting and from "hot head seceshes" like Adam Brewer of Moore County, a self-appointed vigilante who patrolled the woods in search of deserters. Determined to crush Unionism in his community, Brewer was no respecter of gender. Three women who fled from him after preventing his capture of a seventeen-year-old suspected deserter were ordered shot but were spared by the refusal of Brewer's men to heed the command.[43]

Throughout the Piedmont, women encouraged men to desert the army, and they rioted at grain mills and government grain depots. In exasperation, the editors of the Piedmont's major Whig press, the *Greensborough Patriot*, reminded white women that the war was being fought specifically on their behalf and that acts of riot or letters imploring men to return home showed a capricious, selfish side of feminine nature that must be overcome. Any woman who encouraged a man to desert the army bore the burden of guilt for the deserter's "bloody and ignominious" death. The same editors condemned women food rioters as the unchaste female component of "the elements which wage eternal war against society . . . and against which society must wage eternal war."[44]

When not condemning female rioters as degraded and selfish, *Patriot* editors trivialized their motives by labeling them silly, uncultivated girls motivated by greed rather than want. Commenting about a raid on a Georgia textile mill, *Patriot* editors emphasized that it was not bread but calico cloth that the women seized. "Well we are sorry for the gals," the editors wrote in mocking tones, "as they still have to wear homespun or fig leaves. Can't the humane public make up a purse to buy *caliker* frocks for them?" In making a distinction between bread and cloth as "genuine needs," the editors ignored the fact that cotton thread was as hard to obtain during the war as grain and meat.[45]

Disparaging remarks notwithstanding, many female rioters were the mothers, wives, or widows of men serving or killed in the war, and most had children to clothe and feed. In Montgomery County, ten women charged with rioting "with sticks, staves, & clubs" at Sanders' Mill came from long-established yeoman families of the region, including the Hulins and Moores.[46] Although rioters were usually poorly educated, few were ignorant of the world around them. From Alamance County, rioter Nancy Mangum astutely observed that textile mill owner Edwin Holt had so successfully speculated in cloth and thread that "if this war holds on 2 years longer he [will] own all of allamance."[47]

As for the suffering that impelled women to seek the return of husbands, Lincoln County's David Schenck reasoned that even "good livers" lacked meat, sugar, coffee, and butter. He blamed disloyalty not on the desperation and sense of betrayal felt by many common people but on Chief Justice Pearson's release of deserters "on almost every pretext" and on William W. Holden for his "treason" in fomenting a peace movement within the state.[48] Since many citizens shared these sentiments, there was widespread discrimination against Piedmont families of suspected deserters. Governor Vance was compelled on several occasions to assure public millers that it was not official state policy to deny the wives of deserters access to their services, contrary to what many were told by local Confederate officials.[49]

Public rioting and illicit contact with deserters put women at risk with Confederate authorities. In March 1864, a Confederate regiment traveled to Bladensboro "to suppress a mob of low women backed by deserters who have been attempting to plunder government freight trains lately on that road." Yet by no means had all the women harassed by Confederate soldiers been disloyal or defiant before such harassment. Soldiers often made sweeping judgments based on region and class. Lieutenant Colonel Pugh justified his excessive use of force against Piedmont citizens not only because they were disloyal but also because this was a region where "few respectable people live & [where people have] little or no refinement."[50]

The actions of Confederate soldiers roused Nancy Robbins of Randolph County to respond with force. Pointing out that she was the wife of a Confederate soldier, Robbins protested Confederate soldiers' confiscation of her mules. Exasperated, she warned Lieutenant Colonel Alexander McAlister, "If you dont returne the mules I shall be out there in the Morning." Deprived of the preindustrial farmer's most important piece of equipment, she complained, "We air out of bread and [have] nothing to go to mill with; we are out of wood also and not one four[th] of [the] ground [is] plowed yet."[51] Similarly, Sarah Black of Davidson County appeared before the governor to complain that Home Guard soldiers had taken her and Priscilla Miller's chickens, wagons, and horses. In response, Home Guard Major John W. Graham complained that Black had "abused" his soldiers with "union talk" and added that those who defended Unionism or harbored deserters "are not entitled to expect that we shall observe every nicety in our dealings with them."[52]

Governor Vance expressed outrage at the actions of many soldiers against the people of western North Carolina. A native of far western Buncombe County, he understood the fierce independence and resentment of outsiders so characteristic of mountain people. He also understood that military impressment of food and livestock threatened the survival of people who even in the best of times practiced only subsistence farming. Commenting in December 1864 on the murder of two Confederate soldiers by the sons of a woman whose horses they had stolen, Vance accused General J. C. Vaugn of driving mountain citizens to desperation by allowing soldiers to commit numerous robberies and outrages against the local people. He pointed out that there had been "a general stealing of horses & [consequently] an occasional slaughter of the thief." He added, "I am frank to say that I approve of it."[53]

All the sympathy in the world, however, could not end the abuse of western citizens as long as Vance remained committed to a Confederate victory. To allow disloyalty to continue unabated would have required that he defy, not merely chastise, the Confederate government. Vance remained true to the Confederate cause, thus prompting more women to refuse to be its victims any longer. Three months before the war's end, another angry wife of a Confederate soldier threatened the sheriff of Montgomery County with a visit from local deserters if he did not deliver four bushels of grain to her doorstep. "You nasty old whelp," warned Martha Sheets, "you have told lys to get your suns out of this war and you dont care for the rest that is gone nor for ther famelyes. Now you ma[y] depend: if you dont bring that grain to my dore you will sufer, and that bad."[54] County authorities arrested Sheets, but she was eventually acquitted, perhaps because of strong community sympathy.

As the disloyal grew in numbers and boldness, efforts by state and local Confederate leaders to regain control over communities became more desperate. It seemed that no one knew whom to trust, but one thing was certain: the most outspoken Unionists in Montgomery County had long been the devoutly Wesleyan Hulin and Moore families. Long before the war, family patriarchs Hiram Hulin and Valentine Moore had expressed their antislavery views and passed those views on to their children, who intermarried. Two of Hulin's sons had deserted the Confederate army and participated in at least one raid on their Confederate neighbors. At least one of his sons (and perhaps two) refused to enlist in the army.[55]

The Hulin family became the focus for the fears, mistrust, and anger that many loyal citizens felt after having lost sons, fathers, and husbands in the war. In the month following the divisive election of 1864, mobs of Confederate neighbors and former magistrates twice ransacked the home of Hiram Hulin and his second wife, Candace Beaman Hulin. The next month, a Home Guard soldier assaulted Hulin's daughter-in-law Caroline Hulin. Harassment of the family continued until unidentified assailants captured Jesse, John, and William Hulin on January 27, 1865, tied them down in a cold basement until the following morning, and shot them to death. The worst fears of Phebe Crook, Sarah Moore, and Caroline Hulin were realized with these deaths. Crook lost three brothers-in-law; Moore lost three brothers; Hulin lost her husband.[56]

Only one week before these murders, a war-weary citizen of Randolph County had implored editor Robins to consider whether "the people, the bone and sinew of this once great country were ever ligitimately consulted upon the subject of cecession."[57] In the central Piedmont of North Carolina, the polarization and violence that accompanied the Civil War reflected a widespread belief among the yeomanry that, indeed, they had not been consulted. Within this internal schism, the behavior of farm women sprang from their traditional role as protectors of hearth and family and from their religious faiths and political beliefs. Whether Unionists or Confederates, women protected family lives and property with a fierce loyalty.

Women who rioted at grain mills or encouraged menfolk to desert the Confederate army put the needs of family and community ahead of loyalty to the state. The ideals of feminine duty so carefully inculcated in white women from birth—ironically, as a means of ensuring social stability—strengthened the convictions that underlay women's disorderly behavior. As the war increasingly threatened destruction of families, and thus the life's work of many women, some women defied the boundaries of their sphere in the struggle to preserve community autonomy.

The participation of women in the revolt of the North Carolina Piedmont reveals the importance of gender in a struggle otherwise drawn along lines of region and class. Not only did women's behavior significantly alter the balance of power between warring men, but it exposed as myth women's supposed frailty or meekness. Although the concerns that tempted a woman to place the safety of her family above all else might be determined by gender, class and community interests reinforced and politicized this primary devotion to family and propelled her to transcend the narrow limits of gender-appropriate behavior.

By waging a war to save slavery at the expense of nonslaveholders, the Confederacy lost the allegiance of many men and women of the North Carolina yeomanry. The defiance exhibited by women who rioted or harbored deserters attests to the unpopularity of a war that did not serve the interests of the overwhelming majority of its people and that ultimately could not be won without their support.

Epilogue

In keeping with the recent tendency to study history from the bottom up, historians have increasingly made "ordinary" Americans central to studies of Reconstruction. To achieve a more comprehensive history of Reconstruction, many have also turned, as Willie Lee Rose has urged, "to that inglorious kind of historical effort called local history." Local studies enable us to gauge more effectively whether a real transformation of power occurred during Reconstruction, or whether the architects of Reconstruction thwarted significant reforms. If we emphasize the dismal shortcomings of Reconstruction, we forget, as Rose further points out, that the destruction of slavery was indeed a revolution for African Americans.[1]

Eric Foner agrees that Reconstruction, despite its shortcomings, constituted a "Second American Revolution." He emphasizes that the Thirteenth, Fourteenth, and Fifteenth amendments transformed the legal status of African Americans and prompted a profound shift in the national seats of political and economic power. As James M. McPherson reminds us, although a counterrevolution "overthrew the fledgling experiment in racial equality . . . it did not fully restore the old order." McPherson stresses that slavery ended and that the Reconstruction amendments "provided the legal framework for the second Reconstruction of the 1960s."[2]

Numerous important state and local studies of Reconstruction have confirmed the sweep of this Second American Revolution, and they have also explored the counterrevolution that crippled the postwar reforms. Many scholars have broadened our understanding of Reconstruction by moving beyond the struggles of political parties to focus specifically on region, race, class, and gender. Thanks in large part to Eric Foner's masterful synthesis *Reconstruction: America's Unfinished Revolution, 1863–1877*, we now have a much firmer grasp of the complexities of the Reconstruction era.[3]

Although this study closes in 1865, postwar sketches of the six women introduced in Chapter 1 suggest the continuities and changes in the arrangements of gender, race, and class. National reconstruction and the emergence of a New South would reshape the lives of Mary Chambers, Maria Tinnen Murray, Rosetta Hurley, Susan Williford, Winnefred Tyler, and Harriet Smith. Although the abolition of slavery profoundly altered the legal framework of productive relationships and racial arrangements, it did not end the legal, political, and social subordination of women.

Harriet (Smith) personified the slave for whom the Union victory brought "nothing but freedom." After the war, she worked as a maid for her former mistress, Mary Ruffin Smith, in return for food, clothing, and shelter. In freedom as in slavery, Harriet remained estranged from her four daughters, who were fathered by the brothers of Mary Ruffin Smith. Harriet stayed in the same slave cabin while they continued to live, as they had before the war, with Mary Ruffin Smith as servants in the Big House. Lightning struck Harriet's cabin in 1872 and led to her death a few months later.[4]

As Paula Giddings and Jacqueline Jones have shown, the most immediate goal of former slave women was to find paid work, and their options were usually restricted to domestic service and fieldwork. Most former slave women did not receive property from their former masters, but Harriet's daughters were striking exceptions. They benefited from being the nieces of Mary Ruffin Smith, who oversaw their upbringing and education and provided each with a house and one hundred acres of land upon her death around 1885.[5]

The postwar fate of Winnefred Tyler, an antebellum free black, supports Loren Schweninger's argument that blacks in the Upper South who had been free before the war increased their wealth more significantly during Reconstruction than did their Lower South counterparts. It also suggests that previously free blacks perhaps fared better than former slaves. By 1870, seventy-four-year-old Tyler, who lived alone, had increased the value of her real estate to $2,180, compared to $1,500 in 1860. According to Schweninger, such gains occurred because Upper South blacks like Tyler were less economically dependent on the defeated planter class and had closer ties to former slaves. "They could more easily build on their past experiences during the postwar era," he writes, "to advance not only their own cause but the cause of freedmen as well."[6]

To advance the cause of blacks soon proved a dangerous endeavor in the Reconstruction South. By mid-1868, Tyler's kinfolk were locked in a fierce struggle against the Ku Klux Klan. On October 11, 1868, Silas Curtis, Cuffee Mayo, James Anderson, Charles Curtis, Terrell Curtis, William Tyler, and Archibald Kearsey, all of whom had been free blacks before the war, joined others to petition Governor William Holden to punish Klansmen who had committed outrages against blacks in the Tally Ho township. "God in heaven Knows we must have something," they pleaded, "otherwise we will have to give up Gen. Grant and take Seymour [for president] and if I have to do that I am going to take me a Rope and go to the woods."[7]

The Curtises who signed the petition were related not only to Tyler but to four mulatto children of Susan Williford, who was white. Williford does not appear in the public records after 1861, but her son Lunsford was among the petitioners to the governor. Lunsford had married Harriet Curtis the previous year. His participation in the battle against the Klan symbolized the converging interests of poor whites and blacks within the interracial subculture of Granville County. The petitioners framed their demands for a democratic New South in terms of class rather than strictly race. They accused the Conservative Democratic party in North Carolina of trying to "nulify the republican form of Government and place the Colored Race—and labering Class of white people—in the same possion—only wors—As they were before [the war]."[8]

Historians of postwar North Carolina have shown that a different enemy—growing landlessness—confronted the Piedmont yeomanry. Such was the case of Montgomery County's Rosetta Hurley, who headed a household that included her two sisters, Hannah and Ann

Hurley. By 1880, the Hurleys had become impoverished as they slipped into the ranks of the landless.[9]

The hardest blow to the landowning status of the Hurley sisters came from a protracted court battle with James G. Allen, one of the richest men in northeastern Montgomery County. In February 1875, Allen challenged the Hurleys' legal title to 140 of their 160 acres of land, claiming that it was rightfully his through descent from his wife's family. Rosetta Hurley obtained legal defense as a pauper and struggled in vain for more than three years to convince the court that her brother Willis had obtained legal title to the land before transferring ownership to her and her sisters. The Montgomery Superior Court ruled against the Hurleys in the fall of 1878 and gave them until January 1, 1879, to relinquish the land to Allen.[10]

By 1880, the Hurleys had lost the remaining twenty acres of their farm and lived in the nearby town of Ophir, side by side in separate households with their respective children and grandchildren. Eight of their neighbors petitioned county commissioners in 1881 and again in 1882 to grant economic aid to Hannah. "She is 66-years-old," the petitioners explained, "and has not been able to work hardley any in 4 or 5 years on account of a canser on her face and she has nothing to live on onley as she begs it." The commissioners responded by admitting Hannah to the county poorhouse.[11]

As the defeated planter class made its comeback in North Carolina through the Conservative party political coalition, it enshrined white women as the morally pure symbol of its revival. Conservative Democrat and Klan member David Schenck invoked a sentimental glorification of white women in an effort to reinstate paternalistic features of the old slave order in the new postwar setting. "Now ladies," he counseled the 1869 graduates of Lincolnton Female Seminary, "how shall we escape these pernicious influences, which are spreading like locusts and carpetbaggers among us. . . . God and Woman are our only hope!"[12]

Such moral perfection was too heavy a burden, however, for at least one woman from the old planter class. Widowed in 1869 after six years of marriage, twenty-nine-year-old Maria Tinnen Murray was still a vital woman, but she lived in a society in which war had reduced the number of men of marriageable age by 25 percent. She became involved in an illicit affair with William R. White, a married man, by whom she became pregnant in late 1872.[13]

White, fearful that public knowledge of the affair would "ruin" him, obtained from a local doctor a "poison" that would cause premature labor in pregnant women, and he persuaded Maria to take it. In a locked cellar on June 19, 1873, she gave birth three months prematurely to a dead infant. White reportedly left his work in the fields only long enough to supply her with a tub of rags. He concealed the dead infant in a pile of "strong ashes."[14]

David Schenck loathed women like Maria Murray who did not morally elevate southern society. "Nothing is more contemptible than an unworthy woman," he said. "Woman must be adored or despised. There is no middle ground for her."[15] Since such pronouncements had become standard fare by 1873 in the service of creating the Myth of the Lost Cause, Murray had no reason to expect understanding or forgiveness from her peers for having committed adultery and infanticide. She hanged herself nine days after she gave birth. The county coroner, after questioning Murray's neighbors and relatives, concluded that she had killed herself "from a sense of shame and deep disgrace brought upon herself by improper conduct."[16]

More pragmatic problems confronted plantation mistress Mary Chambers after the war as she and her husband turned immediately to the task of maintaining order and production levels on their eight-hundred-acre plantation. Like many former slaveholders in North Carolina, they negotiated work and apprenticeship contracts with their former slaves in an attempt to devise a new labor system. They found that their goals conflicted with those of former slaves. Asa Chambers blamed "a low down set of white people" in neighboring Moore County for "enticing" two black families to leave him and report the low wages he paid to the Freedmen's Bureau. He did not even consider whether the families left of their own accord. When the wife of another former slave refused to leave the Chambers plantation with her husband, however, Asa called her a "good servant" and attributed her decision to the fact that "my wife raised her."[17]

The freed woman, who had four children under the age of five, perhaps had more practical than sentimental reasons for staying with the Chambers family. As Susan Mann and Paula Giddings note, the interests of freed women and freedmen were not identical, especially in regard to the economic constraints placed upon them by white landowners. Although leaving the plantation represented hopes of personal freedom and economic opportunity for many former slaves, it might raise fears of hunger and homelessness among others, particularly mothers with small children. Asa Chambers even acknowledged this in regard to the aforementioned woman: "She says she does not want to go strolling over the World with her children and says she knows she would suffer."[18]

Convinced that they were the stewards of society, former slaveholders like Mary and Asa Chambers did not shrink from coercing their former slaves into submission. In her final will, probated in 1882, the widowed Mary Chambers displayed both authoritarian benevolence and gender awareness by leaving portions of her estate to faithful black servants. To Phillis Chambers, for example, she left a variety of household goods, some livestock, one hundred dollars, and a house on five acres of land "as long as it is kept orderly." She specified, however, that Phillis's husband, Jim Chambers, should "have no control whatever over anything I have given her." To Ben Dillamot, she left forty dollars as a reward for having cared for her husband during his final illness. She also directed that Harry Chambers, another former slave, receive fifty dollars, provided he stayed with her until his contract expired or she died. Mary Chambers's actions represented what Willie Lee Rose has described as "the old familiar mixture of exploitation and kindness."[19]

The Civil War and Reconstruction uprooted many North Carolina women and especially transformed the lives of slave women. The abolition of slavery, however, did not destroy the basic beliefs of white southerners or northerners about the place of blacks and women in the republic.[20] In coming years, the textile and tobacco factories that accompanied the commercialization of agriculture in the Piedmont absorbed many women formerly of the yeoman and poor white classes. African American women struggled to hold families together within the sharecropping system, and many took jobs in the homes of whites.[21] Especially for women who lived outside the charmed circle of southern wealth and power, the heart of their endeavor remained the same: to sustain themselves and their families in a society in which their gender, class, race, and behavior limited their resources in crucial ways.

Notes

Introduction

1. For gender analyses of the relationship between deviancy and social control, see especially Rodmell, "Men, Women and Sexuality"; D'Emilio and Freedman, *Intimate Matters*, pp. 39–52; Stansell, *City of Women*, pp. 171–92; Jowkar, "Honor and Shame"; Schur, *Labeling Women Deviant*; Ross and Rapp, "Sex and Society"; Wyatt-Brown, *Southern Honor*; Walkowitz, *Prostitution and Victorian Society*; Smart and Smart, eds., *Women, Sexuality, and Social Control*; Fox, "Nice Girl"; Douglas, *Purity and Danger*.

2. See Kerber, "Separate Spheres."

3. Hindus, *Prison and Plantation*; Tushnet, *American Law of Slavery*; Ayers, *Vengeance and Justice*. For a study of nineteenth-century law that analyzes gender, see Bardaglio, "An Outrage upon Nature." On slave law in Virginia, see Schwarz, *Twice Condemned*.

4. Grossberg, *Governing the Hearth*, p. 300. For evidence that women made gains in property rights under this judicial patriarchy, see Salmon, *Women and the Law of Property*; and Lebsock, *Free Women of Petersburg*.

5. Rose, *In Slavery and Freedom*, p. 98; Brittan and Maynard, *Sexism, Racism, and Oppression*, p. 212. For an excellent discussion of the need to redefine power from the perspective of the oppressed, see hooks, *Feminist Theory*, p. 83. See also Collins, *Black Feminist Thought*, p. 230; and Lerner, "Reconceptualizing Differences among Women."

6. Gordon, "What's New in Women's History" and *Heroes of Their Own Lives*.

7. Genovese, *Roll, Jordan, Roll*; Blassingame, *Slave Community*; Gutman, *Black Family*; Levine, *Black Culture*; Escott, *Slavery Remembered*; Du Bois, *Souls of Black Folk*. See Harris, "Flowering of Afro-American History," for a fuller treatment of the earliest historiography of slavery.

8. Wyatt-Brown, *Southern Honor*, provides a full treatment of the southern system of honor. See also Ayers, *Vengeance and Justice*, pp. 9–33; and Genovese, *Roll, Jordan, Roll*, passim.

9. For different interpretations of southern paternalism, see especially Genovese, *Roll, Jordan, Roll*; Gutman, *Black Family*; and Faust, *Sacred Circle*. See Tushnet, *American Law of Slavery*, for a discussion of southern law, slavery, and paternalism.

10. See especially Blassingame, *Slave Community*; Davis, "Reflections on the Black Woman's Role in the Community of Slaves"; Gutman, *Black Family*; Escott, *Slavery Remembered*; Jones, *Labor of Love*; Rawick, *From Sundown to Sunup*; Levine, *Black Culture*; White, *Ar'n't I a Woman?*; Farnham, "Sapphire?"; Joyner, *Down by the Riverside*; Stuckey, *Slave Culture*. Many scholars have come under fire for having exaggerated the degree of autonomy in the nineteenth-century slave community. See, for example, Kolchin, "Reevaluating the Antebellum Slave Community." For a recent, more critical assessment of the impact of slavery on black males, see Wyatt-Brown, "Mask of Obedience."

11. Aptheker, *Woman's Legacy*; Davis, *Women, Race, and Class*; hooks, *Ain't I a Woman?*; Giddings, *When and Where I Enter*; White, *Ar'n't I a Woman?*; Jones, *Labor of Love*; Fox-Genovese, *Within the Plantation Household*. For a pioneer work on race and gender in the slave community, see Davis, "Reflections on the Black Woman's Role in the Community of Slaves."

12. Davis, "Reflections on the Black Woman's Role in the Community of Slaves," p. 9; Giddings, *When and Where I Enter*, pp. 33–55; White, *Ar'n't I a Woman?*, pp. 77–80, 27–61; Fox-Genovese, "Strategies and Forms of Resistance," pp. 157–59. See also Fox-Genovese, *Within the Plantation Household*, pp. 291–92.

13. Davis, "The Role of the Black Woman in the Community of Slaves," pp. 12–13. See also hooks, *Ain't I a Woman?*, p. 29. For graphic representations of the sexual oppression of black women, see Jacobs, *Incidents in the Life of a Slave Girl*; and Murray, *Proud Shoes*. On rape and miscegenation in the antebellum South, see Clinton, "Southern Dishonor."

14. On racism in the North, see especially Litwack, *North of Slavery*; and White, "'We Dwell in Safety and Pursue Our Honest Callings.'" For a discussion of northern sexism and racism, see Berthoff, "Conventional Mentality"; and Dudden, *Serving Women*, pp. 32–35.

15. Franklin, *Free Negro in North Carolina*, pp. 56–57. The most comprehensive treatment of southern free blacks is Berlin, *Slaves without Masters*. See also Fields, *Slavery and Freedom on the Middle Ground*, pp. 63–89; Burton, *In My Father's House*, pp. 202–24; Schweninger, "Prosperous Blacks in the South."

16. Lebsock, *Free Women of Petersburg*, pp. 88–103. On free black women as property owners, see also Schweninger, "Property-Owning Free African-American Women"; and Franklin, *Free Negro in North Carolina*, pp. 228–29.

17. Fields, *Slavery and Freedom on the Middle Ground*, p. 88. See also Watson, *Jacksonian Politics*, pp. 43–44; and Burton, *In My Father's House*, pp. 47–57.

18. Long, *Son of Carolina*, p. 47. On upper-class perceptions of poor whites, see Ash, "Poor Whites in the Occupied South"; Wyatt-Brown, *Southern Honor*, p. 46. Evidence that many slaves held poor whites and free blacks in contempt is scattered throughout the WPA ex-slave narratives in Rawick, ed., *American Slave*. See also Blassingame, *Slave Community*, pp. 276, 306–7.

19. Olmsted, *Journey in the Seaboard Slave States*, p. 276. James H. Hammond, a South Carolina slaveholder, also remarked that "somehow—God forgive—I could never bear poor girls. When pretty and pure spirited I pitied but nevertheless avoided them" (quoted in Wyatt-Brown, *Southern Honor*, p. 200). Johnson, *Antebellum North Carolina*, p. 246, notes that poor white women in North Carolina refused almost all but domestic work, despite low wages, because of the disgrace of public work.

20. Johnson, *Antebellum North Carolina*, p. 238. For a fuller treatment of the role of yeoman women in the southern household economy, see McCurry, "Defense of Their World."

21. Dublin, *Women at Work*; Stansell, *City of Women*, p. 100. In contrast, the employment of white women in the antebellum cotton mills of the North Carolina Piedmont apparently did not enhance the status of working white women. See Watson, *Jacksonian Politics*, pp. 43–44; Johnson, *Antebellum North Carolina*, p. 247; and Kenzer, *Kinship and Neighborhood*, p. 30.

22. Carlton, "Revolution from Above"; Escott, *Many Excellent People*; O'Brien, *Legal Fraternity*; Johnson, *Antebellum North Carolina*; Calhoon, *Religion and the American Revolution in North Carolina*. Many southern agricultural presses also extolled the virtues of the busy farm wife. See Bardolph, "North Carolina Farm Journal"; and Hagler, "Ideal Woman in the Antebellum South."

23. Welter, "Cult of True Womanhood"; Friedman, *Enclosed Garden*; Fox-Genovese, *Within the Plantation Household*, pp. 43–44.

24. See especially Welter, "Cult of True Womanhood"; Smith-Rosenberg, "Female World of Love and Ritual"; Cott, *Bonds of Womanhood*; Sklar, *Catharine Beecher*; Epstein, *Politics of Domesticity*; Ryan, *Cradle of the Middle Class*. On the southern cult of ladyhood, see Taylor, *Cavalier and Yankee*, pp. 145–76; Scott, *Southern Lady*; Clinton, *Plantation Mistress*; Fox-Genovese, *Within the Plantation Household*.

25. Scott, *Southern Lady*; Clinton, *Plantation Mistress*. For Fox-Genovese's analysis of the shaping of gender in slaveholding and nonslaveholding households, see *Within the Plantation Household*, pp. 38–99. Stephanie McCurry's "Defense of Their World" also finds that yeoman and planter households in South Carolina were governed by similar principles.

26. Quoted in Faust, ed., *Ideology of Slavery*, p. 78. See Douglas, *Purity and Danger*, for an analysis of the connections between systems of honor and

sexual purity. For effects of the Jezebel stereotype on black women, see White, *Ar'n't I a Woman?*, pp. 30–46; Jones, "'My Mother Was Much of a Woman'"; Jennings, "'Us Colored Women Had to Go through a Plenty.'"

27. D'Emilio and Freedman, *Intimate Matters*, p. xvii.

28. Fox-Genovese, "Strategies and Forms of Resistance," p. 144.

29. On women's marginality, see Smith-Rosenberg, *Disorderly Conduct*. For works that illuminate how race, class, and gender converge to create diverse forms of marginality, see especially Moraga and Anzaldua, *This Bridge Called My Back*; Anzaldua, *Making Face, Making Soul*; hooks, *Feminist Theory*; and Newton, Ryan, and Walkowitz, eds., *Sex and Class in Women's History*.

30. On women and the Confederate home front, see especially Faust, "Altars of Sacrifice"; Rable, *Civil Wars*; Bynum, "'War within a War.'" On class conflict within the Confederacy, see Ash, "Poor Whites in the Occupied South"; Bailey, *Class and Tennessee's Confederate Generation*; Escott, *Many Excellent People*; Auman, "Neighbor against Neighbor"; Paludan, *Victims*.

31. In 1860, women headed sixteen of eighty propertied free black households in Granville County; their per capita wealth was $262, compared to $400 for their male counterparts. Women headed five of twenty-three such households in Orange, where their per capita wealth was $435, compared to $777 for males. Montgomery County had no free black female-headed households (U.S. Federal Manuscript Censuses, 1860, Granville, Orange, and Montgomery counties; Franklin, *Free Negro in North Carolina*, pp. 230–33).

Lebsock, *Free Women of Petersburg*, pp. 100–104, finds that free black women in Petersburg, Virginia, headed over one-half of free black households and claimed just under one-half of free black wealth in 1860. Burton, *In My Father's House*, p. 215, shows that free black women in Edgefield, South Carolina, controlled 82 percent of the real and personal wealth of the free black population in 1860.

Chapter 1

1. Sitterson, *Secession Movement*, p. 1.

2. Johnson, *Antebellum North Carolina*, pp. 59–67.

3. Marriage Bonds, Granville County, North Carolina Department of Archives and History, Raleigh, N.C. (hereafter cited as NCDAH); U.S. Federal Manuscript Census, 1860, Montgomery County; U.S. Federal Manuscript Slave Schedule, 1860, Montgomery County; Tax List, 1851, Montgomery County, NCDAH; Inventory of Estate of Mary A. Chambers, 1882, Estate Records, Montgomery County, NCDAH.

4. U.S. Federal Manuscript Censuses, 1850, 1860, Orange County; U.S. Federal Manuscript Census, Slave Schedule, 1860, Orange County; Wills of

John Walker and David Tinnen, 1844, 1851, Wills, Orange County, NCDAH; Marriage of Maria F. Tinnen and William B. Murray, July 26, 1863, Marriage Bonds, Orange County, NCDAH. That William Murray may have been an older friend of the family is suggested by his designation by John Walker in 1844 as one of four men authorized to appraise the worth of Walker's slaves. Murray also may have been previously married to Elizabeth Reeves. In his will of 1869, he refers to his "sons and daughters"; he and Maria, however, had only one son and one daughter. See marriage of William Murray and Elizabeth Reeves, January 9, 1840, Marriage Bonds, Orange County, NCDAH; and Wills of William Murray, Maria F. Murray, 1869, 1872, Wills, Orange County, NCDAH.

5. U.S. Federal Manuscript Censuses, 1850, 1860, Montgomery County.

6. U.S. Federal Manuscript Censuses, 1850, 1860, Granville County, NCDAH; Apprenticeship Bonds, Granville County, NCDAH. Williford's birth date and illegitimate status are recorded on her apprenticeship bond, November 1822. The illegitimate births and apprenticeships of her children are recorded in the Bastardy Bonds, 1836–49, and Apprenticeship Bonds, 1850–61, Granville County, NCDAH.

7. U.S. Federal Manuscript Census, 1860, Granville County; Marriage of Lemuel Tyler and Winnefred Anderson, 1811, Marriage Bonds, Granville County, NCDAH. The earliest free black Andersons that I found were George and Lewis, who were listed as Granville County taxpayers in 1755. See Ratcliff, comp., *North Carolina Taxpayers*, p. 5.

8. Murray, *Proud Shoes*, pp. 33–48. For an analysis of Murray's book, see Clinton, "Caught in the Web of the Big House."

9. Watson, *Jacksonian Politics*, pp. 59, 70, 318.

10. Kruman, *Parties and Politics in North Carolina*, pp. 222–70; Butts, "Irrepressible Conflict." Many fine studies of the southern yeomanry and the potential for conflict with the planter class have been published in recent years. See especially Watson, *Jacksonian Politics*; Hahn, *Roots of Southern Populism*; Bailey, *Class and Tennessee's Confederate Generation*; Escott, *Many Excellent People*; Harris, *Plain Folk and Gentry in a Slave Society*; and O'Brien, *Legal Fraternity*. The issues addressed in these monographs were anticipated by Genovese, "Yeoman Farmers in a Slaveholders' Democracy"; Goodman, "White over White"; and Bardaglio, "Power and Ideology in the Slave South."

11. On republican womanhood, see especially Kerber, *Women of the Republic*; and Norton, *Liberty's Daughters*.

12. Escott and Crow, "Social Order and Violent Disorder," pp. 378–79.

13. Escott, *Many Excellent People*, pp. 4–9; Watson, "'Old Rip' and a New Era," pp. 217–40. On the limited breadth of entrepreneurial experience among antebellum Piedmont planters, see Carlton, "Revolution from Above," pp. 458–59. For other studies that highlight the regional diversity of North

Carolina in regard to the organization and economic structure of slavery, see Phifer, "Slavery in Microcosm," pp. 77–79; and Inscoe, *Mountain Masters*.

14. O'Brien, *Legal Fraternity*, pp. 139, 145.

15. Johnson, *Antebellum North Carolina*, p. 67; Bardolph, "North Carolina Farm Journal"; Hagler, "Ideal Woman in the Antebellum South."

16. Lefler and Newsome, *North Carolina*, p. 19; Johnson, *Antebellum North Carolina*, pp. 4–13. For a history of Orange County, see Kenzer, *Kinship and Neighborhood*; and Blackwelder, *Age of Orange*, pp. 1–10.

17. Johnson, *Antebellum North Carolina*, pp. 343–58. For an in-depth discussion of Quakers in antebellum North Carolina, see Weeks, *Southern Quakers and Slavery*. For a survey of the expansion of religion throughout North Carolina, see Johnson, *Antebellum North Carolina*, pp. 331–434. On the religious diversity of the Piedmont, see Ainsley and Florin, "North Carolina Piedmont."

18. Wright, *Political Economy of the Cotton South*, pp. 43–47.

19. Escott and Crow, "Social Order and Violent Disorder," p. 374.

20. Olmsted, *Journey through the Back Country*, pp. 178–80, 203, 259, 265, 269–70.

21. Cox, "Freedom during the Frémont Campaign," p. 382; Sitterson, *The Secession Movement*, pp. 104–5.

22. Crooks, *Life of Reverend Adam Crooks*, p. 92. On Hurley's antislavery sentiments, see also Richter, ed., *Heritage of Montgomery County*, pp. 248–50.

23. Quoted in Olmsted, *Journey through the Back Country*, p. 259.

24. Crooks, *Life of Reverend Adam Crooks*, p. 44; Nicholson, *Wesleyan Methodism in the South*, pp. 24–38; *True Wesleyan*, June 1, August 17, October 19, October 26, 1850. McBride regarded North Carolina Quakers and Wesleyans as "co-laborers" in the struggle against slavery. See *True Wesleyan*, May 25, 1850.

25. Auman, "Neighbor against Neighbor," p. 62.

26. *True Wesleyan*, February 8, March 8, 1851.

27. U.S. Federal Manuscript Census, 1860, Montgomery County.

28. *True Wesleyan*, March 8, 1851; Nicholson, *Wesleyan Methodism in the South*, pp. 21–22.

29. Crooks, *Life of Reverend Adam Crooks*, pp. 76–100; Nicholson, *Wesleyan Methodism in the South*, p. 34. The strength of Whig Unionism in Montgomery County is demonstrated by Unionist Alfred Dockery's easy victory over Democrat G. W. Caldwell in the congressional election of the Third District in 1851. "We did our duty," commented an unnamed county official to newspaper editor E. J. Hale, "and gave Secession a death blow" (*Fayetteville Observer*, August 19, 1851). As late as April 3, 1861, citizens of Montgomery County met and declared that they were "devotedly attached to the Union and op-

posed to secession, and will support for a seat in Congress any fit man who is a Union man, irrespective of his former party association" (ibid., April 8, 1861).

30. Letter of William W. Crane, March 20, 1850, in *True Wesleyan*, May 11, 1850. Crane added that slavery destroyed the sanctity of the "family relation," because "to degrade or destroy woman's natural position & chastity was for man to break the chain of order."

31. Mathews, *Religion in the Old South*, pp. 101–2.

32. For more information on the antislavery activities of Delphina Mendenhall and other Quaker women, see Hilty, "North Carolina Quakers and Slavery." See also Weeks, *Southern Quakers and Slavery*, pp. 103–6, 119, 139, 233–83. On the trial of Crooks and McBride, see the *True Wesleyan*, November 9, 1850; Nicholson, *Wesleyan Methodism in the South*, pp. 48–52; and Crooks, *Life of Reverend Adam Crooks*, pp. 57–66.

33. Crooks, *Life of Reverend Adam Crooks*, p. 100; Nicholson, *Wesleyan Methodism in the South*, p. 68; *True Wesleyan*, September 13, 1851. The marriage bond of Jesse Hulin and Caroline Moore is dated December 24, 1855 (Marriage Bonds, Montgomery County, NCDAH). Genealogies for Montgomery County were compiled from Marriage Bonds, Estate Records, Wills, and U.S. Federal Manuscript Censuses of Montgomery County and from Richter, ed., *Heritage of Montgomery County*, passim. On the extensive intermarriage between yeomen as well as planter families, see Wyatt-Brown, *Southern Honor*, pp. 220–21.

34. Editors of the *Fayetteville Observer* quoted the denunciation of the Wesleyan movement by the *Greensborough Patriot* on October 8, 1850. They printed their own denunciations on June 24 and July 1, 1851.

35. W. H. Newman to Governor Reid, August 12, 1851, Governors' Papers, Reid, NCDAH.

36. U.S. Federal Manuscript Census, 1860, Orange County.

37. U.S. Bureau of the Census, *Population of the United States in 1860*; *Agriculture of the United States in 1860*.

38. U.S. Federal Manuscript Census, 1860, Orange County.

39. U.S. Federal Manuscript Censuses, 1860, Granville, Orange, and Montgomery counties; Franklin, *Free Negro in North Carolina*, p. 159.

40. U.S. Bureau of the Census, *Population of the United States in 1860*; *Agriculture in the United States in 1860*.

41. Kenzer, *Kinship and Neighborhood*, p. 30; U.S. Federal Manuscript Census, 1860, Orange County.

42. Jo. Jno. Davis to Bettie [Hargrove], August 29, 1848, Elizabeth R. Hargrove Papers, Special Collections Department, Duke University; Battle, *Memories of an Old-Time Tar Heel*, p. 73. For a partial biography of Dr. James Strudwick Smith, see Murray, *Proud Shoes*, pp. 33–54.

43. Boyd, *Story of Durham*, pp. 1–32; Kenzer, *Kinship and Neighborhood*, p. 33; Blackwelder, *Age of Orange*, p. 7.

44. Alexander Fleming to M. B. Fleming, June 22, 1848 (or 1849), M. B. Fleming Papers, Special Collections Department, Duke University; Davis to Bettie [Hargrove], August 29, 1848, Hargrove Papers.

45. Peter D. Swaim, Esq., to Benjamin P. Elliot, February 22, 1841, Benjamin P. Elliot Papers, Special Collections Department, Duke University.

46. U.S. Bureau of the Census, *Population of the United States in 1860*; *Agriculture of the United States in 1860*.

47. Kenzer, *Kinship and Neighborhood*, pp. 9–10; U.S. Federal Manuscript Census, 1860, Orange County.

48. Bynum, "'War within a War'"; Paludan, *Victims*; Auman, "Neighbor against Neighbor"; Auman and Scarboro, "Heroes of America in Civil War North Carolina."

Chapter 2

1. Gass, "A Felicitous Life."

2. Diary entry, June 30, 1869, David Schenck Books, Southern Historical Collection, Library of North Carolina at Chapel Hill (hereafter cited as SHC, UNC-CH). Despite Schenck's romantic image of slave women's suckling the infants of white women, this practice was not as common as he suggests. See McMillen, *Motherhood in the Old South*, pp. 111–12.

3. White, *Ar'n't I a Woman?*, pp. 27–61.

4. Rawick, ed., *American Slave*, 14:pt. 1, p. 139; Jacobs, *Incidents in the Life of a Slave Girl*, p. 35. Sophronia Horner to James Horner, August 18, 1861, James H. Horner Letters and Papers, Special Collections Department, Duke University. For a vivid account of growing up in slavery as the offspring of a white master, see Murray, *Proud Shoes*.

5. *Culbreath* v. *Culbreath*, 1850, Granville County Divorce Records, NCDAH. For other examples of husbands' flaunting their exploitation of slave women before their wives, see Jones, *Labor of Love*, pp. 26–27.

6. White, *Ar'n't I a Woman?*, pp. 35, 41; Jones, *Labor of Love*, p. 27; Jacobs, *Incidents in the Life of a Slave Girl*, pp. 27–36; Clinton, "Southern Dishonor," p. 64.

7. *Satterwhite* v. *Satterwhite*, September 1871, Divorce Records, Granville County, NCDAH.

8. Ibid. Martha Satterwhite died in 1873.

9. Jacobs, *Incidents in the Life of a Slave Girl*, pp. 27–28, 33–34.

10. Murray, *Proud Shoes*, pp. 45–54.

11. Rawick, ed., *American Slave*, 18:51; White, *Ar'n't I a Woman?*, p. 38.

12. Rawick, ed., *American Slave*, 14:pt. 1, p. 220.

13. White, *Ar'n't I a Woman?*, pp. 27–61.

14. *Fayetteville Observer*, March 6, 1849; Criminal Action Papers, June 3, 1847, Orange County, NCDAH.

15. John H. Cook to Governor Reid, April 22, 1854; John M. Kirkland to Governor Reid, April 23, 1854, both in Governors' Papers, Reid, NCDAH.

16. White, *Ar'n't I a Woman?*, pp. 62–90; Fox-Genovese, "Strategies and Forms of Resistance," pp. 143–65; Fox-Genovese, *Within the Plantation Household*, pp. 303–33.

17. *State* v. *Hannah, a Slave*, March 1836, Criminal Actions Concerning Slaves and Free Persons of Color, Granville County, NCDAH; Lovejoy, "Fugitive Slaves," p. 73.

18. Criminal Actions Concerning Slaves and Free Persons of Color, Fall 1843, Granville County; Criminal Action Papers, March 1845, June 1846, January 1853, Orange County, all in NCDAH.

19. Minutes of the Wardens of the Poor, Orange County, NCDAH. See Criminal Action Papers, 1840–60, Granville, Orange, and Montgomery counties, NCDAH, for many other examples of slaves who were charged with behaving as if they were free.

20. *Lucas* v. *Nichols*, Spring 1858–Fall 1859, Superior Court of Montgomery County, North Carolina, Civil Action Papers, 1859–62, NCDAH; *Lucas* v. *Nichols*, 52 N.C. 50 (1859).

21. *Lucas* v. *Nichols*, 52 N.C. 50 (1859).

22. *McBrayer* v. *Hill*, 52 N.C. 102 (1843).

23. For evidence of the troubled social and financial status of Joel Lucas, the plaintiff's father, see Civil Action Papers, June 20, 1855, August 1855, and February 26, 1856, Montgomery County, NCDAH. I determined Candace Lucas's age by using the U.S. Federal Manuscript Censuses, 1850, 1860, Montgomery County.

24. Civil Action Papers, 1854–56, 1857–59, Montgomery County, NCDAH; Bastardy Bond of Willoughby Lucas, May 13, 1857; Letter of Joel Lucas to Justice of the Peace John McLennan, July 6, 1857, both in Bastardy Bonds of Montgomery County, NCDAH.

25. U.S. Federal Manuscript Census, 1860, Montgomery County; *Lucas* v. *Nichols*, Civil Action Papers, 1859–62, Montgomery County, NCDAH.

26. *Lucas* v. *Nichols*, Civil Action Papers, 1859–62, Montgomery County, NCDAH.

27. *Haltom* v. *Lucas*, Civil Action Papers, Fall 1860, Montgomery County, NCDAH. After Joel Lucas declared himself financially insolvent on January 18, 1861, Thomas C. Haltom sued Lucas's security, son Fincher Lucas, for

payment of debts owed him (Civil Action Papers, April 1862, Montgomery County, NCDAH).

28. Throughout her suit, Candace Lucas regularly objected to the court's pronouncements in favor of Nichols. She pursued her case for almost two years (*Lucas* v. *Nichols*, 1859–62, Civil Action Papers, NCDAH; *Lucas* v. *Nichols*, 52 N.C. 50 [1859]). On the relationship between personal reputation and the credibility of one's courtroom testimony, see Friedman, *History of American Law*, p. 347, and Wyatt-Brown, *Southern Honor*, p. 364.

29. *McBrayer* v. *Hill*, 26 N.C. 102 (1843).

30. Clinton, *Plantation Mistress*, p. 85; Wyatt-Brown, *Southern Honor*, p. 229. For contemporary views on marriage, see "A Plea for Marriage," reprinted from Dr. Hall's *Journal of Health*, in the March 8, 1858, issue of the *Fayetteville Observer*. The author noted that unmarried people lived shorter lives and that "there are more insane single persons in our asylums, in proportion, than of married." See the *Hillsborough Recorder*, June 15, 1859, for a call to end the custom of announcing weddings as "Miss A married Mr. B" because the woman "does not marry the man—the man marries her." For a satirical account of how a father might marry off an aging daughter by presenting her as a widow instead of a spinster, see "How to Make a Young Wife of an Old Maid," *Hillsborough Recorder*, May 16, 1838.

31. Anna Jane Bingham to Mary Lynch, March 2, 1846, Thomas Lynch and Mary Lynch Letters, Special Collections Department, Duke University.

32. Clinton, *Plantation Mistress*, p. 121; Wyatt-Brown, *Southern Honor*, p. 221; Scott, *Southern Lady*, pp. 20–21; Johnson, *Antebellum North Carolina*, pp. 192–96.

33. Clinton, *Plantation Mistress*, p. 210. In *Purity and Danger*, anthropologist Mary Douglas provides interesting insights into how beliefs concerning the "dangerous contagion" of those outside the boundaries of society function to uphold the moral values and system of relationships within a society. As Phyllis M. Palmer notes, "The dualism of good/bad was usually connected with race and class but it could be used to chastise any woman moving out of her assigned place." See Palmer, "White Women/Black Women," p. 157.

34. *George W. Trice* v. *Luther, Zachariah, and Jason Trice and John Davis*, Spring 1846, Criminal Action Papers, Orange County, NCDAH.

35. Criminal Action Papers, September and November 1852, Orange County; J. Roberts to Governor Holden, March 10, 1869, Governors' Papers, Holden; *Strong* v. *Strong*, Divorce Records, Granville County; Criminal Actions Concerning Slaves and Free Persons of Color, Fall 1842, Granville County, all in NCDAH. In both of the above cases, whites pulled rank and manipulated the racial biases of court magistrates to try to punish their black associates.

36. Rawick, ed., *American Slave*, 15:pt. 2, pp. 3, 273.

37. Ibid., p. 343.

38. Johnson, *Antebellum North Carolina*, pp. 209–17; Watson, *Jacksonian Politics*, p. 44.

39. *Hillsborough Recorder*, June 20, 1849, August 22, 1839; *Fayetteville Observer*, July 10, 1849, May 25, 1857; *Greensborough Patriot*, June 4, 1858.

40. Johnson, *Antebellum North Carolina*, pp. 20–79; Blackwelder, *Age of Orange*, pp. 1–10, 83; Norton, *Democratic Party in Antebellum North Carolina*, p. 3; Taylor, *Slaveholding in North Carolina*, pp. 52–59.

41. Scott, *Southern Lady*, pp. 23–44; Johnson, *Antebellum North Carolina*, p. 231; James Norcom to daughter, August 19, 1846, James Norcom Family Papers, NCDAH.

42. *Fayetteville Observer*, March 5, 26, 1850, March 20, 1849.

43. Ibid., July 10, 1849.

44. Ibid., July 24, 1849, June 17, 1851.

45. Sitterson, *Secession Movement*, pp. 98–99; Norton, *Democratic Party in Antebellum North Carolina*, pp. 109–13; Butts, "Challenge to Planter Rule."

46. Butts, "Challenge to Planter Rule," pp. 1–25.

47. *Fayetteville Observer*, October 1, 29, 1850.

48. Ibid., April 30, 1850, July 8, 1851.

49. For a similar suggestion, see Lebsock, *Free Women of Petersburg*, pp. 240–41.

50. In the North Carolina Piedmont, the movement toward greater education for women reflected the Quaker and Moravian influence. See Johnson, *Antebellum North Carolina*, pp. 302–8. It was also part of a general nationwide elevation of the role of mothers in building a strong republic. This movement has been studied by historians of American women. See especially Sklar, *Catharine Beecher*; Cott, *Bonds of Womanhood*; Kerber, *Women of the Republic*. For evidence of similar ideals in the North Carolina Piedmont, see the *Fayetteville Observer*, March 29, May 14, June 4, 1858, and the *Hillsborough Recorder*, May 16, 1860.

51. *Fayetteville Observer*, July 2, November 5, 1850.

52. Johnson, *Antebellum North Carolina*, pp. 424–26, 402–9, 560–70; Sterling Ruffin to Thomas Ruffin, June 1804, in Hamilton, ed., *Papers of Thomas Ruffin*, 1:54–55; Caldwell, "Churches of Granville County," pp. 1–22.

53. Sowle, "North Carolina Manumission Society," pp. 53–60.

54. Nuermberger, *Free Produce Movement*, pp. 458–62, 561; Sowle, "North Carolina Manumission Society," pp. 53–60.

55. *Newlin* v. *Freeman*, 23 N.C. 405 (1841); *Thompson* v. *Newlin*, 42 N.C. 338 (1844). Judge Gaston advised the 1832 graduating class of the University of North Carolina that it was their duty to provide for the "mitigation" of slavery

and what he hoped would be the "ultimate extirpation of the worst evil that affects the southern part of our Confederacy" (quoted in Johnson, *Antebellum North Carolina*, p. 563).

56. *Thompson* v. *Newlin*, 42 N.C. 338 (1844). For further discussion of this case, see Tushnet, *American Law of Slavery*, pp. 206–7, 246.

57. *True Wesleyan*, April 12, 1851; Whitener, *Prohibition in North Carolina*, pp. 13–31.

58. Johnson, *Antebellum North Carolina*, pp. 453–58; Whitener, *Prohibition in North Carolina*, p. 31; Peter Swaim to Benjamin P. Elliot, May 11, 1842, Elliot Papers; J. T. Davis to Bettie [Hargrove], July 21, 1848, Hargrove Papers. On Orange County's participation in the temperance movement, see Blackwelder, *Age of Orange*, p. 97.

59. Whitener, *Prohibition in North Carolina*, pp. 30, 39, 42; Johnson, *Antebellum North Carolina*, p. 458; Blackwelder, *Age of Orange*, p. 97.

60. *Fayetteville Observer*, April 13, 1857. See also the issue of May 11, 1857, in which the same editors admitted that drunkenness was a problem in Piedmont society but blamed it on the importation of "cheap" and "chemical" liquors from outside the state.

61. Ibid., February 16, May 25, 1857. Similar laments were issued in the North. See Dublin, *Women at Work*, p. 55.

62. *Greensborough Patriot*, May 14, 1858.

63. "Address by James A. Long, Esq., before the Young Ladies of Edgeworth," May 27, 1858, printed in the *Greensborough Patriot*, June 25, 1858.

Chapter 3

1. Inventory of estate of Sally Fain (Fane), 1855; Inventory of estate of Jacob Fain (Fane), 1838, both in Estate Records, Granville County, NCDAH. John Bullock was the administrator of the estates of both Jacob and Sally Fane.

2. Marriage contract of Sarah E. Ware and Edwin J. Nuttall, October 30, 1851, Sarah Ware Nuttall Letters, Miscellaneous Records, Granville County, NCDAH; *Sarah Ware* v. *Henry F. Ware*, September 1839, March 1846, Divorce Records, Granville County, NCDAH.

3. Edwin Nuttall was charged with numerous assaults and batteries by various citizens throughout the 1830s. See Criminal Action Papers, 1834, 1835, 1836, 1837, Granville County, NCDAH. Nuttall was convicted of manslaughter for the shooting death of Mansfield Jenkins (Criminal Action Papers, 1837–38, Granville County, NCDAH). Evidence that Nuttall was denied all but a token inheritance from his father was found in the 1832 will of John Nuttall (Wills, Granville County, NCDAH). For reference to Nuttall being

"drunk one-half of the time" and the struggle to keep him sober, see letter written by his stepson, J. B. Ware, to Augustis Landis, September 28, 1861, Nuttall Letters.

4. Frustration with her trustee, Augustis Landis, caused Sarah Nuttall to write in 1864, "I have always placed the greatest confidence in your friendship untill you neglected answering my letters and not sending me My Money" (Nuttall to Landis, February 1, 1864). Letters dated February 22, 1864, and July 1, 1864, expressed similar frustration, all in Nuttall Letters.

5. Jacob Fane purchased his freedom on May 1, 1805. An undated petition indicates he sought the emancipation of Sally (his then future wife), a slave of Sarah Smith, and James Fane (his brother), a slave of William Bullock, on grounds of their faithfulness and meritorious service to their masters. He was apparently forced instead to purchase Sally and James Fane and emancipate them himself in September 1822. All three petitions are in Miscellaneous Records of Slaves and Free Persons of Color, Granville County, NCDAH.

6. Quoted in Salmon, "Equality or Submersion?," p. 94. For a more general discussion of separate estates, see Salmon, "Women and Property in South Carolina."

7. On the opinion that women had more power within the family than the law suggested, see Johnson, *Antebellum North Carolina*, p. 243. For evidence that women had greater formal as well as informal control over property during the colonial era in New York and Virginia, see Gunderson and Gampel, "Married Women's Legal Status."

8. *Joyner* v. *Joyner*, 59 N.C. 331 (1862).

9. U.S. Federal Manuscript Censuses, 1860, Granville, Orange, and Montgomery counties.

10. Friedman, *History of American Law*; Grossberg, *Governing the Hearth*, pp. 1–17. For a comparison of the development of the law North and South, see Hindus, *Prison and Plantation*. North Carolina was not as "medieval" in its adherence to outmoded marriage and property laws as South Carolina, but the application of the law was deeply influenced by slavery.

11. Grossberg, "Who Gets the Child?"

12. Friedman, *History of American Law*, pp. 180–90; Salmon, "Equality or Submersion?"; Salmon, "Women and Property in South Carolina," p. 657.

13. In a single tax year, 1854, women in Granville and Montgomery counties owned 8.1 percent and 9.5 percent of all taxable property, respectively. Unfortunately, their marital status is indeterminable (List of Taxables and tax list, 1854, Granville and Montgomery counties, NCDAH). The 1854 tax list for Orange County is not extant, and there is no year in the 1850s for which all three counties' tax lists exist.

14. Friedman, *History of American Law*, p. 22. In Orange County, the wills probated between 1851 and 1861 reveal that of the forty-nine men who left

property to their widows, only seven left property in fee simple; the rest chose to leave their wives "life estates" (Estate Records, Orange County, NCDAH).

15. This was especially evident in letters written by Sarah Nuttall to Augustis Landis between January 7, 1864, and March 27, 1865, after Nuttall had moved to Guilford County (Nuttall Letters).

16. Lebsock, *Free Women of Petersburg*, p. 109.

17. Estate Papers of Dill Delaney, December 8, 1853, Estate Records, Montgomery County, NCDAH.

18. Ibid.; Rawick, ed., *American Slave*, 14:pt. 1, pp. 360–61. On the relations of African American women and men under slavery, see Stevenson, "Distress and Discord in Virginia Slave Families."

19. The General Assembly of North Carolina granted the state's first divorce in 1794. In 1814, the legislature authorized the superior courts to share the power of granting divorce with the assembly. In 1827, it granted sole power to grant divorce to the superior court, as well as the right to consider offenses other than impotence and adultery. The supreme court was simultaneously empowered to hear appeals of suits of divorce (Ferrell, "Notes and Comments," pp. 604–11; Act of 1814, N.C. Rev. St., ch. 869).

20. Cott, "Divorce and the Changing Status of Women"; Friedman, *American Law*, pp. 181–84.

21. Friedman, *American Law*, p. 183.

22. Fox-Genovese, *Within the Plantation Household*, p. 203; Kerber, *Women of the Republic*, pp. 183–84.

23. D'Emilio and Freedman, *Intimate Matters*, p. 95; Clinton, *Plantation Mistress*, pp. 87–89.

24. Butts, "Irrepressible Conflict," p. 3; Johnson, *Antebellum North Carolina*, pp. 239–40.

25. Miscellaneous Records, 1832, Granville County, NCDAH.

26. Salmon, "Equality or Submersion?," pp. 95–96; Salmon, "Women and Property in South Carolina," p. 657.

27. Salmon, "Women and Property in South Carolina," p. 659. Milnes, *On the Property of Married Women*, pp. 351–53, states that the "principle" of separate estate existed in varying degrees in Maine, Rhode Island, Michigan, Indiana, Wisconsin, North Carolina, Tennessee, Kentucky, Mississippi, Florida, Arkansas, Louisiana, Texas, and California.

28. *Barfield* v. *Combs*, 15 N.C. 422 (1834).

29. *Kerns* v. *Peeler*, 49 N.C. 224 (1856).

30. *Watson* v. *Cox*, 36 N.C. 312 (1841). The court also ruled in *Miller* v. *Bingham*, 36 N.C. 58 (1841), that if a widow remarried, a second deed of separate estate must be filed or the estate would vest in the second husband.

31. *Bason* v. *Holt*, 47 N.C. 312 (1855). Flexibility was shown on at least one occasion. In *Davis* v. *Cain*, 36 N.C. 248 (1840), the court held that although

the word "separate" was preferred, other "sufficiently plain" and appropriate words could be accepted.

32. *Saunders* v. *Ferrill*, 23 N.C. 72 (1840).

33. *Worth* v. *York*, 35 N.C. 195 (1851).

34. Act of 1848, N.C. Rev. St., ch. 39, sec. 12.

35. See *Gray* v. *Mathis*, 52 N.C. 526 (1860), in which the court voided a deed that conveyed to another the separate estate of Susannah Mathis because her husband's name, although "affixed after the signature of the wife," was not contained in the body of the deed of sale.

36. *Frazier* v. *Brownlow*, 33 N.C. 184 (1844).

37. *Harris* v. *Harris*, 42 N.C. 107 (1850).

38. Ibid.

39. *Houston* v. *Brown* (1859), quoted in Johnson, *Antebellum North Carolina*, pp. 240–41. See also *Draper, Knox and Co.* v. *Jordan*, 58 N.C. 189 (1859).

40. *Felton* v. *Reid*, 52 N.C. 290 (1859).

41. Lebsock, "Radical Reconstruction and the Property Rights of Southern Women."

42. *Thompson* v. *Newlin*, 38 N.C. 338 (1844); Act of 1830, N.C. Rev. St., ch. 101.

43. *Worth* v. *York*, 35 N.C. 195 (1851).

44. See especially the early letters of Sterling Ruffin to his son Thomas Ruffin, in Hamilton, ed., *Papers of Thomas Ruffin*, 1:54–55.

45. *Wood* v. *Wood*, 27 N.C. 553 (1845); *Whittington* v. *Whittington*, 19 N.C. 65 (1836). See also *Hansley* v. *Hansley*, 32 N.C. 365 (1848), for Ruffin's statement that strict divorce laws were "intended to protect the public morals and promote public policy." In "Family and Female Identity in the Antebellum South," Elizabeth Fox-Genovese argues forcibly that the family was the Old South's "central metaphor."

46. Ferrell, "Notes and Comments."

47. The divorce suits, cited individually throughout the chapter, were taken from *North Carolina Reports*, vols. 13–33.

48. *Scroggins* v. *Scroggins*, 14 N.C. 567 (1832).

49. Ibid. Later that year, Ruffin conceded to "the deeprooted and virtuous prejudices of the community" by granting Jesse Barden, whose wife had also mothered a mulatto child, a new trial (*Barden* v. *Barden*, 14 N.C. 580 [1832]).

50. *Whittington* v. *Whittington*, 19 N.C. 65 (1836). The superior court of Caswell County had also denied a divorce to Andrew Whittington (Divorce Records, Caswell County, NCDAH).

51. *Moss* v. *Moss*, 24 N.C. 44 (1841). For discussions of both paternalism and the Ruffin court in regard to slaves, see Genovese, *Roll, Jordan, Roll*, pp. 3–7, 35–36.

52. *State* v. *Mann*, 13 N.C. 229 (1829). For analyses of antebellum southern

courts and slavery in the colonial period, see Higginbotham, *In the Matter of Color*. On the nineteenth century, see Tushnet, *American Law of Slavery*; Schwarz, *Twice Condemned*; Yanuck, "Thomas Ruffin and North Carolina Slave Law," p. 456; and Nash, "A More Equitable Past?," p. 197.

53. *State* v. *Hussey*, 44 N.C. 124 (1852).

54. *State* v. *Mann*, 13 N.C. 229 (1829).

55. Quoted in Johnson, *Antebellum North Carolina*, p. 242.

56. Caldwell and 238 petitioners advocated clemency for Martin Icehower and David Weant of Mecklenburg County, both of whom had been convicted of manslaughter for beating to death one of the men's slaves who had resisted their efforts to whip him for "neglect of work." The men were sentenced to three months' imprisonment and fined $750 and $250, respectively. In response to the petition, Governor Thomas Bragg left the fines intact but commuted both men's sentences (G. W. Caldwell to Governor Bragg, June 12, 1858, Governors' Papers, Bragg, NCDAH).

57. Wyatt-Brown, *Southern Honor*, pp. 462–93.

58. *Hansley* v. *Hansley*, 32 N.C. 365 (1849). In dealing with a couple as miserable as the Hansleys, Ruffin warned against the possibility of collusion. By law, divorce was a reward for an injured party, not a solution to mutual misery created by both parties.

59. *Barbee* v. *Armstead et al.*, 32 N.C. 382 (1849).

60. *Foy* v. *Foy*, 35 N.C. 89 (1851).

61. *Everton* v. *Everton*, 50 N.C. 202 (1857).

62. *Earp* v. *Earp*, 54 N.C. 223 (1854).

63. *Coble* v. *Coble*, 55 N.C. 366 (1856).

64. Censer, "Smiling through Her Tears," reaches similar conclusions.

65. Henry Ware's misconduct had occurred in Fluvanna, Virginia, where he and his wife lived before returning to Granville County (*Sarah Ware* v. *Henry Ware*, 1839, 1846, Divorce Records, Orange County, NCDAH).

66. On the impact of one's social position on the outcome of court cases, see Wyatt-Brown, *Southern Honor*, p. 303. There are interesting gaps in the records of the otherwise extremely well-documented suit of *Trice* v. *Trice*. All of the depositions taken in favor of Martha Trice at the home of her father, John Strayhorn, are missing from the file (*Trice* v. *Trice*, Fall 1839–Fall 1842, Divorce Records, Orange County, NCDAH).

67. The 1842 will of John Strayhorn specified that Martha Trice be left the bed and furniture of her choice, a chopping ax, cooking utensils, and "all the cloth and bed clothing she has made since she has been living with me" (Wills, Orange County, NCDAH).

68. *Mitchell* v. *Mitchell*, 1831, Divorce Records, Granville County, NCDAH.

69. *Phillips* v. *Phillips and Lemay*, 1837, Divorce Records, Granville County, NCDAH. Margaret Strother, the sister of Susan Phillips, sued her husband,

Christopher Strother, and John Lemay in a suit identical to her sister's. Strother went so far as to have the court first apprentice her children to two of her brothers, apparently to keep her estranged husband from gaining custody of them (Apprenticeship Bonds, May 1836, Granville County, NCDAH; *Strother* v. *Strother*, 1837, Divorce Records, Granville County, NCDAH).

70. *Cape* v. *Cape*, September 1833–May 1834, Divorce Records, Orange County, NCDAH. It is uncertain whether Martha Cape ever received her divorce. She entered the poorhouse as Mrs. Thomas Cape on September 7, 1846 (Minutes of the Warden of the Poor, Orange County, NCDAH). During the divorce trial of Martha and Zachariah Trice, Cornelius Cook testified that Martha's verbal abuse of her first husband, Sampson Moore, had caused Moore to beat her with a wagon whip on one occasion (*Trice* v. *Trice*, 1839–42, Divorce Records, Orange County, NCDAH).

71. *Cooke* v. *Cooke*, 1845, Divorce Records, Granville County, NCDAH. Many divorce petitions filed by women similarly cited years of drunken and violent abuse.

72. *O'Fairhill* v. *O'Fairhill*, 1830, Divorce Records, Orange County, NCDAH.

73. In Granville County, for example, Mary Stanfield, Frances Davis, Nancy Hunt, and Ella Ann Royster had instituted peace warrants against their husbands before filing for divorce (Criminal Action Papers, June 1840, December 1846, July 1851, July 1852, Granville County, NCDAH).

74. *Richardson* v. *Richardson*, March 1857, Minute Docket of the Superior Court, Granville County, NCDAH. Richardson's race was determined from his apprenticeship contract of May 1835 (Apprenticeship Bonds, Granville County, NCDAH).

75. Criminal Action Papers, Granville and Orange counties, NCDAH.

76. Will of George Anderson, 1771, recorded in Owen, *Granville County*.

77. Will of Lewis Anderson, 1814, Wills, Granville County, NCDAH. Marriages between free blacks of Granville County are interspersed with those of whites in Holcomb, *Marriages of Granville County*. I have deduced the race of the couples listed therein from a variety of sources: wills, estate records, and manuscript censuses. These sources identify the race of many individuals and reveal that apparently the surnames Chavis, Bass, Kearsey, Taborn, and Pettiford belonged exclusively to free blacks. Although not exclusively belonging to free blacks, the surnames Anderson, Mitchell, and Tyler are seldom found among nineteenth-century whites in the county. On intermarriages among free black families, see Franklin, *Free Negro in North Carolina*, p. 183.

78. U.S. Federal Manuscript Census, 1860, Granville County. The number of free black property holders is listed in Franklin, *Free Negro in North Carolina*, pp. 230–31.

79. U.S. Federal Manuscript Census, 1860, Orange County; Franklin, *Free Negro in North Carolina*, pp. 230–31.

80. Quoted in Murray, *Proud Shoes*, p. 39.

81. Reuben Day, Sr., farmed ten acres of land in the Flat River-Durham neighborhood during the 1830s and claimed property valued at $50 in 1850. By 1860, the property had passed to his widow, Nancy Day (Land Entry Book, June 7, 1830, May 5, 1835, pp. 8, 119, Orange County, NCDAH). Murray, *Proud Shoes*, pp. 40–43, suggests that Reuben Day, Jr., was chased off the Chapel Hill plantation of James S. Smith, where his slave wife, Harriet, lived, in 1842. This probably occurred closer to 1840, since Day married Mary Brooks, a free black, on January 21, 1841. He may have left Chapel Hill permanently, but he did not, as Murray contends, move out of the county (Marriage of Reuben Day and Mary Brooks, January 21, 1841, Marriage Records, Orange County, NCDAH). The court charged Day with fornicating with white women Lucinda Woodrow and Lotty Vaughn in 1851 and 1867, respectively (Criminal Action Papers, Orange County, NCDAH; Sally Walker to Governor Holden, June 14, 1869, Governors' Papers, Holden, NCDAH).

82. Petition for emancipation of Jacob Fane, 1805; petition for emancipation of James Fane, 1822; both in Miscellaneous Records of Slaves and Free Persons of Color, Granville County, NCDAH; Criminal Actions Concerning Slaves and Free Persons of Color, Granville County, NCDAH. On the connections between free blacks and influential whites in another county, see Jacobs, *Incidents in the Life of a Slave Girl*, p. 29 and passim.

83. Lebsock, *Free Women of Petersburg*, pp. 99–101. Franklin, *Free Negro in North Carolina*, pp. 135, 143, lists 413 servants, many of whom were women, 412 washers, and 175 seamstresses among the free blacks of North Carolina included in the 1860 census. Most of these women lived in counties with large free black populations. In Montgomery and Orange counties, where the free black population was relatively small, very few free black women were listed in such occupations. In Granville County, however, there were 6 female domestic servants, 9 washers, 3 female weavers, and 1 seamstress among the substantially larger free black population (U.S. Federal Manuscript Censuses, 1860, Granville, Orange, and Montgomery counties). On Nancy Anderson, see Criminal Action Papers, Granville County, NCDAH.

84. Only one free black woman was charged with prostitution in Orange County during the 1850s. A free black couple, Patsey and James Huckabee, was indicted for maintaining a disorderly house in June 1850. Silvia Chavis initiated the suit against Sam, a slave of Chuza Hopkins, in April 1841 (Criminal Action Papers, Orange County, NCDAH).

85. According to the Granville County list of taxables for 1854, there were two Nancy Andersons. I have been unable to determine if one or both of them accounted for the numerous appearances of the name in court. In 1840, Nancy Anderson was also convicted of trading goods with a slave. In 1852, she was charged with stealing a heifer from Phebe Morris, a white woman, and in

May 1854 and February 1857, with participating in frays that included numerous members of the Bass, Anderson, and Taborn families (Criminal Actions Concerning Slaves and Free Persons of Color, and Criminal Action Papers, Granville County, NCDAH).

86. Criminal Action Papers and Criminal Actions Concerning Slaves and Free Persons of Color, Granville County, NCDAH; Stansell, *City of Women*, p. 59.

87. White women initiated peace warrants in Granville County six times as often as did black women, although roughly equal numbers from both groups participated in crimes of violence. Peace warrants were initiated against Harriet and Anderson Chavis in November 1859, against Isabella and James Chavis in November 1859, and against Ephraim and Peggy Anderson in July 1859 (Criminal Action Papers, 1840–60, Granville County, NCDAH).

88. For insights into the behavior of free blacks see Johnson and Roark, "Strategies of Survival," and Horton, "Freedom's Yoke." The assertiveness of free black women does not suggest the existence of a "black matriarchy." As Suzanne Lebsock notes, "Women are called matriarchs when the power they exercise relative to the men of their own group is in some respect greater than that defined as appropriate by the dominant group" *(Free Women of Petersburg*, p. 88). Psychologist Jean Baker Miller has made a similar observation: "Dominant groups tend to characterize even subordinates' initial small resistance to dominant control as demands for an excessive amount of power" (*Toward a New Psychology of Women*, p. 117).

89. Criminal Action Papers and Minute Dockets of the Superior Courts, 1830–60, Granville, Orange, and Montgomery counties, NCDAH.

90. In at least four of the six cases in which blacks were charged with murdering white men, executions were carried out. There is no evidence, however, that any of the four white men accused of killing blacks were executed for their crime. Only one, Obediah Christmas, was even charged with first-degree murder. Although Orange County's superior court sentenced Christmas to hang, the state supreme court overturned his conviction (Criminal Action Papers, 1858, Orange County, NCDAH). Requests that the governor pardon white men convicted of manslaughter of black men were common. See especially the letters of William J. Wilson, September 26, 1846, Asa Briggs, June 26, 1849, and the petition of Union County citizens, April 1847, all in Governors' Papers, Graham, NCDAH. On the different treatment accorded black and white men accused of murder, see Wyatt-Brown, *Southern Honor*, pp. 387–88, and Johnson, *Antebellum North Carolina*, pp. 503–4.

91. For general attitudes toward wife-beating, see the *Fayetteville Observer*'s endorsement of a Richmond County judge who fined Stephen Cole $500 and sentenced him to ten days' imprisonment for beating his wife in a "cruel and brutal manner" (April 6, 1857). See also "A Brute Served Rightly," in the

Hillsborough Recorder, June 1, 1859, wherein the editors applauded a man who attacked his sister's husband for having beaten the sister. See also Wyatt-Brown, *Southern Honor*, pp. 281–82.

92. *State* v. *Preslar*, 48 N.C. 417 (1856). Requests for clemency included a petition dated December 20, 1856, and letters written by D. A. Covington, J. M. Steward, and Samuel Walkup, all dated December 15, 1856, to the governor, all in Governors' Papers, Bragg, NCDAH.

93. *State* v. *Preslar*, 48 N.C. 417 (1856).

94. W. Lander to Governor Bragg, December 20, 1856 Bragg granted the temporary reprieve on December 22, 1856 (Governors' Papers, Bragg; Governors' Letter Book, Bragg, NCDAH). I have been unable to determine whether Preslar was ever executed, but he did not appear in the 1860 U.S. Federal Manuscript Census for Union County.

95. In an earlier case in which Achelius Durham had been convicted of manslaughter in the beating death of his wife, petitioners also argued that Durham should be pardoned because he had used no weapon and had been intoxicated at the time of the murder. Governor Reid granted the pardon (Petition to Governor Reid, May 5, 1852, Governors' Papers, Reid; Governors' Letter Book, Reid, NCDAH). On violence in the Old South, see Bruce, *Violence and Culture in the Antebellum South*, and Ayers, *Vengeance and Justice*.

96. Wyatt-Brown, *Southern Honor*, pp. 281–83.

97. Petition to Governor Bragg, April 1857, Governors' Papers, Bragg, NCDAH.

98. T. Ruffin, Jr., to Governor Bragg, December 3, 1858, Governors' Paper, Bragg, NCDAH.

99. Petition of P. Murphy to Governor Bragg, May 10, 1858, letter of Raiford Harris to Governor Bragg, January 31, 1850, ibid.

100. J. C. Badham to Governor Bragg, November 5, 1858, ibid.

101. The state supreme court overturned the conviction (*State* v. *Obediah Christmas*, March 1859, Criminal Action Papers, Orange County, NCDAH).

102. *State* v. *Sewell*, 48 N.C. 248 (1855).

103. Battle, *Memories of an Old-Time Tar Heel*, pp. 90–91.

104. *State* v. *Mary Meadows*, Spring 1849, Criminal Action Papers, Orange County, NCDAH; *State* v. *George*, 30 N.C. 237 (1848).

105. *State* v. *Mary Meadows*, Spring 1849, Criminal Action Papers, Orange County, NCDAH.

106. Ibid.

Chapter 4

1. The court apprenticed all seven of Williford's children—Thomas, William, Augustine, and Lunsford in February 1850; Mary in November

1856; Nancy and Louisa in February 1861 (Affidavit of Susan Williford, April 8, 1862, Apprenticeship Bonds, Granville County, NCDAH).

2. Apprenticeship Bonds, 1840–60, Granville, Orange, and Montgomery counties, NCDAH.

3. Apprenticeship Bond of Susan Williford, November 6, 1821, Apprenticeship Bonds, Granville County, NCDAH. On the yeoman background of Elizabeth Williford, see Deed Book F, 1746–65, pp. 239–40, which records that William and Elizabeth Williford, possibly Susan's grandparents or great-grandparents, sold two hundred acres of land to John Bird on February 7, 1763. See also Deed Book I, 1821–23, p. 297, which records a transfer of land to Elizabeth Williford on February 1, 1823. Both are in Gwynn, *Kinfolks*, pp. 230, 246.

Other Willifords of the Knapp of Reeds neighborhood included Lewis, a forty-four-year-old farmer with combined real and personal property worth $930, and David, age thirty-eight, who had personal property valued at $100. James, age twenty-two and propertyless, may have been an illegitimate child of Elizabeth's. Betsy Williford, age sixty, was living with him and his wife in 1860. If this is the same Elizabeth, she would have been fifteen at the time of Susan's birth (U.S. Federal Manuscript Census, 1860, Granville County, NCDAH).

4. Apprentice Bond of Susan Williford, November 6, 1821, and November 1822, Apprenticeship Bonds, Granville County, NCDAH.

5. Wyatt-Brown, *Southern Honor*, p. 369.

6. On the issue of labeling women as deviant according to their race, class, or behavior, see D'Emilio and Freedman, *Intimate Matters*, pp. 85–108; Stansell, *City of Women*, pp. 171–216; and Palmer, "White Women/Black Women," p. 157.

7. For example, Thomas Curtis was apprenticed to James Hobgood in 1830 and Eliza Ann Curtis to Hezekiah Hobgood in 1833 (Apprenticeship Bonds, Granville County, NCDAH).

8. Bastardy Bond of Susan Williford, July 1836, Bastardy Bonds, Granville County, NCDAH. The court did not charge Parthenia Melton with bastardy until 1847, although she gave birth to the first of five, perhaps seven, children by John R. Hobgood in 1837. This child, Nancy, was apprenticed in 1851 (Apprenticeship Bonds, Granville County, NCDAH).

9. Murder of Shelton Hobgood, 1828, Coroners' Inquests, Granville County, NCDAH. On the yeoman origins of the Hobgoods, see the estate papers of their father, Thomas Hobgood, 1818; Shelton Hobgood, 1829; Hezekiah Hobgood, 1841; and Joseph D. Hobgood, 1862, all in Estate Records, Granville County, NCDAH.

10. Bastardy Bond of Parthenia Melton, November 1847, Bastardy Bonds, Granville County, NCDAH. The court charged Melton and Hobgood with

fornication in March 1841 and again in the spring of 1855 (Criminal Action Papers, Granville County, NCDAH). The court apprenticed Albert Melton in August 1850 and Nancy Melton in February 1851. It sent William, Galinda, and Joanna Melton to the poorhouse in February 1851. In 1870, Parthenia had two additional children living with her: David, age thirteen, and Sallie, age eleven. Whether their father was John R. Hobgood is unclear. Indeed, they may not have been Parthenia's children (Apprenticeship Bonds, Granville County, NCDAH; U.S. Federal Manuscript Censuses, 1860, 1870, Granville County).

11. An 1835 amendment to the North Carolina constitution forbade marriage between whites and persons descended from a black ancestor to the fourth generation. The Act of 1838, c. 24, made attempted marriages between blacks and whites punishable by imprisonment for four months to ten years and subject to fines at the discretion of the court. The act left interracial cohabitation punishable as fornication under N.C. Rev. St., ch. 34, sec. 46. Fornication convictions stemming from miscegenous liaisons were upheld by the state supreme court in *State* v. *Fore*, 23 N.C. 299 (1841), and *State* v. *Watters*, 25 N.C. 388 (1843). Williford and Curtis were charged with fornication in August 1852, May 1855, and February 1861. The witnesses against them were Fielding Harris and Walter A. Bullock, the same men Williford had accused of forcibly taking two of her children before the court apprenticed them to Harris (Criminal Action Papers, Granville County, NCDAH).

12. The court charged Samuel Jackson with beating up Williford in November 1840 and February 1841 (Criminal Action Papers, Granville County, NCDAH). Williford's son Augustus married Laura Jane Curtis on December 26, 1865, and her daughter Mary married John Wright on December 8, 1867. Her son Lunsford married Harriet Curtis on December 21, 1867 (Marriage Bonds, Granville County, NCDAH). All three of the Willifords' spouses were members of pre–Civil War free black families of the Tally Ho neighborhood (U.S. Federal Manuscript Census, 1860, Granville County).

In both Granville and Orange counties, where many propertyless women headed households, nonspousal assaults and batteries of women by men occurred in far greater numbers than in Montgomery County. In Granville County, forty-six such attacks were reported between 1840 and 1860 (twenty of them on black women). In Orange County, thirty-six such assaults were reported (thirty-one of them on white women). Montgomery County reported only seven such attacks (all on white women). Of the total eighty-nine assaults, seventeen were on women who had previously been charged with sexual misbehavior.

13. See especially the indictment of Nancy Anderson, May 1856, Criminal Action Papers, Granville County, NCDAH. Indictments for keeping a "bawdy house," which involved only the selling of sexual favors, were much rarer. One

example was that of Elvira Short and Sally Short in spring 1852 (Criminal Action Papers, Orange County, NCDAH).

14. For example, the 1860 U.S. Federal Manuscript Census for Orange County identified white women Betsie Warren and Nancy Warren as prostitutes. That the courts never indicted them suggests a grudging acceptance of their profession. The 1850 U.S. Federal Manuscript Census shows Betsie Warren to have been the wife of Thomas Warren, a cooper. Nancy was one of six children listed in the couple's household.

15. The indictment against Elvira Short and Sally Short in spring 1852 for keeping a "bawdy house" accused them of committing "dreadfully filthy and lewd offences" with white, free black, and slave men (Criminal Action Papers, Granville County, NCDAH).

16. Criminal Action Papers, August 28, 30, 1847, Granville County, NCDAH.

17. The court apprenticed Huckabee's child in August 1841, Woodrow's in 1852, and King's three children in November 1855 (Apprenticeship Bonds, Orange County, NCDAH). Glasgow's children were apprenticed in February 1840. The court charged Short with bastardy in August 1837, although it did not apprentice a child of hers (Apprenticeship Bonds, Granville County, NCDAH). In 1850, eleven-year-old Mary Perry was living with Edmond Ivey's family, which suggests her apprenticeship to Ivey. In 1850, twelve-year-old Catherine Mincey lived with forty-four-year-old Sally Mincey, the head of household and probably her mother. There is no evidence that Sally Mincey ever married. The presence of seventy-three-year-old Thomas Mincey in the home suggests that three generations were living together. Mary Perry and Catherine Mincey were only sixteen and seventeen years old when charged together in 1855 for rioting and prostitution (U.S. Federal Manuscript Census, 1850, Orange County; Criminal Action Papers, Orange County, NCDAH).

18. Only ten of the nineteen women indicted for keeping either a "disorderly house" or "bawdy house" between 1850 and 1860 could be positively identified through records. Of these ten, at least three owned property. The 1860 U.S. Federal Manuscript Census for Granville County reported Martha Mangum, a white woman, to have combined personal and real property valued at $90. Estate Records for Orange County reveal that Parthenia Crabtree, a white woman who died in 1858, left an estate valued at $900 and was the widowed mother of six children. Finally, the 1854 List of Taxables for Granville County indicates that Nancy Anderson owned at least 340 acres of land in Oxford, making her one of the wealthiest of the free black Andersons.

19. Criminal Action Papers, Spring 1856, Granville County, NCDAH.

20. *State* v. *Samuel G. Reed*, January 1856, Criminal Action Papers, Orange County, NCDAH. Other women indicted for crimes involving prostitution who also became involved in crimes of violence include, in Granville, Sally

Short, Elvira Short, and Martha Mangum, and in Orange, Lucinda Woodrow, Catherine Mincey, and Mary Perry (Criminal Action Papers, August 1847, September 1856, May 1855, Granville County; January 1852, April 1855, Orange County, NCDAH).

21. In 68 of the 112 fornication indictments for the period 1840–60, both partners can be identified by race and status of freedom. Of these indictments, 24 were for illegal cohabitation between slaves and free blacks, 17 for interracial sexual intercourse, and 27 for sexual intercourse between whites not married to one another (Criminal Action Papers, 1840–60, Granville, Orange, and Montgomery counties, Criminal Actions Concerning Slaves and Free Persons of Color, Granville County, 1840–60, NCDAH).

22. Slaves and free blacks who formed marital alliances were charged with illegal cohabitation, a special category of fornication predicated on the illegality of such marriages. The law stated that "no free person of color can be married to a slave, and every such marriage is void, unless the consent of the owner or master of the slave be had in writing" (quoted in Swaim, *North Carolina Justice*, p. 313).

23. Sarah Boon to James Boon, November 27, 1849, July 11, 1850, James Boon Papers, NCDAH.

24. Marriage license of James Boon and Mahala Buffalo, May 14, 1854, ibid.

25. Rawick, ed., *American Slave*, 15:pt. 2, p. 325.

26. Lebsock, *Free Women of Petersburg*, p. 104, suggests that the free black women of Petersburg, Virginia, because of an uneven sex ratio, the law, and poverty, married in fewer numbers than did white women. A much higher rate of apprenticeship among children of free black women than among those of white women suggests the same for North Carolina (Apprenticeship Bonds, Granville, Orange, and Montgomery counties, NCDAH).

27. Bowles and Allen, a slave of Nancy Hilliard, were accused in fall 1851 of fornication (illegal cohabitation). Evidence that Bowles purchased Allen is in the settlement of her estate in 1862 (Criminal Action Papers, Estate Records, and Wills, Orange County, NCDAH).

28. For similar observations about free black women and their marital options, see Johnson and Roark, "Strategies of Survival," pp. 92–93. Mary, Nancy, and Emily Durham, ages four, six, and thirteen, respectively, the daughters of Kate Durham, a free black woman, were apprenticed to Horace H. Rowland, a white planter, in November 1861. Stephen M. Durham, age nine, had been apprenticed eight years earlier to the same Rowland (August 1853) and was likely the son of Mary Durham and Stephen, a slave of James W. Brame. Both women and their slave mates were charged separately with fornication (illegal cohabitation) in August 1864. After the war, Kate Durham and freedman London Brame legitimized their marriage and sued both

Horace H. Rowland and James W. Brame for custody of their apprenticed children (Apprenticeship Bonds, Criminal Actions Concerning Slaves and Free Persons of Color, Granville County, NCDAH).

29. Of seventeen indictments for fornication between 1840 and 1860 that can be identified as involving interracial couples, only four consisted of white men and black women. Miscegenous unions were automatically regarded as fornication because interracial marriages were illegal (Criminal Action Papers and Criminal Actions Concerning Slaves and Free Persons of Color, Granville County, NCDAH; N.C. Rev. St. c. 34, p. 46).

30. Wyatt-Brown, *Southern Honor*, pp. 295–98; Clinton, *Plantation Mistress*, p. 88.

31. Wyatt-Brown, *Southern Honor*, pp. 307–8, 314.

32. Indictment of Thomas Peace and Tabby Chavous for fornication, May 1844; *State* v. *Dickerson Peace*, March 1854, both in Criminal Action Papers, Granville County, NCDAH. Dickerson Peace died in jail, allegedly from illness precipitated by depression over the murder. July 5, 1854 (Coroners' Inquest, Granville County, NCDAH).

33. Clinton, *Plantation Mistress*, pp. 37, 60, 88; Wyatt-Brown, *Southern Honor*, pp. 208–9, 296.

34. For a general discussion of the "fallen woman" in the antebellum South, see Clinton, *Plantation Mistress*, pp. 110–22. On white women and miscegenation, see Wyatt-Brown, *Southern Honor*, pp. 315–18. Unfortunately, Wyatt-Brown perpetuates stereotypes by arguing that white women who consorted with black men displayed a "defective" notion of their social position and by suggesting that many may have been "mentally retarded."

35. For example, at least seven of the eighteen white couples indicted for fornication in Orange County between 1840 and 1860 included married men and single women. Of the eighteen white women, only one, Parthenia Crabtree, charged in 1853 with keeping a "disorderly house," can be identified as formerly married as well as propertied. At least nine of the eighteen women were propertyless. Martha Trice may have charged her husband, Zachariah Trice, with fornication in September 1839 to establish grounds for her divorce suit that same year. Nancy Hunt initiated a fornication suit against James Hunt two years after suing him for divorce, perhaps to prove him an unfit father. He had threatened to have their children apprenticed if Nancy divorced him. All indictments for fornication are in Criminal Action Papers, 1840–60, Orange County, NCDAH; *Hunt* v. *Hunt*, 1851, Divorce Records, Granville County, NCDAH.

36. Bastardy Bond of Susan Mason and William S. Moore, April 1848, Bastardy Bonds, Orange County, NCDAH; *State* v. *William S. Moore*, 1848, Criminal Action Papers, Orange County, NCDAH.

37. The defendant in this case was Stanford Moore. I have deduced that

Stanford Moore and William S. Moore are the same man because of the link of Susan Mason and because the 1860 U.S. Federal Manuscript Census for Orange County lists a William S. Moore but no Stanford Moore. See *State* v. *Hardy Horn and William Pickett*, February 1856, Criminal Action Papers, Orange County, NCDAH.

38. Indictment of Levi Nichols and Hannah Cotton for fornication (illegal cohabitation), spring 1858, Criminal Action Papers, Montgomery County, NCDAH. Nichols was the uncle of Mary Jane Nelson, who had charged Willoughby Lucas with bastardy the previous year.

39. John Hussey, age sixty-eight in 1860, was the son of Samuel Hussey, an Englishman, and his wife, Milly Turner, a mulatto woman who passed and was received as white in the Marion district of South Carolina from which the Hussey family migrated. An affidavit to that effect was filed in Montgomery County Court on August 9, 1860. Hussey and his wife settled in Montgomery County sometime before 1850. Their children—Barfield, Samuel, Eleanor (Nelly), Lindsay, and Emilia (Milly)—all married white citizens of the county. Although the 1850 U.S. Federal Manuscript Census had listed the Husseys as mulatto, the 1860 census identified them as white. Shortly after the outbreak of the Civil War, however, their race became an issue in the community, and all six couples were indicted (and later acquitted) for fornication (Fall 1861–January 1864, Miscellaneous Records, Montgomery County, NCDAH; U.S. Federal Manuscript Censuses, 1850, 1860, Montgomery County).

40. Not only did this interracial marriage go unchallenged, but the children born to the couple were apparently never apprenticed (U.S. Federal Manuscript Census, 1860, Montgomery County; Apprenticeship Bonds, Montgomery County, NCDAH).

41. Swaim, *North Carolina Justice*, pp. 56–57. See also Keyser, "Apprenticeship System in North Carolina." Keyser notes that apprenticeship was a refinement of colonial statutes that required mulatto children of white servant women to be bound until age thirty-one and provided that all free black children be bound.

42. Swaim, *North Carolina Justice*, pp. 235–39; Gunderson and Gampel, "Married Women's Legal Status," pp. 114–34.

43. Apprenticeship Bonds, Granville, Orange, and Montgomery counties, NCDAH; U.S. Federal Manuscript Censuses, 1860, Granville, Orange, and Montgomery counties.

44. A. D. Dickinson [attorney] on behalf of Cassandra Pollard to Governor Graham, July 20, 1848, Governors' Papers, Graham, NCDAH.

45. Notice of Sarah Jackson, April 20, 1839, Apprenticeship Bonds, Orange County, NCDAH.

46. Between 1840 and 1860, eleven white mothers petitioned the courts to cancel their children's apprenticeship contracts. In seven other cases, court

officials who sought to remove white children from their homes noted that the children were "not to be found" (Apprenticeship Bonds, Granville, Orange, and Montgomery counties, NCDAH).

47. *Midgett* v. *McBride*, 48 N.C. 36 (1855).

48. Criminal Action Papers, Granville County, NCDAH; U.S. Federal Manuscript Census, 1860, Granville County. For positive features of the apprentice system, see Franklin, *Free Negro in North Carolina*, pp. 129–30.

49. Petition of Lusey Morgan, February 25, 1828, Apprenticeship Bonds, Orange County, NCDAH. (As late as 1850, Lusey Morgan's son Jefferson still lived in the household of William Chamblee, according to the Federal Manuscript Census.) Petition of Milly Richerson, July 10, 1858; petition of Rigdon Valentine for Leaney Mitchell, February 2, 1836, Apprenticeship Bonds, Granville County, NCDAH.

50. *State* v. *Reuben Day Sr. and Nancy Day*, 1824, Criminal Actions Concerning Slaves and Free People of Color, Granville County, NCDAH. On the apprenticeships of Sterling and Leonidas Day to their uncle Jeremiah Day, see Petition to Governor Clark, August 22, 1861, Governors' Papers, Clark, NCDAH.

51. Apprenticeship Bonds, 1830–60, Granville and Orange counties, NCDAH.

52. Franklin, *Free Negro in North Carolina*, p. 126.

53. *State* v. *Patton*, 27 N.C. 147 (1844).

54. N.C. Rev. St., ch. 31, sec. 37; *State* v. *Pate*, 47 N.C. 14 (1854).

55. Swaim, *North Carolina Justice*, pp. 83–88.

56. *State* v. *Patton*, 27 N.C. 147 (1844). In *State* v. *Floyd*, 35 N.C. 354 (1852), Ruffin cited the Bastardy Acts of 1850–51 which allowed evidence concerning a woman's character to be submitted in bastardy suits.

57. Clinton, *Plantation Mistress*, pp. 110–22; Wyatt-Brown, *Southern Honor*, p. 119.

58. Minutes of the Wardens of the Poor, March 25, 1857. October 1832, October 1834, September 1836, Orange County, NCDAH. In September 1853, the Orange County poorhouse had thirty-one inmates. Only sixteen were women, including Nancy Carroll, whose illegitimate child was "idiotic," and Betsy Baldwin, who had been a ward of the poorhouse since infancy. Montgomery County did not build a poorhouse until 1853, depending until then on the "letting out system," in which the indigent were auctioned off to the lowest bidders for their support. By October 1857, the Montgomery County poorhouse had thirteen inmates, eleven of whom were women whose unfamiliar surnames suggest they lacked kinfolk as well as money. See ibid., September 5, 1853; Minutes of the Wardens of the Poor, October 1857, Montgomery County, NCDAH.

59. Willoughby Lucas was bonded for bastardy on May 13, 1857; Joel Lu-

cas's letter to John McLennan is dated July 6, 1857, both in Bastardy Bonds, Montgomery County, NCDAH.

60. Nelson's pregnancy became part of the ongoing feud between the Nichols and Lucas families. Between 1850 and 1860, thirteen of the forty-two women charged with bastardy in Montgomery County accepted out-of-court settlements from the fathers of their children, compared with only six out of ninety-four in Orange and none in Granville. The cash payments ranged from $20 to $60 (Bastardy Bonds, 1850–60, Granville, Orange, and Montgomery counties, NCDAH).

61. Of 169 women charged with bastardy between 1850 and 1860 in the three counties, 29 refused to name the fathers of their children. All but two of these women lived in Orange or Montgomery County. This is consistent with Granville County's reluctance to prosecute more controversial cases of bastardy. Martha Day's testimony, given in November 1845, is in Bastardy Bonds, Granville County, NCDAH.

62. Bond of Mary McQuean, September 1859, Bastardy Bonds, Montgomery County, NCDAH.

63. Bonds of Susan Clemmons (Clements), December 1856, February 1858, Bastardy Bonds, Orange County, NCDAH. In return for her silence, Bartlett Durham posted Clements's bond in 1856. He died before her second court appearance for bastardy. Copies of Clements's unsuccessful suit against Durham's estate are contained in his estate settlement of 1857. The same year that Durham died, Clements entered the poorhouse. By 1860, Clements and her two sons had left the poorhouse and were living with Sallie Clements, age forty-five, probably her mother. See Estate Records of Orange County; Minutes of the Wardens of the Poor, May 25, 1857, Orange County, NCDAH; U.S. Federal Manuscript Census, 1860, Orange County; *Clements* v. *Durham,* 52 N.C. 119 (1859).

64. Despite the many illegitimate free black children who can be identified through the apprenticeship records between 1840 and 1860, only one interracial and two free black couples were charged with bastardy in Granville County; in Orange, five interracial and two free black couples faced similar charges (Bastardy Bonds, Granville and Orange counties, NCDAH).

65. I make this inference from the high number of free blacks who were apprenticed in Granville County, coupled with the comparatively small number of men and women charged with bastardy (one-third the number in Orange).

66. On the eve of the Civil War, eleven of forty-two inmates of the three county poorhouses were black. Of these eleven, there were six aged seventy-five or older, one aged sixty-five, and two who were below the normal age of apprenticeship (U.S. Federal Manuscript Censuses, 1860, Granville, Orange,

and Montgomery counties). See also Franklin, *Free Negro in North Carolina*, p. 237, and Lebsock, *Free Women of Petersburg*, p. 102.

67. *State* v. *Long*, 31 N.C. 340 (1848); *State* v. *Haithcock*, 33 N.C. 34 (1850).

68. There were at least seven families headed by Hurleys in the nearby vicinity of the Hurley sisters in 1850 and 1860. The Hurley name appears in the earliest extant records of Montgomery County and is still prominent in the community today (U.S. Federal Manuscript Censuses, 1850, 1860, Montgomery County; Richter, ed., *Heritage of Montgomery County*, pp. 248–50).

69. *Rosetta Hurley* v. *Pinckney Shaw*, August 1850, Minute Docket of the Superior Court, Montgomery County, NCDAH; *Hannah Hurley* v. *Frederick F. Steed*, April 1849, Minute Docket of the County Court, Montgomery County, NCDAH.

70. *McAulay* v. *Birckhead*, August 1850, Civil Action Papers, Montgomery County, NCDAH; *McAulay* v. *Birckhead*, 35 N.C. 33 (1851).

71. N.C. Rev. Code, ch. 31, sec. 78. See also *Briggs* v. *Evans*, 27 N.C. 13 (1844).

72. Wyatt-Brown, *Southern Honor*, p. 297; Clinton, *Plantation Mistress*, p. 121.

73. Petition of J. R. J. Daniel to Governor Reid, May 24, 1851, Governors' Papers, Reid, NCDAH. See also the petition of Samuel T. Bond to Governor Reid, October 28, 1850, ibid. Bond requested the release of Jesse Blanchard—in prison for cowhiding his wife and assaulting two aunts who harbored her—on grounds the beatings were provoked by the "abusive and provoking language" of his wife and her "meddlesome" aunts.

74. *State* v. *Hussey*, 44 N.C. 124 (1852).

75. Wyatt-Brown, *Southern Honor*, p. 297; Clinton, "Southern Dishonor," p. 65. During the 1850s the courts of Granville, Orange, and Montgomery counties recorded only one indictment for a rape of a black woman and three indictments for rapes committed or attempted on white women. In April 1856, Sarah Ware Nuttall charged a "slave boy" belonging to Mary Wagstaff with having raped her slave Rosa, described in the indictment as "under the age of 10 years" (Criminal Action Papers, Granville, Orange, and Montgomery counties, NCDAH).

76. Letter of J. L. G. Gulley and accompanying petition to Governor Bragg, April 1, 1856, Governors' Papers, Bragg, NCDAH. There were, however, also those who viewed the pardoning of a black man for raping *any* white woman as a threat to "the most sacred ties that bind us to our mothers, wives, sisters, and daughters." See H. B. Williams to Governor Graham, September 6, 1846, Governors' Papers, Graham, NCDAH. Fifteen petitioners protested in 1860 that speculators stood to gain from the pardon of slaves found guilty of rape who were then ordered sold out of the state. See Petition to Governor Ellis, April 17, 1860, Governors' Papers, Ellis, NCDAH. Few free black men accused

of rape ever had white citizens petition for their pardon (if they were fortunate to survive a lynch mob to gain a trial). See Wyatt-Brown, *Southern Honor*, pp. 436–39. There is a recorded case of the pardon of a free black man for the crime of attempted rape, however. William Boon of Sampson County received a pardon in 1852 for a conviction that, according to Attorney General William Eaton, had been decided on "a bare possibility of guilt" (Wm. Eaton to Governor Reid, July 22, 1852, Governors' Papers, Reid, NCDAH).

Chapter 5

1. For recent works that highlight southern women's opposition to the Civil War, see especially Faust, "Altars of Sacrifice"; Rable, *Civil Wars*; and Paludan, *Victims*.

2. "Poor women" refers primarily to women from landless households during the first two years of the war. By 1863, even many women of the yeomanry had become impoverished as a result of the war. The North Carolina yeomanry's revolt against the Confederacy is recounted in Auman, "Neighbor against Neighbor"; Escott, *Many Excellent People*; and Bynum, " 'War within a War.' "

3. Rawick, ed., *American Slave*, 14:pt. 1, p. 357. See also Escott, *Slavery Remembered*, p. 121.

4. Rawick, ed., *American Slave*, 15:pt. 2, pp. 102–3.

5. Ibid., 19:165–66, 174–75. On the sexual exploitation of slave women by masters, see White, *Ar'n't I a Woman?*; and Jennings, " 'Us Colored Women Had to Go through a Plenty.' "

6. Mag Bingham to brother, October 30, 1862, Lynch Letters. See also Escott, *Slavery Remembered*, p. 122.

7. *State* v. *Massey and Joe*, Spring 1857, Criminal Actions Concerning Slaves and Free Persons of Color, Granville County, NCDAH; *State* v. *Jim, Dick, and Clary*, Fall 1860, Miscellaneous Records, Montgomery County, NCDAH. The attempted slave insurrection in Orange County was reported to Governor Bragg on December 24, 1856, by five county justices of the peace (Governors' Papers, Bragg, NCDAH).

8. *State* v. *Joe and Massey*, Spring 1857, Criminal Actions Concerning Slaves and Free Persons of Color, Granville County, NCDAH.

9. Ibid.; Rawick, ed., *American Slave*, 15:pt. 2, pp. 46–50.

10. Rawick, ed., *American Slave*, 15:pt. 2, pp. 47–50.

11. *State* v. *Jim, Dick, and Clary*, Fall 1860, Miscellaneous Records, Montgomery County, NCDAH.

12. Ibid.

13. Ibid.

14. On the symbolism of the "death bird" in black folk culture, see Levine, *Black Culture and Black Consciousness*, pp. 56, 63, 66. On slave women's resistance, see White, *Ar'n't I a Woman?*, pp. 76–84, and Fox-Genovese, "Strategies and Forms of Resistance."

15. For comments by Royster's contemporaries on his fears of being murdered by his slaves, see his estate papers, 1863, in Estate Records, Granville County, NCDAH. On the separate murders of John Lockhart and Isaac H. Stroud by their slaves, see *State* v. *America, Dan, and Solomon*, February 1863, and *State* v. *Lucian and Allen*, March 1863; both in Criminal Action Papers, Orange County, NCDAH. For correspondence concerning the murders, see Paul C. Cameron to Governor Vance, February 19, 23, 1863; Henry K. Nash to Governor Vance, February 20, 1863; H. B. Guthrie to Governor Vance, February 21, 1863, all in Governors' Papers, Vance, NCDAH.

16. Emily Jenkins to Governor Clark, November 11, 1861, Governors' Papers, Clark, NCDAH; Sarah A. Elliot to Governor Vance, January 6, 1864, Governors' Papers, Vance, NCDAH. There were unsubstantiated reports of a slave conspiracy that extended from Troy, in Montgomery County, to Society Hill, South Carolina (H[enry] Nutt to Governor Vance, December 12, 1864, in Yearns and Barrett, eds., *North Carolina Civil War Documentary*, pp. 257–58).

17. For an excellent analysis of the way in which sexual stereotyping of black males provided a tool for whites' regaining and maintaining power during Reconstruction, see Hall, "'The Mind That Burns in Each Body,'" pp. 329–33.

18. Petition to Governor Vance, September 1, 1864, Governors' Papers, Vance, NCDAH.

19. *State* v. *Elias*, November 1864, and C. Stephens to Orange County Court, March 7, 1865, Criminal Action Papers, Orange County, NCDAH.

20. Governor Vance granted clemency to Sam, a slave who raped Melitia Pullen, a free black woman, on July 1, 1864. A copy of the document is in Governors' Papers, Worth, NCDAH.

21. Petition to Governor Clark, August 23, 1861, Governors' Papers, Clark, NCDAH. On the pardon of Gray, see Governors' Letter Books, p. 80, Clark, NCDAH.

22. *Belvin* v. *Belvin*, Fall 1866, Divorce Records, Granville County, NCDAH; *Wells* v. *Wells*, Spring 1866, Divorce Records, Orange County, NCDAH.

23. *Couch* v. *Couch*, Fall 1867; *Bowling* v. *Bowling*, Spring 1866, both in Divorce Records, Orange County, NCDAH.

24. Ibid.; *Belvin* v. *Belvin*, Fall 1866, Divorce Records, Granville County, NCDAH.

25. A. K. Lane to Governor Worth, n.d., Governors' Papers, Worth, NCDAH.

26. Escott, *Many Excellent People*, p. 54; E. T. Graham to Governor Clark, November 20, 1861, Governors' Papers, Clark, NCDAH.

27. Copy of "An Act to Prevent, during the existing War, Monopolies, Extortions and Speculation in Breadstuffs and Other Articles of general use and consumption, and to make such acts criminal, and to provide penalties for the same," December 14, 1861, Governors' Papers, Clark, NCDAH. For evidence of the act's failure, see Henry T. Farmer to Governor Clark, April 17, 1862, and Major Archibald McLean to Governor Clark, May 17, 1862, ibid.

28. *State* v. *Gideon Canaday, Sally Canaday, and Mary Canaday*, November 1861; *State* v. *Anderson Day*, November 1863; *State* v. *Sophia Day*, February 1864, all in Criminal Action Papers, Orange County, NCDAH. Nancy Day, as head of the Day household in 1860, claimed $50 in personal property but owned no land. She was the widow of Reuben Day, Sr., and the mother of Reuben Day, Jr. (U.S. Federal Manuscript Census, 1860, Orange County).

29. The dead woman's husband was George W. Johnson, who was incarcerated at the military prison in Wilmington. In response to her death, Governor Vance recommended Johnson's release from prison (Ralph P. Buxton to General W. H. C. Whiting, November 27, 1863, Governors' Papers, Vance, NCDAH).

30. Franklin, "Enslavement of Free Negroes in North Carolina," p. 425. See also Franklin, *Free Negro in North Carolina*, pp. 218–20.

31. Mitchell, *Legal Aspects of Conscription and Exemption in North Carolina*, p. 64.

32. Wilson Williams, age forty-three, was ordered into Confederate military service in April 1862. He applied for exemption on May 30, 1864, and was recommended by Lieutenant T. H. Haughton for detail duty on July 11, 1864. D. C. Pearson approved the exemption on July 20, 1864, but his superior, Josiah Jones, overturned the decision nine days later. Williams was ordered to camp on July 30, 1864 (County Court Minutes, April 1862, Montgomery County, NCDAH; Ms., Vol. 1, Files 21, 38, Letter Book of the Chief Enrolling Office, Seventh Congressional District, Lexington, North Carolina, Confederate Conscript Papers, SHC, UNC-CH).

33. File 13, Letter Book of the Chief Enrolling Office, Seventh Congressional District, Lexington, North Carolina, Confederate Conscript Papers, SHC, UNC-CH.

34. Franklin, *Free Negro in North Carolina*, pp. 186–88. Antebellum accusations against whites and free blacks for trading illegally with slaves are scattered throughout the Criminal Action Papers and Minute Dockets of the County Courts of the three counties in this study. For Granville County, see also Criminal Actions Concerning Slaves and Free Persons of Color, NCDAH.

35. Rawick, ed., *American Slave*, 14:pt. 1, pp. 60, 266, 15:pt. 2, p. 52.

36. Auman, "Neighbor against Neighbor"; *State* v. *Jane Deaton*, Spring 1865,

Criminal Action Papers, Montgomery County, NCDAH; *State* v. *Elizabeth Wright, Sarah Wright, Nancy Wright, and Milly Floyd,* Fall 1864, ibid. The U.S. Federal Manuscript Census, 1860, lists Elizabeth Wright as a forty-five-year-old widow who headed a household of six. She owned real estate valued at $140 and personal property valued at $25. The description of Margaret Church was given by Major E. A. Carr, Fifth U.S. Cavalry, to Brigadier General J. A. Campbell, General Military Commander of North Carolina. Army Command Letters, Vol. 69, pp. 101–14, ser. 3276, Record Group 393, National Archives, Washington, D.C.

37. In May 1863, Kearsey was charged with stealing four wagon tires from Susan Green and a buggy harness from Sheriff Philpott. In the fall of 1864, Kearsey's brother-in-law William Tyler was charged with "aiding, assisting and maintaining" Kearsey, who was enrolled in the Confederate army but refused to serve (Criminal Action Papers, Granville County, NCDAH). Kearsey was an unusually prosperous free black. In 1860, he claimed $1,800 in real estate and $600 in personal property (U.S. Federal Manuscript Census, 1860, Granville County).

38. Petition to Governor Worth, October 1867, Governors' Papers, Worth, NCDAH.

39. Ibid.

40. *State* v. *Leonard and Stewart,* Fall 1860, Criminal Action Papers, Granville County, NCDAH.

41. *State* v. *Hussey and Dunn*; *State* v. *Hussey and Burroughs*; *State* v. *Hussey and Freeman*; *State* v. *Bean and Hussey*; *State* v. *Freeman and Hussey,* Fall 1861–January 1864, Miscellaneous Records, Montgomery County, NCDAH; *State* v. *John Hussey,* Spring 1863, Criminal Action Papers, Montgomery County, NCDAH. The Husseys appear never to have personally identified themselves as African American. Besides marrying a white woman, John Hussey owned eleven slaves. In 1883 his son Lindsay sued his wife for divorce; among his charges was that his wife's sister had had a child by a "coal-black negro" (U.S. Federal Manuscript Census, Slave Schedule, 1860, Montgomery County; Divorce Records, Montgomery County, NCDAH).

42. Escott, "Poverty and Governmental Aid for the Poor"; Kenzer, *Kinship and Neighborhood,* pp. 84–92.

43. Gates, *Agriculture and the Civil War,* pp. 38–40. For a vivid commentary on the famous riot in Richmond, Virginia, see the *Richmond Whig,* April 6, 1863.

44. *Greensborough Patriot,* April 16, 1863.

45. Ibid., April 9, 1863.

46. Magnolia Lee and company to Governor Vance, January 16, 1863; L. N. Brassfield to Governor Vance, March 27, 1863, Governors' Papers, Vance, NCDAH. In 1860, Brassfield's husband, James W. Brassfield, claimed $250 in

personal property but no land (U.S. Federal Manuscript Census, 1860, Orange County).

47. Harriet Dickey to Governor Vance, June 24, 1863, and Mary C. Clayton to Governor Vance, July 11, 1863, Governors' Papers, Vance, NCDAH. Harriet Dickey's husband claimed $75 in personal property and no land. The 1860 census did not include Mary Clayton, but she claimed in her letter to be landless (U.S. Federal Manuscript Census, 1860, Orange County).

48. Martha A. Allen to Governor Vance, May 6, 1863, and Jehial Atwater to Governor Vance, May 18, 1863, Governors' Papers, Vance, NCDAH. Two Martha Allens appear in the 1860 census; one was married to Ruffin Allen, a farm laborer, and the other to David Allen, who claimed $100 in personal property. Both households were landless. In 1860, Jehial Atwater owned $5,000 in real estate and $34,555 in personal property (U.S. Federal Manuscript Census, 1860, Orange County). For statistics on Orange County relief, see Escott, "Poverty and Governmental Aid for the Poor," pp. 477–78.

49. Louena Cates to Governor Vance, July 25, 1863, and Lucinda Glenn to Governor Vance, October 29, 1863, Governors' Papers, Vance, NCDAH. In 1860, Louena was married to Willie Cates, who owned $75 in real estate. At that time the couple had four children ranging in age from two to eight years. Unmarried at the time of the census, Glenn, whose maiden name was Batchelor, lived in a propertyless household of four spinners that probably included her mother and sisters (U.S. Federal Manuscript Census, 1860, Orange County).

50. *Fayetteville Observer*, March 30, 1863.

51. Margaret Guess and Bettie Horner to Governor Vance, August 6, 1863, and Martha A. Veazey to Governor Vance, December 21, 1863, Governors' Papers, Vance, NCDAH. In 1850 Margaret Guess was the wife of William Guess, a farmer who did not own property in his own name. The Guesses were probably related to William W. Guess, a nearby miller, who was shunned by secessionists during the war because of his Unionist views. See testimony of William W. Guess, claim of John Cole, no. 12789, 1877, in Claims of Loyal Citizens for Supplies Furnished during the Rebellion, Orange County, Southern Claims Commission, National Archives, Washington, D.C. According to the 1860 census, Bettie Horner was a landless farmer who headed a household of five and claimed $300 in personal property. I did not find Martha Veazey listed in either census (U.S. Federal Manuscript Censuses, 1850, 1860, Orange County).

52. Margaret Guess and Bettie Horner to Governor Vance, August 6, 1863, C. W. Walker to Governor Vance, May 8, 1863, Governors' Papers, Vance, NCDAH. Neither Walker nor her husband, W. J. Walker, appeared in the U.S. Federal Manuscript Census, 1860, Orange County; W. J. Walker, however, was listed in the slave schedule of the same census as the owner of two slaves.

53. *State* v. *Rebecca Davis, Nancy Bowers, Nancy Carroll*, Spring 1865, Criminal Action Papers, Orange County, NCDAH; U.S. Federal Manuscript Census, 1860, Orange County. William McCown was listed in the 1850 Federal Manuscript Census for Orange County as a thirty-seven-year-old farmer with property worth $4,500.

54. *State* v. *Martha Briggs, Lucy Fuller, Sally Fuller*, May 1864, Criminal Action Papers, Granville County. Charges were eventually dropped against all but Sally Fuller. The description of the elder Coghill's battle with the two women is in J. F. Coghill to Mit Coghill, March 28, 1864, James O. Coghill Papers, Special Collections Department, Duke University. Martha Briggs did not appear in the 1860 census. The Fullers lived with their parents, John and Rebecca Fuller. J. O. Coghill owned land worth $1,142 and had personal property valued at $900 (U.S. Federal Manuscript Census, 1860, Granville County).

55. *State* v. *Henry Henly, Luvenia Pratty, Arena Holmes, Elizabeth May, Celestia Hays, Judy Peace, Jacksey Harp, Frances Morton, Calvin May, Mrs. William Ball, Mrs. Alexander Morton, Mrs. Benjamin Catlett, Mrs. Samuel Evans*, Fall 1865, Criminal Action Papers, Granville County, NCDAH. Marriage records and the 1860 census for Granville County reveal the rioters' kinship ties and modest yeoman backgrounds. Henly was the maiden name of both Luvenia Pratty and Arena Holmes. The census recorded two Henry Henlys: one a farm laborer, the other a farmer with land worth $100. May was the maiden name of Celestia Hays, and Elizabeth May was the wife of William May, a farmer who owned land valued at $225 and personal property worth $50. Peace was the maiden name of Frances Morton. Elizabeth Ball was the wife of William Ball, who owned $500 worth of personal property but no land in 1860. Mrs. Samuel (Martha) Evans, whose maiden name was Catlett, was apparently the sister-in-law of Mrs. Benjamin Catlett. Martha Catlett, unmarried in August 1860, lived with Benjamin Catlett in the propertyless household of William Catlett, probably their father. Samuel Evans, whom Martha Catlett married in September 1860, owned land worth $125. In contrast to his robbers, Stephen Dement owned land valued at $3,498 and personal property worth $2,500 (Marriage Bonds, Granville County, NCDAH; U.S. Federal Manuscript Census, 1860, Granville County).

56. Escott, *Many Excellent People*; Bynum, "'War within a War.'"

Chapter 6

1. Easter Robins to M. S. Robins, December 28, 1864, Marmaduke S. Robins Papers, SHC, UNC-CH.

2. Yearns and Barrett, eds., *North Carolina Civil War Documentary*, pp. xii, 94.

3. Auman, "Neighbor against Neighbor," p. 69.

4. Sitterson, *Secession Movement*, pp. 196–97; Randall and Donald, *The Civil War and Reconstruction*, pp. 186–87; Yates, *The Confederacy and Zeb Vance*, p. 16.

5. Butts, "Irrepressible Conflict," pp. 44–66; Kruman, *Parties and Politics in North Carolina*; Auman, "Neighbor against Neighbor"; Escott, *Many Excellent People*; Honey, "War within the Confederacy."

6. Escott and Crow, "Social Order and Violent Disorder." The percentage of population in slaves for the following Piedmont counties, in contrast to a state average of 33.3 percent, was as follows: Randolph, 9.8; Moore, 22.0; Montgomery, 23.8; Chatham, 32.7; Davidson, 18.5; Guilford, 18.0; and Alamance, 29.0.

7. Unsigned, undated poem to Governor Zebulon Vance, Governors' Papers, Vance, NCDAH.

8. Robins to Robins, December 28, 1864, Robins Papers.

9. Davis, "Women on Top," pp. 130, 136, 147, 149–50.

10. Enrolling Officer P. H. Williamson to Captain D. C. Pearson, August 5, 1864, Confederate Conscript Papers, SHC, UNC-CH.

11. Elizabeth Flowers to Governor Ellis, June 20, 1861, Governors' Papers, Ellis, NCDAH.

12. Martha Coletrane to Governor Vance, November 18, 1862, John A. Beaman to Governor Vance, n.d., both in Governors' Papers, Vance, NCDAH. Beaman enlisted in Company K, Thirty-fourth North Carolina Regiment, on March 5, 1863, and deserted with his brother Jackson Beaman on May 13, 1863 (Adjutant General's Roll of Honor, NCDAH). For Beaman's relationship with the Wesleyan Unionists of Montgomery County, see Chart 6.1.

13. Anonymous letter from Bryant Swamp in Bladen County to Governor Vance, February 18, 1863, Governors' Papers, Vance, NCDAH.

14. Petition to Governor Vance, April 13, 1864, Governors' Papers, Vance, NCDAH. The petition asked for the pardon of five women convicted of breaking into the grain warehouse at the Bladenboro depot in broad daylight.

15. Yearns and Barrett, eds., *North Carolina Civil War Documentary*, pp. 219–22.

16. "A Poor Woman and children" to Governor Vance, January 10, 1865, Governors' Papers, Vance, NCDAH.

17. Nancy Hines, Margaret M. Smith, and M. W. Harrel[?] to Governor Vance, February 9, 1863, Governors' Papers, Vance, NCDAH. For evidence of even higher prices, see Escott, *Many Excellent People*, p. 54.

18. Ransom and Sutch, *One Kind of Freedom*, p. 159.

19. For an account of the Laurel Valley murders, see Paludan, *Victims*. Letters detailing the murders are scattered throughout the Governors' Papers from the war and reconstruction years. See especially Augustus T. Merriman to Governor Vance, February 24, 1863, Governors' Papers, Vance, NCDAH.

The testimony of Nancy Franklin on the murder of her sons is in Governors' Papers, Worth, NCDAH. An account of the entire episode is in the papers of William Woods Holden, Special Collections Department, Duke University. For a sensationalized account of the massacre, see Wilson, *Brief History of the Cruelties and Atrocities of the Rebellion*.

20. Petition of Judah Shelton, Marthy Jane Shelton, Elizabeth Shelton, Polly Shelton, Margret Shelton, Rody Hall, Sarah Shelton, Rachel Shelton, Nancy King, Liney Norton, and Emeline Riddle to Governor Vance, May 29, 1863, Governors' Papers, Vance, NCDAH; Paludan, *Victims*, pp. 126–33.

21. Sitterson, *Secession Movement*, p. 22.

22. Auman, "Neighbor against Neighbor," p. 66.

23. Ibid., p. 59.

24. On March 2, 1860, the Hulins, Hurleys, and Moores were indicted along with Daniel Wilson and Hugh Baker, who were Wesleyan leaders from Guilford County, for passing "incendiary" literature (*State* v. *Daniel Wilson, Hugh Baker, Hiram Hulin, Jesse Hulin, Nelson Hulin, William Hurley, Sr., William Hurley, Jr., and Spencer Moore*, Criminal Action Papers, Montgomery County, NCDAH). On the participation of the Hulins, Moores, and Hurleys in the southern antislavery movement, see also Crooks, *Life of Reverend Adam Crooks*, pp. 28–105, and Nicholson, *Wesleyan Methodism in the South*, pp. 53–76, 106–13. For evidence that other branches of the Hurley and Moore families served the Confederacy, see Adjutant General's Roll of Honor, Co. C, Twenty-third North Carolina Regiment, and Co. K, Thirty-fourth North Carolina Regiment, NCDAH, and Lassiter, "*Pattern of Timeless Moments*," pp. 315–43.

25. J. P. Aldridge to Governor Ellis, June 22, 1861, Governors' Papers, Ellis, NCDAH; Marinda Moore to her mother, August 25, 1861, Branson Family Papers, NCDAH.

26. James Moore to Governor Clark, July 18, 1861, Governors' Papers, Clark, NCDAH. John Hilton, the alleged leader of this association, indicates that this was the secret pro-Union organization, the Heroes of America. For an excellent history of this long-maligned group, see Auman and Scarboro, "Heroes of America." See also Honey, "War within the Confederacy," pp. 82–83. Various regions of the state reported Unionist organizing after secession. See petition from Durham's Creek in Beaufort County, reporting that certain citizens were ready to hoist a United States flag and defend it with arms (Petition to Governor Ellis, August 9, 1861, Governors' Papers, Ellis, NCDAH). From Polk County, Alexander J. Cansler reported that Confederate families feared the large number of Unionists in the area. "What I have said in relation to this county," he added, "is true in relation to the entire West" (Cansler to Governor Ellis, August 20, 1861, ibid.).

27. The names of deserters from Montgomery County were compiled from the Adjutant General's Roll of Honor, NCDAH; Confederate Conscript Pa-

pers, SHC, UNC-CH; Miscellaneous Records, Montgomery County, NCDAH; and the papers of Alexander Carey McAlister, SHC, UNC-CH.

28. Household and family links were compiled from the U.S. Federal Manuscript Censuses of 1850 and 1860, Estate Records, Wills, and Marriage Bonds, all for Montgomery County, NCDAH.

29. Ibid.

30. Yearns and Barrett, eds., *North Carolina Civil War Documentary*, pp. 100–102. Emily Branson of Randolph County wrote Governor Vance on April 21, 1863, that "deserters are so numerous that we dare not go alone to the nearest neighbor's house" (Governors' Papers, Vance, NCDAH).

31. Governor Vance to Secretary of War James A. Seddon, December 21, 1863, Vance to Lt. Col. J. Hargrave, August 29, 1864, both in Governors' Papers, Vance, NCDAH.

32. Auman, "Neighbor against Neighbor," p. 87.

33. Richter, ed., *Heritage of Montgomery County*, pp. 316–17.

34. Auman, "Neighbor against Neighbor," p. 87.

35. Auman, "North Carolina's Inner Civil War," p. 82.

36. First Lt. William A. Pugh to Major Archer Anderson, March 21, 1863, Governors' Papers, Vance, NCDAH. For further evidence of the importance of kinship among deserters, see Report of Lt. Col. A. C. McAlister to General Robert E. Lee, March 16, 1865, McAlister Papers.

37. Phebe Crook to Governor Vance, June 19, 1863, Governors' Papers, Vance, NCDAH. Phebe Crook's sister Clarinda was married to Hiram Hulin's son Nelson. In 1860, Phebe lived with her sister and brother-in-law in Montgomery County. The women's parents were William, a schoolteacher, and Rachel Crook (U.S. Federal Manuscript Censuses 1850, 1860; Marriage Bonds, Montgomery County, NCDAH).

38. Richter, ed., *Heritage of Montgomery County*, pp. 316–17.

39. Thomas Settle to Governor Vance, October 4, 1864, reprinted in Yearns and Barrett, eds., *North Carolina Civil War Documentary*, pp. 103–14. In Montgomery County, the Owens band murdered slaveholder Pleasant Simmons and secessionist Jacob Sanders in June 1864, the same month that Mary Chambers recommended amnesty for deserters (*State* v. *William Owens, Riley Cagle, John Latham and Murphy Owens*, Criminal Action Papers, Montgomery County, NCDAH). For further details, see [Representative] J. T. Leach to Governor Holden, April 5 and September 1, 1869, and J. R. Bulla to Governor Holden, March 27, 1868, Governors' Papers, Holden, NCDAH.

40. Auman, "Inner Civil War," p. 188; Phebe Crook to Governor Vance, June 19, 1863; Phebe's sister Clarinda Hulin wrote a similar letter to Governor Vance on November 19, 1863; both in Governors' Papers, Vance, NCDAH; Honey, "War within the Confederacy," p. 83.

41. M. J. Hogan to Governor Vance, n.d., Governors' Papers, Vance,

NCDAH. Slaveholder Mary Chambers took a different tack. She urged Governor Vance to issue another proclamation of amnesty to deserters as a means to lessen depredations (M. A. Chambers to Governor Vance, June 25, 1864, Governors' Papers, Vance, NCDAH).

42. Miss M. M. McMasters to Marmaduke S. Robins, Robins Papers; letter of Jane Sugg, quoted in Auman, "Neighbor against Neighbor," p. 83.

43. Alexander K. Pearce to Bryan Tyson, October 24, 1864, Bryan Tyson Papers, Special Collections Department, Duke University; Thomas W. Ritter to Governor Vance, January 25, 1864, Governors' Papers, Vance, NCDAH.

44. *Greensborough Patriot*, February 19, March 12, 1863.

45. Ibid., April 16, 23, 1863.

46. Fall 1865, Criminal Action Papers, Montgomery County, NCDAH. Perninia Trogden, Mary Lucas, Sarah Moore, Amy Latham, Lilia Crowder, Mishail Wright, Sarah Hulin, Union Vuncannon, Ally Nichols, and Eliza Jackson perpetrated the riot on May 1, 1865. With the exceptions of Nichols and Lucas, all of the women came from families in Montgomery and Randolph counties that were known as Unionists or deserters. Sarah Moore was the wife of deserter Elisha Moore and the sister of deserters John, Jesse, and William Hulin. Mary Lucas was either the wife or daughter of slaveholder Willoughby Lucas. Sisters Ally Nichols and Amy Latham, the wife of yeoman farmer Harvey Latham, were daughters of yeoman farmer John Nichols. Lilia Crowder's maiden name was Moore so she and Sarah Moore were probably related. Eliza Jackson was a propertyless widow who was living in 1860 with the Unionist Bryant Beaman family, to whom she was related by marriage. (See Richter, ed., *Heritage of Montgomery County*, passim; Marriage Bonds, Montgomery County, NCDAH; and U.S. Federal Manuscript Census, 1860, Montgomery County.) On May 24 of the previous year, a special court session was held to consider punishing deserters' wives. No official action was taken (Minute Docket of the County Court, Montgomery County, NCDAH).

47. Nancy Mangum to Governor Vance, April 9, 1863, reprinted in Yearns and Barrett, eds., *North Carolina Civil War Documentary*, p. 221. Although the war itself may not have enriched the Holt family, their wartime methods of doing business enabled them to survive the disruption of the economy. After the war, Edwin Holt and his son Thomas Holt exploited the northern capital that Reconstruction made available and became one of North Carolina's most successful New South families. For accounts of the Holts' successful postwar careers, see Beatty, "Edwin Holt Family"; Billings, *Planters and the Making of a "New South,"* p. 65; and Escott, *Many Excellent People*, p. 199.

48. Diary entry in David Schenck Books, December 12, 1863. Schenck's claim that even upper-class citizens of North Carolina suffered from a lack of basic supplies is contradicted by the reminiscences of Tempie Herndon Durham, a slave of wealthy planter George Herndon of Chatham County. Dur-

ham claimed that even slaves on the Herndon plantation had access to chickens, geese, flour, milk, and butter (Rawick, ed., *American Slave*, 14:pt. 1, p. 285).

Justice Pearson and Holden had statewide reputations for their hostility to the Confederacy. Pearson issued numerous writs of habeas corpus on behalf of men charged with desertion. Many Confederate leaders feared that he would declare the conscript laws unconstitutional if given the chance. See, for example, R. T. Armfield to Governor Vance, February 19, 1863, Governors' Papers, Vance, NCDAH. Holden had a long and varied political career in North Carolina that began with the powerful editorship of the *Raleigh Standard* and ended with his impeachment as the state's governor during Reconstruction in 1871. His wartime leadership of North Carolina's Peace Movement earned him the lasting hatred of slaveholders. See Harris, "William Woods Holden."

49. Letters of J. S. Patterson and William Thomas to Governor Vance, June 15, 1863, and August 11, 1864, both in Governors' Papers, Vance, NCDAH.

50. First Lt. William A. Pugh to Major Archer Anderson, March 21, 1863, Governors' Papers, Vance, NCDAH.

51. Nancy L. Robbins and J. W. Conner, Jr., to A. C. McAlister, March 16, 1865, McAlister Papers.

52. Major John W. Graham, Thirty-sixth North Carolina Regiment, to Governor Vance, December 6, 1863, Governors' Papers, Vance, NCDAH.

53. Governor Vance to General J. C. Vaugn, December 17, 1864, Governors' Letter Books, Vance, pp. 311–12, NCDAH.

54. Martha A. Sheets to Sheriff Aaron H. Sanders, January 27, 1865, Criminal Action Papers, Montgomery County, NCDAH.

55. William and John Hulin had enlisted in the Confederate army on March 1, 1862, in the Forty-fourth North Carolina Regiment. See Lassiter, "*Pattern of Timeless Moments*," p. 330. On Jesse Hulin's refusal to enlist, see Richter, ed., *Heritage of Montgomery County*, pp. 316–17. Nelson Hulin, aged thirty-two in 1862, never served in the army and may have evaded the draft.

56. Candace Beaman Hulin was the daughter of Effarilla Moore Beaman, a sister of Valentine Moore (see Chart 6.1). Hiram and Candace Hulin were robbed twice in August 1864, once by sixteen men who forced their way into their home, and again by five men of planter backgrounds. See *State* v. *David Barringer, Dumas Coggin, Harris Russell, and Thos. Haltom* and *State* v. *Thomas C. Haltom, Spencer Haltom, Dumas Coggin, et al.*, 1864, Criminal Action Papers, Montgomery County, NCDAH. Caroline Hulin, the wife of Jesse Hulin, was arrested and assaulted by Martin Overton, a private in the Home Guard, on September 1, 1864. Overton filed an affidavit at his trial claiming he had acted under orders of Major R. Anderson, commander of his Home Guard bat-

talion (*State* v. *Martin Overton*, Spring 1867, Criminal Action Papers, Montgomery County, NCDAH).

Dias Hulin, a younger son of Hiram Hulin who was under the legal age of conscription, was assaulted and battered sometime late in the war by Davidson Barringer and James Cotton, members of prominent planter families (*State* v. *Davidson Barringer and James Cotton*, Special Court of Oyer and Terminer, 1865, Criminal Action Papers, Montgomery County, NCDAH).

Hiram Hulin detailed the murders of his three sons in a letter to Colonel M. Cogwell, September 28, 1867, reprinted in McPherson, ed., "Letters from North Carolina to Andrew Johnson," pp. 118–19. My thanks to William T. Auman for calling this letter to my attention. Hulin named Captain Henry Plott of Cabarrus County as the man who ordered the killings. In the fall of 1866, Plott was charged with assault and battery with intent to kill the Hulin brothers, but there is no record of conviction (*State* v. *Henry Plott*, Criminal Action Papers, Montgomery County, NCDAH). See also Richter, ed., *Heritage of Montgomery County*, pp. 316–17; Auman, "Inner Civil War," p. 89; and Nicholson, *Wesleyan Methodism in the South*, p. 111.

57. E. Beckerdite to M. S. Robins, January 21, 1865, Robins Papers.

Epilogue

1. Rose, *In Slavery and Freedom*, pp. 100–101. For a collection of state studies that focus on the political history of Reconstruction, see Olsen, ed., *Reconstruction and Redemption in the South*. See also Burton and McMath, eds., *Toward a New South?*; and Magdol, *A Right to the Land*.

2. Foner, *Nothing but Freedom*; McPherson, *Abraham Lincoln and the Second American Revolution*, p. 22.

3. For a sampling of the recent literature on Reconstruction, see especially Fields, *Slavery and Freedom on the Middle Ground*; Escott, *Many Excellent People*; Alexander, *North Carolina Faces the Freedmen*; Ash, *Middle Tennessee Society Transformed*; Wallenstein, *From Slave South to New South*; Giddings, *When and Where I Enter*, pp. 57–74; Jones, *Labor of Love*, pp. 44–78; Rable, *Civil Wars*, pp. 240–64.

4. Murray, *Proud Shoes*, pp. 164, 231. On the treatment of former slaves in North Carolina immediately after the war, see Alexander, *North Carolina Faces the Freedmen*.

5. Giddings, *When and Where I Enter*, p. 59; Jones, *Labor of Love*, p. 53; Murray, *Proud Shoes*, p. 242; Estate Papers of Mary Ruffin Smith, Estate Records, Orange County, NCDAH. On postwar black struggles in general, see Litwack, *Been in the Storm So Long*; and Harding, *There Is a River*, pp. 242–332.

6. Schweninger, "Prosperous Blacks in the South," pp. 51–53; U.S. Federal Manuscript Census, 1870, Granville County.

7. Petition to Governor Holden, October 11, 1868, Governors' Papers, Holden, NCDAH. Mayo, one of the petitioners, served in the North Carolina legislature that same year (Balanoff, "Negro Legislators in the North Carolina General Assembly," p. 23).

8. Petition to Governor Holden, August 11, 1869, Governors' Papers, Holden, NCDAH. On the Klan in North Carolina during Reconstruction, see Escott, *Many Excellent People*, pp. 154–64; Trelease, *White Terror*, pp. 189–338; Olsen, *Carpetbagger's Crusade*. Information on the Klan's activities is scattered throughout the Governors' Papers, Holden, NCDAH. See also the William Woods Holden Collection. For a study of Granville County women's use of the courts to combat sexual violence during Reconstruction, see Edwards, "Sexual Violence, Gender, and Reconstruction."

9. U.S. Federal Manuscript Censuses, 1870, 1880, Montgomery County. For an excellent discussion of growing landlessness among the yeomanry after the war, see Hahn, *Roots of Southern Populism*, pp. 158–65. On Orange County, see Kenzer, *Kinship and Neighborhood*, pp. 111–14. For North Carolina, see Nathans, *Quest for Progress*, pp. 10–13.

10. *James G. Allen* v. *Rosetta Hurley, Ann Hurley, and Hannah Hurley*, February 1875–Fall 1877, Civil Action Papers Concerning Land, 1870–80, and Minute Docket of the Superior Court, Fall 1878, both in Montgomery County, NCDAH. In 1860, Allen had real estate valued at $800 and personal property at $6,000. The family operated a store, grist mill, and cotton gin. Allen was married to Jane Saunders, whose family's lands adjoined the Hurleys'. In 1860, the Hurley sisters' household was headed by their father, Stephen, who owned $125 in real estate. In 1870, the household was headed by Rosetta Hurley, and the value of its real estate had dropped to $30. In 1873, Rosetta was taxed on 160 acres of land valued at $218. This represented an increased value of $188 in real estate since 1870 as a result of Willis Hurley's transfer of 140 acres to his sisters (U.S. Federal Manuscript Censuses, 1860, 1870, Montgomery County; Richter, ed., *Heritage of Montgomery County*, p. 105; Tax Levies on Land, 1873–80, Montgomery County, NCDAH).

11. U.S. Federal Manuscript Census, 1880, Montgomery County, NCDAH; Minutes of the Wardens of the Poor and Paupers Records, 1843–1910, in Officials' Bonds and Records, 1837–1918, Montgomery County, NCDAH.

12. Clipping of address to the Lincolnton Female Seminary, 1869, in Schenck Books. On Schenck's membership in the Klan, see Trelease, *White Terror*, pp. 197–98.

13. Will of William B. Murray, 1869, Wills, Orange County, NCDAH; Kenzer, *Kinship and Neighborhood*, p. 97; Testimonies of Joby Vincent, David T.

Clark, and Dr. T. J. Wilson, regarding the death of Maria Murray, June 29, 1873, all in Coroners' Reports, Orange County, NCDAH.

14. Testimonies of Joby Vincent, David T. Clark, and Dr. T. J. Wilson, regarding the death of Maria Murray, June 29, 1873, Coroners' Reports, Orange County, NCDAH.

15. Clipping of address to the Lincolnton Female Seminary, 1869, Schenck Books.

16. Coroner's Report on the Death of Maria Murray, June 29, 1873, Coroners' Reports, Orange County, NCDAH. Two days before her suicide, Murray drew up a will in which she gave custody of her children to their paternal grandparents and directed that her property be distributed among her two children. She concluded the will with a suicide note: "Good bye to all, forgive me dear friends. I've toiled hard for my little children. Now in a moment of unthoughtedness have ruined them forever, but God will have mercy on them" (Will of Maria F. Murray, June 26, 1873, Wills, Orange County, NCDAH).

17. Asa Chambers to [attorney] Ralph Gorrell, March 25, 1866, Ralph Gorrell Papers, SHC, UNC-CH; Apprenticeships of Dick, Joe, Howell, and Jennie, October 1866, and Nancy, Harry, and Tamer to Mary A. Chambers, April 1868, all in Minute Docket of the County Court, Montgomery County, NCDAH. On the North Carolina legislature's approval of work and apprenticeship contracts for former slaves, see Alexander, *North Carolina Faces the Freedmen*, pp. 38–48. On apprenticeship, see Scott, "Battle over the Child," pp. 101–13; and Gutman, *Black Family in Slavery and Freedom*, pp. 402–12.

18. Mann, "Slavery, Sharecropping, and Sexual Inequality"; Giddings, *When and Where I Enter*, pp. 57–74; Chambers to Gorrell, March 25, 1866, Gorrell Papers. For an analysis of conflict between African American women and men under slavery, see Stevenson, "Distress and Discord in Virginia Slave Families."

19. Will of Mary A. Chambers, Wills, Montgomery County, NCDAH. Rose, *In Slavery and Freedom*, p. 88.

20. Berthoff, "Conventional Mentality"; Rable, *Civil Wars*, pp. 265–68. For a more favorable assessment of the progress of propertied white women toward equality in the postwar South, see Scott, *Southern Lady*, pp. 105–84.

21. For excellent studies of the effects of postwar commercial patterns on the lives of North Carolina women, see Janiewski, *Sisterhood Denied*; Hall et al., *Like a Family*. On black women, see especially Giddings, *When and Where I Enter*, pp. 57–74; Jones, *Labor of Love*, pp. 44–78; Burton, *In My Father's House*, p. 302; Gutman, *Black Family in Slavery and Freedom*, pp. 432–50.

Bibliography

Primary Sources

Manuscripts

Chapel Hill, North Carolina
Southern Historical Collection, Library of the University of North Carolina at Chapel Hill (SHC, UNC-CH)
Rufus Amis Papers
Battle Family Papers
Carrie H. Clack Papers
Confederate Conscript Papers
Confederate Papers
Ralph Gorrell Papers
Hobbs-Mendenhall Papers
John Kelly Family Papers
Reminiscences of Jacob Alson Long
Alexander Carey McAlister Papers
James N. Patterson Papers
Richmond Pearson Papers
Marmaduke S. Robins Papers
Thomas Ruffin Papers and Books
David Schenck Books
Jonathan Worth Papers
Durham, North Carolina
Special Collections Department, Duke University
John Allen Papers
Frances N. Bennett Papers
James Bennitt Papers
John Berry Papers
Benjamin W. Brookshire Collections
Hugh Conway Browning Papers

James O. Coghill Papers
John Couch Papers
William A. Couch Papers
James A. Crewes Papers
Benjamin P. Elliot Papers
M. B. Fleming Papers
William Alexander Graham Papers
William H. Gregory Papers
Elizabeth R. Hargrove Papers
John Willis Hays Letters and Papers
Archibald Erskine Henderson Papers
William Woods Holden Collection
James H. Horner Letters and Papers
Elias Hurley Papers
Ku Klux Klan Collection
Thomas Lloyd Papers
Thomas Lynch and Mary Lynch Letters
Adolphus W. Mangum Papers
Benjamin Markham Papers
Scarborough Family Papers
James Strudwick Smith and Thomas John Faddis Daybook
Lewis O. Sugg Letters
John J. Taylor Papers
George W. Trice Papers
Michael H. Turrentine Papers
Bryan Tyson Papers
Abraham Watkins Venable Scrapbook
James K. Wilkerson Papers
Raleigh, North Carolina
North Carolina Department of Archives and History (NCDAH)
Oscar W. Blacknall Papers
James Boon Papers
Branson Family Papers
Atlas Cochran Collection
Eben Ingram Collection
James Norcom Family Papers
Zebulon Baird Vance and Harriet N. Espy Vance Letters

Public Documents and Records

Raleigh, North Carolina
North Carolina Department of Archives and History
Adjutant General's Roll of Honor, 1861–63

Apprentice Bonds, Granville County
———, Montgomery County
———, Orange County
Apprentice Docket, Granville County
Bastardy Bonds, Granville County
———, Montgomery County
———, Orange County
Civil Action Papers, Montgomery County
Civil Action Papers Concerning Land, Montgomery County
Coroners' Inquests, Granville County
Coroners' Reports, Orange County
County Court Minutes, Granville County
———, Montgomery County
———, Orange County
Criminal Action Papers, Granville County
———, Montgomery County
———, Orange County
Criminal Actions Concerning Slaves and Free Persons of Color, Granville County
Divorce Records, Caswell County
———, Granville County
———, Montgomery County
———, Orange County
Enon Baptist Church, Tally Ho Township Minutes, Granville County
Equity Minutes of the Superior Court, Granville County
———, Montgomery County
———, Orange County
Estate Records, Granville County
———, Montgomery County
———, Orange County
Governors' Letter Books, 1840–71
Governors' Papers, 1841–70
Land Entry Book, Orange County
Lauril Hill Baptist Church, Montgomery County
List of Taxables, 1854, Granville County
Marriage Bonds, Granville County
———, Montgomery County
———, Orange County
Minute Dockets of the County Court, Granville County
———, Montgomery County
———, Orange County
Minute Dockets of the Superior Court, Granville County

———, Montgomery County
———, Orange County
Minutes of the Wardens of the Poor, Montgomery County
———, Orange County
Miscellaneous Records, Granville County
———, Montgomery County
———, Orange County
Miscellaneous Records of Slaves and Free Persons of Color, Granville County
Officials' Bonds and Records, 1837–1918, Montgomery County
Special Tax List, 1873, Montgomery County
Tax Levies on Land, 1873–80, Montgomery County
Tax Lists, 1851, 1854, Montgomery County
Wills, Granville County
———, Montgomery County
———, Orange County
Washington, D.C.
National Archives
Army Command Letters, vol. 69, ser. 3276, Record Group 393
Southern Claims Commission: Records of the General Accounting Office, Third Auditor's Office, Record Group 217

Published and Unpublished U.S. Censuses and Census Reports

U.S. Bureau of the Census, Federal Manuscript Censuses, 1850, 1860, 1870, 1880, Granville, Montgomery, Orange, Randolph, and Union counties. Microfilm.

U.S. Bureau of the Census. *The Seventh Census of the United States: 1850. Embracing a Statistical View of Each of the States and Territories, Arranged by Counties, Towns, etc., under the Following Divisions*. Washington, D.C.: Robert Armstrong, 1853.

———. *Agriculture of the United States in 1860; Compiled from the Original Returns of the Eighth Census under the Direction of the Secretary of the Interior.* Washington, D.C.: Government Printing Office, 1864.

———. *Manufactures of the United States in 1860; Compiled from the Original Returns of the Eighth Census under the Direction of the Secretary of the Interior.* Washington D.C.: Government Printing Office, 1865.

———. *Population of the United States in 1860; Compiled from the Original Returns of the Eighth Census under the Direction of the Secretary of the Interior.* Washington D.C.: Government Printing Office, 1864.

———. *Statistics of the United States, (Including Mortality, Property, etc.,) in 1860; Compiled from the Original Returns and Being the Final Exhibit of the*

Eighth Census under the Direction of the Secretary of the Interior. Washington, D.C.: Government Printing Office, 1866.

Newspapers

Fayetteville Observer, Fayetteville, North Carolina
Greensborough Patriot, Greensboro, North Carolina
Hillsborough Recorder, Hillsborough, North Carolina
Richmond Whig, Richmond, Virginia
True Wesleyan, New York, New York

Books

Bassett, John Spencer. *Anti-Slavery Leaders of North Carolina*. Baltimore: Johns Hopkins Press, 1898.

Battle, Kemp Plummer. *Memories of an Old-Time Tar Heel*. Edited by William James Battle. Chapel Hill: University of North Carolina Press, 1945.

Crooks, Mrs. E. W. *Life of Reverend Adam Crooks, A.M.* Syracuse: Wesleyan Methodist Publishing Company, 1871.

Hamilton, J. G. de Roulhac, ed. *The Papers of Thomas Ruffin*. 4 vols. Raleigh: Edwards and Broughton, 1918–20.

Harper, Chancellor, Governor Hammond, Dr. Simms, Professor Dew. *The Proslavery Argument as Maintained by the Most Distinguished Writers of the Southern States*. 1852. Reprint. New York: Negro Universities Press, 1968.

Holcomb, Brent H. *Marriages of Granville County, North Carolina, 1753–1868*. Baltimore: Genealogical Publishing Company, 1981.

Jacobs, Harriet. *Incidents in the Life of a Slave Girl, Written by Herself* (1861). Edited with an Introduction by Jean Fagin Yellin. Cambridge, Mass.: Harvard University Press, 1987.

Long, Augustus White. *Son of Carolina*. Durham: Duke University Press, 1939.

Milnes, Monckton. *On the Property of Married Women and the Law of Divorce: A Collection of Documents*. N.p., 1857. Facsimile Reprint. William S. Hein & Company, 1975.

North Carolina Reports: Cases Argued and Determined by the Supreme Court of North Carolina. Vols. 13–59. Richmond: James E. Goode, 1898.

Olmsted, Frederick Law. *Journey in the Seaboard Slave States*. Westport, Conn.: Greenwood Press, 1968.

———. *Journey through the Back Country*. New York: Mason, 1860.

Owen, Thomas McAdory. *Granville County, North Carolina: Notes and Memoranda for the History and Genealogy of*. Montgomery, Ala.: N.p., 190[?].

Ratcliff, Clarence E., comp. *North Carolina Taxpayers, 1701–1786*. Baltimore: Genealogical Publishing Company, 1984.

Rawick, George P., ed. *The American Slave: A Composite Autobiography*. 19 vols., 12 vols. in supplement. Westport, Conn.: Greenwood, 1972.

Swaim, Benjamin. *The North Carolina Justice*. Raleigh: Henry D. Turner, 1846.

Taylor, Susie King. *Reminiscences of My Life: A Black Woman's Civil War Memoirs*. Edited by Patricia W. Romero and Willie Lee Rose. New York: Markus Weiner, 1988.

Tolbert, Noble. *The Papers of John W. Ellis*. 2 vols. Raleigh: North Carolina Department of Archives and History, 1964.

Weeks, Steven B. *Southern Quakers and Slavery: A Study in Institutional History*. New York: Bergman, 1896.

Wilson, Thomas L., comp. *A Brief History of the Cruelties and Atrocities of the Rebellion: Compiled from the Most Authentic Sources*. Washington, D.C.: McGill and Witherow, 1864.

Yearns, W. Buck, and John G. Barrett, eds. *North Carolina Civil War Documentary*. Chapel Hill: University of North Carolina Press, 1980.

Secondary Sources

Books, Dissertations, and Theses

Alexander, Roberta Sue. *North Carolina Faces the Freedmen: Race Relations during Presidential Reconstruction, 1865–67*. Durham: Duke University Press, 1985.

Anzaldua, Gloria. *Making Face, Making Soul, Haciendo Caras: Creative and Critical Perspectives by Women of Color*. San Francisco: Aunt Lute Foundation Books, 1990.

Aptheker, Bettina. *Woman's Legacy: Essays on Race, Sex, and Class in American History*. Amherst: University of Massachusetts Press, 1982.

Ash, Stephen. *Middle Tennessee Society Transformed, 1860–1870: War and Peace in the Upper South*. Baton Rouge: Louisiana State University Press, 1987.

Auman, William T. "Neighbor against Neighbor: The Inner Civil War in the Central Counties of Confederate North Carolina." Ph.D. dissertation, University of North Carolina at Chapel Hill, 1988.

———. "North Carolina's Inner Civil War: Randolph County." M.A. thesis, University of North Carolina, Greensboro, 1978.

Ayers, Edward L. *Vengeance and Justice: Crime and Punishment in the 19th-Century American South*. New York: Oxford University Press, 1984.

Bailey, Fred. *Class and Tennessee's Confederate Generation*. Chapel Hill: University of North Carolina Press, 1986.

Bardaglio, Peter. "'An Outrage upon Nature': Incest and the Law in the Nineteenth-Century South." In *In Joy and in Sorrow: Women, Family, and Marriage in the Victorian South, 1830–1900*, edited by Carol Bleser, pp. 32–51. New York: Oxford University Press, 1991.

Barrett, John Gilchrist. *North Carolina as a Civil War Battleground, 1861–1865*. Raleigh: North Carolina Department of Cultural Resources, Division of Archives and History, 1980.

Berlin, Ira. *Slaves without Masters: The Free Negro in the Antebellum South*. New York: Pantheon, 1974.

Billings, Dwight B., Jr. *Planters and the Making of a "New South": Class, Politics, and Development in North Carolina, 1865–1900*. Chapel Hill: University of North Carolina Press, 1979.

Blackwelder, Ruth. *The Age of Orange: Political and Intellectual Leadership in North Carolina, 1752–1861*. Charlotte: W. Loftin, 1961.

Blassingame, John. *The Slave Community: Plantation Life in the Antebellum South*. New York: Oxford University Press, 1972.

Boyd, William. *The Story of Durham, City of the New South*. Durham: Seeman Printery, 1925.

Brittan, Arthur, and Mary Maynard. *Sexism, Racism, and Oppression*. Oxford: Basil Blackwell, 1984.

Bruce, Dickson D., Jr. *Violence and Culture in the Antebellum South*. Austin: University of Texas Press, 1979.

Burton, Orville Vernon. *In My Father's House Are Many Mansions: Family and Community in Edgefield, South Carolina*. Chapel Hill: University of North Carolina Press, 1985.

Burton, Orville, and Robert McMath, eds. *Toward a New South? Studies in Post–Civil War Southern Communities*. Westport, Conn.: Greenwood Press, 1982.

Butler, Lindley S., and Alan D. Watson. *The North Carolina Experience: An Interpretative and Documentary History*. Chapel Hill: University of North Carolina Press, 1984.

Butts, Donald C. "A Challenge to Planter Rule: The Controversy over the Ad-Valorem Taxation of Slaves in North Carolina, 1858–1862." Ph.D. dissertation, Duke University, 1978.

Caldwell, James R., Jr. "The Churches of Granville County, North Carolina, in the Eighteenth Century." In *Studies in Southern History*, edited by Joseph C. Sitterson. Chapel Hill: University of North Carolina Press, 1957.

Calhoon, Robert M. *Religion and the American Revolution in North Carolina*. Raleigh: North Carolina Department of Cultural Resources, Division of Archives and History, 1976.

Campbell, Randolph B. *A Southern Community in Crisis: Harrison County, Texas, 1850–1880*. Austin: Texas State Historical Association, 1983.

Cash, Wilbur J. *The Mind of the South*. New York: Knopf, 1941.

Cashin, Joan E. *A Family Venture: Men and Women on the Southern Frontier*. New York: Oxford University Press, 1991.

Cathey, Cornelius Oliver. *Agricultural Developments in North Carolina, 1783–1860*. Chapel Hill: University of North Carolina Press, 1956.

Censer, Jane Turner. *North Carolina Planters and Their Children, 1800–1860*. Baton Rouge: Louisiana State University Press, 1984.

Chambers-Schiller, Lee Virginia. *Liberty a Better Husband: Single Women in America, the Generations of 1780–1849*. New Haven: Yale University Press, 1984.

Cimprich, John. *Slavery's End in Tennessee, 1861–1865*. Tuscaloosa: University of Alabama Press, 1986.

Clinton, Catherine. "Caught in the Web of the Big House: Women and Slavery." In *The Web of Southern Social Relations: Women, Family, and Education*, edited by Walter J. Fraser, Jr., Frank Saunders, Jr., and Jon L. Wakelyn, pp. 19–34. Athens: University of Georgia Press, 1985.

———. *The Other Civil War: American Women in the Nineteenth Century*. New York: Hill and Wang, 1984.

———. *The Plantation Mistress: Woman's World in the Old South*. New York: Pantheon, 1983.

———. "'Southern Dishonor': Flesh, Blood, Race, and Bondage." In *In Joy and in Sorrow: Women, Family, and Marriage in the Victorian South, 1830–1900*, edited by Carol Bleser, pp. 52–68. New York: Oxford University Press, 1991.

Collins, Patricia Hill. *Black Feminist Thought: Knowledge, Consciousness, and the Politics of Empowerment*. Boston: Unwin Hyman, 1990.

Cott, Nancy F. *The Bonds of Womanhood: "Women's Sphere" in New England, 1780–1835*. New Haven: Yale University Press, 1977.

Davis, Angela. *Women, Race, and Class*. New York: Random House, 1981.

Davis, Natalie Zemon. "Women on Top." In her *Society and Culture in Early Modern France*, pp. 124–51. Stanford: Stanford University Press, 1974.

D'Emilio, John, and Estelle B. Freedman. *Intimate Matters: A History of Sexuality in America*. New York: Harper & Row, 1988.

Douglas, Mary. *Purity and Danger: An Analysis of Concepts of Pollution and Taboo*. London: Routledge & Kegan Paul, 1966.

Dublin, Thomas. *Women at Work: The Transformation of Work and Community in Lowell, Massachusetts, 1820–1860*. New York: Columbia University Press, 1979.

Du Bois, W. E. B. *The Souls of Black Folk: Essays and Sketches*. 1903. Reprint. Greenwich, Conn.: Fawcett, 1961.

Dudden, Faye E. *Serving Women: Household Service in Nineteenth Century America*. Middletown, Conn.: Wesleyan University Press, 1985.

Epstein, Barbara L. *The Politics of Domesticity: Women, Evangelism, and Temperance in Nineteenth Century America*. Middletown, Conn.: Wesleyan University Press, 1981.

Escott, Paul D. *Many Excellent People: Power and Privilege in North Carolina, 1850–1900*. Chapel Hill: University of North Carolina Press, 1985.

______. *Slavery Remembered: A Record of Twentieth-Century Slave Narratives*. Chapel Hill: University of North Carolina Press, 1979.

Faragher, John Mack. *Sugar Creek: Life on the Illinois Prairie*. New Haven: Yale University Press, 1986.

______. *Women and Men on the Overland Trail*. New Haven: Yale University Press, 1979.

Farnham, Christie. "'Sapphire?': The Issue of Dominance in the Slave Family, 1830–1865." In *"To Toil the Livelong Day": America's Women at Work, 1780–1980*, edited by Carol Groneman and Mary Beth Norton, pp. 68–83. Ithaca: Cornell University Press, 1987.

Faust, Drew Gilpin. *James Henry Hammond and the Old South: A Design for Mastery*. Baton Rouge: Louisiana State University Press, 1982.

______. *A Sacred Circle: The Dilemma of the Intellectual in the Old South, 1840–1860*. Baltimore: Johns Hopkins University Press, 1977.

______, ed. *The Ideology of Slavery: Proslavery Thought in the Antebellum South, 1830–1860*. Baton Rouge: Louisiana State University Press, 1981.

Fellman, Michael. *Inside War: The Guerrilla Conflict in Missouri during the American Civil War*. New York: Oxford University Press, 1989.

Fields, Barbara Jeanne. *Slavery and Freedom on the Middle Ground: Maryland during the Nineteenth Century*. New Haven: Yale University Press, 1985.

Foner, Eric. *Nothing but Freedom: Emancipation and Its Legacy*. Baton Rouge: Louisiana State University Press, 1983.

______. *Reconstruction: America's Unfinished Revolution, 1863–1877*. New York: Harper & Row, 1988.

Fox-Genovese, Elizabeth. "Family and Female Identity in the Antebellum South: Sarah Gayle and Her Family." In *In Joy and in Sorrow: Women, Family, and Marriage in the Victorian South, 1830–1900*, edited by Carol Bleser, pp. 15–31. New York: Oxford University Press, 1991.

______. "Strategies and Forms of Resistance: Focus on Slave Women in the United States." In *In Resistance: Studies in African, Caribbean, and Afro-American History*, edited by Gary Y. Okihiro, pp. 143–65. Amherst: University of Massachusetts Press, 1986.

______. *Within the Plantation Household: Black and White Women of the Old South*. Chapel Hill: University of North Carolina Press, 1988.

Franklin, John Hope. *The Free Negro in North Carolina, 1790–1860*. New York: Russell and Russell, 1943.

Fraser, Walter J., Jr., and Winfred B. Moore, Jr., eds. *The Southern Enigma: Essays on Race, Class, and Folk Culture*. Westport, Conn.: Greenwood Press, 1981.

Friedman, Jean. *The Enclosed Garden: Women and Community in the Evangelical South, 1830–1900*. Chapel Hill: University of North Carolina Press, 1985.

Friedman, Lawrence M. *A History of American Law*. New York: Touchstone Books, 1973.

Gates, Paul. *Agriculture and the Civil War*. New York: Knopf, 1965.

Genovese, Eugene. *The Political Economy of Slavery: Studies in the Economy and Society of the Slave South*. New York: Vintage, 1967.

———. *Roll, Jordan, Roll: The World the Slaves Made*. New York: Pantheon, 1974.

Giddings, Paula. *When and Where I Enter: The Impact of Black Women on Race and Sex in America*. New York: Bantam, 1985.

Gilpatrick, Delbert Harold. *Jeffersonian Democracy in North Carolina, 1789–1816*. New York: Columbia University Press, 1931.

Gordon, Linda. *Heroes of Their Own Lives: The Politics and History of Family Violence, Boston, 1880–1960*. New York: Penguin, 1989.

———. "What's New in Women's History." In *Feminist Studies, Critical Studies*, edited by Teresa de Lauretis, pp. 20–30. Bloomington: Indiana University Press, 1986.

Grossberg, Michael. *Governing the Hearth: Law and the Family in Nineteenth-Century America*. Chapel Hill: University of North Carolina Press, 1985.

Gutman, Herbert G. *The Black Family in Slavery and Freedom, 1750–1925*. New York: Random House, 1976.

Gwynn, Zae Hargett. *Kinfolks of Granville County, North Carolina, 1765–1826*. Rocky Mount, N.C.: J. W. Watson, 1974.

Hahn, Steven. *Roots of Southern Populism: Yeoman Farmers and the Transformation of the Georgia Upcountry, 1850–1890*. New York: Oxford University Press, 1983.

Hahn, Steven H., and Jonathan Prude, eds. *The Countryside in the Age of Capitalist Transformation: Essays in the Social History of Rural America*. Chapel Hill: University of North Carolina Press, 1985.

Hall, Jacquelyn Dowd. "'The Mind That Burns in Each Body': Women, Rape, and Racial Violence." In *Powers of Desire: The Politics of Sexuality*, edited by Ann Snitow, Christine Stansell, and Sharon Thompson, pp. 328–49. New York: Monthly Review Press, 1983.

Hall, Jacquelyn Dowd, James Leloudis, Robert Korstad, Mary Murphy, LuAnn Jones, and Christopher B. Daly. *Like a Family: The Making of a*

Southern Cotton Mill World. Chapel Hill: University of North Carolina Press, 1987.

Harding, Vincent. *There Is a River: The Black Struggle for Freedom in America*. New York: Vintage, 1983.

Harris, J. William. *Plain Folk and Gentry in a Slave Society: White Liberty and Black Slavery in Augusta's Hinterlands*. Middletown, Conn.: Wesleyan University Press, 1985.

Higginbotham, Leon, Jr. *In the Matter of Color: Race and the American Legal Process*. New York: Oxford University Press, 1977.

Hilty, Hiram. "North Carolina Quakers and Slavery." Ph.D. dissertation, Duke University, 1969.

Hindus, Michael S. *Prison and Plantation: Crime, Justice, and Authority in Massachusetts and South Carolina, 1767–1878*. Chapel Hill: University of North Carolina Press, 1980.

hooks, bell. *Ain't I a Woman?: Black Women and Feminism*. Boston: South End Press, 1981.

______. *Feminist Theory from Margin to Center*. Boston: South End Press, 1984.

Inscoe, John. *Mountain Masters, Slavery, and the Sectional Crisis in Western North Carolina*. Knoxville: University of Tennessee Press, 1989.

Janiewski, Dolores E. *Sisterhood Denied: Race, Gender, and Class in a New South Community*. Philadelphia: Temple University Press, 1985.

Johnson, Guion Griffis. *Antebellum North Carolina: A Social History*. Chapel Hill: University of North Carolina Press, 1937.

Johnson, Michael P., and James L. Roark. "Strategies of Survival: Free Negro Families and the Problem of Slavery." In *In Joy and in Sorrow: Women, Family, and Marriage in the Victorian South, 1830–1900*, edited by Carol Bleser, pp. 88–102. New York: Oxford University Press, 1991.

Jones, Jacquelyn. *Labor of Love, Labor of Sorrow: Black Women, Work, and the Family from Slavery to the Present*. New York: Basic Books, 1985.

Joyner, Charles. *Down by the Riverside: A South Carolina Slave Community*. Urbana: University of Illinois Press, 1984.

Kenzer, Robert C. *Kinship and Neighborhood in a Southern Community: Orange County, North Carolina, 1849–1881*. Knoxville: University of Tennessee Press, 1987.

______. "Portrait of a Southern Community, 1850–1880." Ph.D. dissertation, Harvard University, 1982.

Kerber, Linda. *Women of the Republic: Intellect and Ideology in Revolutionary America*. Chapel Hill: University of North Carolina Press, 1980.

Keyser, Stanley R. "The Apprenticeship System in North Carolina to 1840." M.A. thesis, Duke University, 1950.

Kruman, Marc W. *Parties and Politics in North Carolina, 1836–1865*. Baton Rouge: Louisiana State University Press, 1983.

Lancaster, James Lawrence. "The Scalawags of North Carolina, 1850–1868." Ph.D. dissertation, Princeton University, 1974.

Lassiter, Mable S. *"Pattern of Timeless Moments": A History of Montgomery County*. Troy, N.C.: Bicentennial Committee, Montgomery County Finances Office, 1978.

Lebsock, Suzanne D. *The Free Women of Petersburg: Status and Culture in a Southern Town, 1784–1860*. New York: Norton, 1984.

Lefler, Hugh T. *Orange County, 1752–1952*. Chapel Hill: University of North Carolina Press, 1953.

Lefler, Hugh T., and Albert R. Newsome. *North Carolina: The History of a Southern State*. 3d ed. Chapel Hill: University of North Carolina Press, 1973.

Lerner, Gerda. *The Creation of Patriarchy*. New York: Oxford University Press, 1986.

———, ed. *Black Women in White America: A Documentary History*. New York: Pantheon, 1972.

Levine, Lawrence W. *Black Culture and Black Consciousness: Afro-American Folk Thought from Slavery to Freedom*. New York: Oxford University Press, 1977.

Litwack, Leon. *Been in the Storm So Long: The Aftermath of Slavery*. New York: Knopf, 1979.

———. *North of Slavery: The Negro in the Free States, 1790–1860*. Chicago: University of Chicago Press, 1961.

Lovejoy, Paul. "Fugitive Slaves: Resistance to Slavery in the Sokoto Caliphate." In *In Resistance: Studies in African, Caribbean, and Afro-American History*, edited by Gary Y. Okihiro, pp. 71–95. Amherst: University of Massachusetts Press, 1986.

McCurry, Stephanie. "Defense of Their World: Gender, Class, and the Yeomanry of the South Carolina Low Country, 1820–1860." Ph.D. dissertation, State University of New York at Binghamton, 1988.

McMillen, Sally G. *Motherhood in the Old South: Pregnancy, Childbirth, and Infant Rearing*. Baton Rouge: Louisiana State University Press, 1990.

McPherson, James M. *Abraham Lincoln and the Second American Revolution*. New York: Oxford University Press, 1990.

Magdol, Edward. *A Right to the Land: Essays on the Freedmen's Community*. Westport, Conn.: Greenwood Press, 1977.

Mathews, Donald G. *Religion in the Old South*. Chicago: University of Chicago Press, 1977.

Miller, Jean Baker. *Toward a New Psychology of Women*. Boston: Beacon Press, 1976.

Mitchell, Memory F. *Legal Aspects of Conscription and Exemption in North Carolina, 1861–1865*. Chapel Hill: University of North Carolina Press, 1965.

Moraga, Cherrie, and Gloria Anzaldua, eds. *This Bridge Called My Back: Writings by Radical Women of Color*. Watertown, Mass.: Persephone Press, 1981.

Morrison, Toni. *Beloved*. New York: Knopf, 1987.

Murray, Pauli. *Proud Shoes: The Story of an American Family*. New York: Harper & Row, 1956.

Nathans, Sydney. *The Quest for Progress: The Way We Lived in North Carolina, 1870–1920*. Chapel Hill: University of North Carolina Press, 1983.

Newton, Judith L., Mary P. Ryan, and Judith R. Walkowitz, eds. *Sex and Class in Women's History*. London: Routledge & Kegan Paul, 1983.

Nicholson, Ray S. *Wesleyan Methodism in the South*. Syracuse: Wesleyan Methodist Publishing House, 1933.

Nixon, Joseph R. *The German Settlers in Lincoln County and Western North Carolina*. Chapel Hill: University of North Carolina Press, 1912.

North, Douglass. *The Economic Growth of the United States, 1790–1860*. New York: Norton, 1966.

Norton, Clarence C. *The Democratic Party in Antebellum North Carolina, 1835–1861*. Chapel Hill: University of North Carolina Press, 1930.

Norton, Mary Beth. *Liberty's Daughters: The Revolutionary Experience of American Women, 1750–1800*. Boston: Little, Brown, 1980.

Nuermberger, Ruth Anna. *The Free Produce Movement: A Quaker Protest against Slavery*. Durham: Duke University Press, 1942.

Oakes, James. *The Ruling Race: A History of American Slaveholders*. New York: Knopf, 1982.

O'Brien, Gail Williams. *The Legal Fraternity and the Making of a New South Community, 1848–1882*. Athens: University of Georgia Press, 1986.

Olsen, Otto H. *Carpetbagger's Crusade: The Life of Albion Winegar Tourgée*. Baltimore: Johns Hopkins Press, 1965.

———, ed. *Reconstruction and Redemption in the South*. Baton Rouge: Louisiana State University Press, 1980.

Owsley, Frank L. *Plain Folk of the Old South*. Baton Rouge: Louisiana State University Press, 1949.

Painter, Nell Irvin. Introduction to *The Secret Eye: The Journal of Ella Gertrude Clanton Thomas, 1848–1889*, edited by Virginia Ingraham Burr, pp. 1–67. Chapel Hill: University of North Carolina Press, 1990.

Paludan, Phillip Shaw. *Victims: A True Story of the Civil War*. Knoxville: University of Tennessee Press, 1981.

Pleck, Elizabeth. *Domestic Tyranny: The Making of American Social Policy against Family Violence from Colonial Times to the Present*. New York: Oxford University Press, 1987.

Rabinowitz, Howard N., ed. *Southern Black Leaders of the Reconstruction Era.* Urbana: University of Illinois Press, 1982.

Rable, George C. *Civil Wars: Women and the Crisis of Southern Nationalism.* Urbana: University of Illinois Press, 1989.

Randall, James G., and David H. Donald. *The Civil War and Reconstruction.* Lexington, Mass.: D. C. Heath, 1969.

Ransom, Roger L., and Richard Sutch. *One Kind of Freedom: The Economic Consequences of Emancipation.* New York: Cambridge University Press, 1977.

Rawick, George P. *From Sundown to Sunup: The Making of the Black Community.* Westport, Conn.: Greenwood Press, 1972.

Reiter, Rayna R., ed. *Toward an Anthropology of Women.* New York: Monthly Review Press, 1975.

Richter, Winnie, ed. *The Heritage of Montgomery County, North Carolina.* Troy, N.C.: Montgomery County Historical Society, 1981.

Riley, Glenda. *The Female Frontier: A Comparative View of Women on the Prairie and the Plains.* Lawrence: University of Kansas Press, 1988.

Rodmell, Sue. "Men, Women and Sexuality: A Feminist Critique of the Sociology of Deviance." In *Radical Voices: A Decade of Feminist Resistance,* edited by Renate D. Klein and Deborah Lynn Steinberg, pp. 80–92. New York: Pergamon Press, 1989.

Rose, Willie Lee. *In Slavery and Freedom.* Edited by William W. Freehling. New York: Oxford University Press, 1982.

Rosengarten, Theodore. *Tombee: Portrait of a Cotton Planter.* New York: McGraw-Hill, 1987.

Ross, Ellen, and Rayna Rapp. "Sex and Society: A Research Note from Social History and Anthropology." In *Powers of Desire: The Politics of Sexuality,* edited by Ann Snitow, Christine Stansell, and Sharon Thompson, pp. 51–73. New York: Monthly Review Press, 1983.

Ryan, Mary P. *Cradle of the Middle Class: The Family in Oneida County, New York, 1790–1865.* New York: Cambridge University Press, 1981.

Salmon, Marylynn. "Equality or Submersion? Feme Covert Status in Early Pennsylvania." In *Women of America: A History,* edited by Carol Ruth Berkin and Mary Beth Norton, pp. 92–113. Boston: Houghton Mifflin, 1979.

———. *Women and the Law of Property in Early America.* Chapel Hill: University of North Carolina Press, 1986.

Sargent, Lydia, ed. *Women and Revolution.* Boston: South End Press, 1981.

Schur, Edwin M. *Labeling Women Deviant: Gender, Stigma, and Social Control.* New York: Random House, 1984.

Schwarz, Philip J. *Twice Condemned: Slaves and the Criminal Laws of Virginia, 1705–1865.* Baton Rouge: Louisiana State University Press, 1988.

Scott, Anne Firor. *The Southern Lady: From Pedestal to Politics, 1830–1930*. Chicago: University of Chicago Press, 1970.

Simkins, Francis Butler, and James Welch Patton. *The Women of the Confederacy*. New York: Garret and Massie, 1936.

Sitterson, Joseph C. *The Secession Movement in North Carolina*. Chapel Hill: University of North Carolina Press, 1939.

Sklar, Kathryn Kish. *Catharine Beecher: A Study in American Domesticity*. New York: Norton, 1973.

Smart, Carol, and Barry Smart, eds. *Women, Sexuality, and Social Control*. London: Routledge & Kegan Paul, 1978.

Smith-Rosenberg, Carroll. *Disorderly Conduct: Visions of Gender in Victorian America*. New York: Knopf, 1985.

Snitow, Ann, Christine Stansell, and Sharon Thompson, eds. *Powers of Desire: The Politics of Sexuality*. New York: Monthly Review Press, 1983.

Stansell, Christine. *City of Women: Sex and Class in New York, 1789–1860*. Urbana: University of Illinois Press, 1987.

Sterling, Dorothy, ed. *We Are Your Sisters: Black Women in the Nineteenth Century*. New York: Norton, 1984.

Stevenson, Brenda. "Distress and Discord in Virginia Slave Families, 1830–1860." In *In Joy and in Sorrow: Women, Family, and Marriage in the Victorian South, 1830–1900*, edited by Carol Bleser, pp. 103–24. New York: Oxford University Press, 1991.

Stuckey, Sterling. *Slave Culture: Nationalist Theory and the Foundations of Black America*. New York: Oxford University Press, 1987.

Taylor, Rosser H. *The Free Negro in North Carolina*. Chapel Hill: James Sprunt Historical Publications, 1920.

———. *Slaveholding in North Carolina: An Economic View*. Chapel Hill: University of North Carolina Press, 1926.

Taylor, William R. *Cavalier and Yankee: The Old South and National Character*. New York: George Braziller, 1961.

Thornton, J. Mills, III. *Politics and Power in a Slave Society: Alabama, 1800–1860*. Baton Rouge: Louisiana State University Press, 1978.

Tilley, Nannie May. *The Brightleaf Tobacco Industry, 1860–1929*. Chapel Hill: University of North Carolina Press, 1948.

Trelease, Allen W. *White Terror: The Ku Klux Klan Conspiracy and Southern Reconstruction*. New York: Harper & Row, 1971.

Tunnell, Ted. *Crucible of Reconstruction: War, Radicalism, and Race in Louisiana, 1862–1877*. Baton Rouge: Louisiana State University Press, 1984.

Tushnet, Mark V. *The American Law of Slavery, 1810–1860: Considerations of Humanity and Interest*. Princeton: Princeton University Press, 1981.

Walkowitz, Judith R. *Prostitution and Victorian Society: Women, Class and the State*. New York: Cambridge University Press, 1980.

Wallenstein, Peter. *From Slave South to New South: Public Policy in Nineteenth-Century Georgia*. Chapel Hill: University of North Carolina Press, 1987.

Watson, Harry L. *Jacksonian Politics and Community Conflict: The Emergence of the Second American Party System in Cumberland County, North Carolina*. Baton Rouge: Louisiana State University Press, 1981.

———. "'Old Rip' and a New Era." In *The North Carolina Experience: An Interpretive and Documentary History*, edited by Lindley S. Butler and Alan D. Watson, pp. 217–40. Chapel Hill: University of North Carolina Press, 1984.

White, Deborah Gray. *Ar'n't I a Woman?: Female Slaves in the Plantation South*. New York: Norton, 1985.

Whitener, Daniel. *Prohibition in North Carolina, 1715–1945*. Chapel Hill: University of North Carolina Press, 1945.

Williamson, Joel. *New People: Miscegenation and Mulattoes in the United States*. New York: Free Press, 1980.

Wood, Peter. *Black Majority: Negroes in Colonial South Carolina from 1670 through the Stono Rebellion*. New York: Norton, 1974.

Woodward, C. Vann. *Origins of the New South, 1877–1913*. Baton Rouge: Louisiana State University Press, 1951.

Wright, Gavin. *The Political Economy of the Cotton South: Households, Markets, and Wealth in the Nineteenth Century*. New York: Norton, 1978.

Wyatt-Brown, Bertram. *Southern Honor: Ethics and Behavior in the Old South*. New York: Oxford University Press, 1982.

Yates, Richard E. *The Confederacy and Zeb Vance*. Tuscaloosa, Ala.: Confederate Publishing Company, 1958.

Zuber, Richard L. *North Carolina during Reconstruction*. Raleigh: North Carolina Department of Cultural Resources, Division of Archives and History, 1975.

Articles

Ainsley, W. Frank, and John W. Florin. "The North Carolina Piedmont: An Island of Religious Diversity." *Studies in the Social Sciences* 12 (June 1973): 30–35.

Ash, Stephen V. "Poor Whites in the Occupied South, 1861–1865." *Journal of Southern History* 57 (February 1991): 39–62.

Auman, William T. "Neighbor against Neighbor: The Inner Civil War in the Randolph County Area of Confederate North Carolina." *North Carolina Historical Review* 61 (January 1984): 60–90.

Auman, William T., and David D. Scarboro. "The Heroes of America in Civil War North Carolina." *North Carolina Historical Review* 58 (October 1981): 327–63.

Balanoff, Elizabeth. "Negro Legislators in the North Carolina General Assembly, July, 1868–February, 1872." *North Carolina Historical Review* 49 (January 1972): 22–55.

Bardaglio, Peter W. "Power and Ideology in the Slave South: Eugene Genovese and His Critics." *Maryland Historian* 12 (Fall 1981): 23–39.

Bardolph, Richard. "A North Carolina Farm Journal of the Mid-1950s." *North Carolina Historical Review* 25 (January 1948): 57–89.

Beatty, Bess. "The Edwin Holt Family: Nineteenth Century Capitalists in North Carolina." *North Carolina Historical Review* 63 (October 1986): 511–35.

______. "The Lowells of the South: Northern Influences on the Nineteenth Century North Carolina Textile Industry." *Journal of Southern History* 53 (February 1987): 37–62.

Berthoff, Rowland. "Conventional Mentality: Free Blacks, Women, and Business Corporations as Unequal Persons, 1820–1870." *Journal of American History* 76 (December 1989): 753–84.

Butts, Donald. "The Irrepressible Conflict: Slave Taxation and North Carolina's Gubernatorial Election of 1860." *North Carolina Historical Review* 58 (January 1981): 44–66.

Bynum, Victoria. "On the Lowest Rung: Court Control over Poor White and Free Black Women." *Southern Exposure* 12 (November–December 1984): 40–44.

______. "'War within a War': Women's Participation in the Revolt of the North Carolina Piedmont, 1863–1865." *Frontiers: A Journal of Women Studies* 9, no. 3 (1987): 43–49.

Carlton, David L. "The Revolution from Above: The National Market and the Beginnings of Industrialization in North Carolina." *Journal of American History* 77 (September 1990): 445–75.

Cashin, Joan E. "The Structure of Antebellum Planter Families: 'The Ties That Bound Us Was Strong.'" *Journal of Southern History* 55 (February 1990): 55–70.

Censer, Jane Turner. "Smiling through Her Tears: Antebellum Southern Women and Divorce." *American Journal of Legal History* 25 (January 1981): 24–47.

Connor, Paul. "Patriarchy: Old World and New." *American Quarterly* 17 (1965): 48–62.

Cott, Nancy F. "Divorce and the Changing Status of Women in Eighteenth-Century Massachusetts." *William and Mary Quarterly* 33 (October 1976): 586–614.

Cox, Monty W. "Freedom during the Frémont Campaign: North Carolina Republicans in 1856." *North Carolina Historical Review* 45 (October 1968): 357–83.

Crawford, Martin. "Political Society in a Southern Mountain Community:

Ashe County, North Carolina, 1850–1861." *Journal of Southern History* 55 (August 1989): 373–90.

Crow, Jeffrey J. "Slave Rebelliousness and Social Conflict in North Carolina, 1775–1802." *William and Mary Quarterly* 37 (January 1980): 79–102.

Davis, Angela. "Reflections on the Black Woman's Role in the Community of Slaves." *Black Scholar* 2 (December 1971): 2–15.

Edwards, Laura. "Sexual Violence, Gender, and Reconstruction in Granville County, North Carolina." *North Carolina Historical Review* 68 (July 1991): 237–60.

Escott, Paul D. "Poverty and Governmental Aid for the Poor in Confederate North Carolina." *North Carolina Historical Review* 61 (October 1984): 462–80.

Escott, Paul D., and Jeffrey J. Crow. "The Social Order and Violent Disorder: An Analysis of North Carolina in the Revolution and the Civil War." *Journal of Southern History* 52 (August 1986): 373–402.

Faust, Drew Gilpin. "Altars of Sacrifice: Confederate Women and the Narratives of War." *Journal of American History* 76 (March 1990): 1200–1228.

Ferrell, Joseph S. "Notes and Comments." *North Carolina Law Review* 41 (1962–63): 604–16.

Fox, Greer Litton. "Nice Girl: Social Control of Women through a Value Construct." *Signs: Journal of Women in Culture and Society* 2 (Summer 1977): 805–17.

Fox-Genovese, Elizabeth. "Antebellum Southern Households: A New Perspective on a Familiar Question." *Review* 7 (Fall 1983): 215–53.

Franklin, John Hope. "The Enslavement of Free Negroes in North Carolina." *Journal of Negro History* 29 (October 1944): 401–28.

———. "The Free Negro in the Economic Life of Antebellum North Carolina." *North Carolina Historical Review* 19 (October 1942): 239–59, 359–75.

Gass, W. Conrad. "A Felicitous Life: Lucy Martin Battle, 1805–1874." *North Carolina Historical Review* 58 (Autumn 1975): 367–93.

Genovese, Eugene. "Yeoman Farmers in a Slaveholders' Democracy." *Agricultural History* 49 (April 1975): 331–42.

Goodman, Paul. "White over White: Planters, Yeomen, and the Coming of the Civil War, A Review Essay." *Agricultural History* 54 (July 1980): 446–52.

Grossberg, Michael. "Who Gets the Child?: Custody, Guardianship, and the Rise of a Judicial Patriarchy in Nineteenth-Century America." *Feminist Studies* 9 (Summer 1983): 235–60.

Gundersen, Joan R., and Gwen Victor Gampel. "Married Women's Legal Status in Eighteenth-Century New York and Virginia." *William and Mary Quarterly* 39 (January 1982): 114–34.

Hagler, D. Harland. "The Ideal Woman in the Antebellum South: Lady or Farmwife?" *Journal of Southern History* 46 (August 1980): 405–18.

Harris, Robert L., Jr. "The Flowering of Afro-American History." *American Historical Review* 92 (December 1987): 1150–61.

Harris, William C. "William Woods Holden: In Search of Vindication." *North Carolina Historical Review* 59 (October 1982): 354–72.

Honey, Michael K. "The War within the Confederacy: White Unionists of North Carolina." *Prologue* (Summer 1986): 75–93.

Horton, James Oliver. "Freedom's Yoke: Gender Conventions among Antebellum Free Blacks." *Feminist Studies* 12 (Spring 1986): 51–76.

Hudson, G. H. "John Chavis, 1763–1838: A Social-Psychological Study." *Journal of Negro History* 64 (Spring 1979): 142–56.

Inscoe, John C. "Mountain Masters: Slaveholding in Western North Carolina." *North Carolina Historical Review* 55 (April 1978): 143–73.

Jeffrey, Thomas E. "Internal Improvements and Political Parties in Antebellum North Carolina." *North Carolina Historical Review* 55 (April 1978): 111–56.

Jennings, Thelma. "'Us Colored Women Had to Go through a Plenty': Sexual Exploitation of African-American Slave Women." *Journal of Women's History* 1 (Winter 1990): 45–74.

Johnson, Michael P. "Planters and Patriarchy: Charleston, 1800–1860." *Journal of Southern History* 46 (February 1980): 45–72.

Jones, Jacqueline. "'My Mother Was Much of a Woman': Black Women, Work, and the Family under Slavery." *Feminist Studies* 8 (Summer 1982): 235–69.

Jowkar, Forouz. "Honor and Shame: A Feminist View from Within." *Feminist Issues* 6 (Spring 1986): 45–65.

Kerber, Linda K. "Separate Spheres, Female Worlds, Woman's Place: The Rhetoric of Women's History." *Journal of American History* 75 (June 1988): 9–39.

Kolchin, Peter. "Reevaluating the Antebellum Slave Community: A Comparative Perspective." *Journal of American History* 70 (December 1983): 579–601.

Lebsock, Suzanne. "Free Black Women and the Question of Matriarchy: Petersburg, Virginia, 1784–1820." *Feminist Studies* 8 (Summer 1982): 270–92.

______. "Radical Reconstruction and the Property Rights of Southern Women." *Journal of Southern History* 43 (May 1977): 195–216.

Lerner, Gerda. "Reconceptualizing Differences among Women." *Journal of Women's History* 1 (Winter 1990): 106–22.

McPherson, Elizabeth Gregory, ed. "Letters from North Carolina to Andrew Johnson." *North Carolina Historical Review* 49 (January 1972): 22–55.

Mann, Susan A. "Slavery, Sharecropping, and Sexual Inequality." *Signs: Journal of Women in Culture and Society* 14 (Summer 1989): 776–98.
Menius, Arthur C., III. "James Bennitt: Portrait of an Antebellum Yeoman." *North Carolina Historical Review* 58 (October 1981): 305–26.
Merrill, Michael. "Cash Is Good to Eat: Self-Sufficiency and Exchange in the Rural Economy of the United States." *Radical History Review* 3 (Winter 1977): 42–71.
Mills, Gary B. "Miscegenation and the Free Negro in Antebellum 'Anglo' Alabama: A Reexamination of Southern Race Relations." *Journal of American History* 68 (June 1981): 16–34.
Moser, Harold D. "Reaction in North Carolina to the Emancipation Proclamation." *North Carolina Historical Review* 44 (Winter 1967): 53–72.
Nash, A. E. Keir. "A More Equitable Past?: Southern Supreme Courts and the Protection of the Antebellum Negro." *North Carolina Law Review* 48 (February 1970): 197–241.
Norton, Mary Beth. "The Evolution of White Women's Experience in Early America." *American Historical Review* 89 (June 1984): 593–619.
Opper, Peter Kent. "North Carolina Quakers: Reluctant Slaveholders." *North Carolina Historical Review* 52 (January 1975): 37–58.
Painter, Nell Irvin. "French Theories in American Settings: Some Thoughts on Transferability." *Journal of Women's History* 1 (Spring 1989): 92–95.
Palmer, Phyllis M. "White Women/Black Women: The Dualism of Female Identity and Experience in the United States." *Feminist Studies* 9 (Spring 1983): 152–69.
Phifer, Edward W. "Slavery in Microcosm: Burke County, North Carolina." *Journal of Southern History* 28 (March 1962): 137–65.
Rapp, Rayna, Ellen Ross, and Renate Bridenthal. "Examining Family History." *Feminist Studies* 5 (Spring 1979): 174–200.
Reid, Richard. "A Test Case of the 'Crying Evil': Desertion among North Carolina Troops during the Civil War." *North Carolina Historical Review* 58 (Summer 1981): 234–62.
Roberts, A. Sellew. "The Peace Movement in North Carolina." *Mississippi Valley Historical Review* 11 (June 1924): 190–99.
Salmon, Marylynn. "Women and Property in South Carolina: The Evidence from Marriage Settlements, 1730–1830." *William and Mary Quarterly* 4 (October 1982): 655–85.
Schweninger, Loren. "Property-Owning Free African-American Women in the South, 1800–1870." *Journal of Women's History* 1 (Winter 1990): 13–44.
———. "Prosperous Blacks in the South, 1790–1880." *American Historical Review* 95 (February 1990): 31–56.

Scott, Anne Firor. "Women's Perspective on the Patriarchy in the 1850s." *Journal of American History* 61 (June 1974): 52–64.

Scott, Joan W. "Gender: A Useful Category of Historical Analysis." *American Historical Review* 91 (December 1986): 1053–75.

Scott, Rebecca. "The Battle over the Child: Child Apprenticeship and the Freedmen's Bureau in North Carolina." *Prologue* 10 (Summer 1978): 101–13.

Smith-Rosenberg, Carroll. "The Female World of Love and Ritual." *Signs: Journal of Women in Culture and Society* 1 (Autumn 1975): 1–29.

Sowle, Patrick. "The North Carolina Manumission Society, 1816–1834." *North Carolina Historical Review* 42 (1965): 47–69.

Standard, Diffee W., and Richard W. Griffin. "The Cotton Textile Industry in Antebellum North Carolina." *North Carolina Historical Review* 34 (January 1957): 15–35.

Thompson, E. P. "The Moral Economy of the Crowd." *Past and Present* 50 (1971): 76–136.

Watson, Alan D. "Women in Colonial North Carolina: Overlooked and Underestimated." *North Carolina Historical Review* 58 (Winter 1981): 1–22.

Welter, Barbara. "The Cult of True Womanhood, 1820–1860." *American Quarterly* 18 (Summer 1966): 151–74.

White, Deborah Gray. "The Lives of Slave Women." *Southern Exposure* 12 (November–December 1984): 32–39.

White, Shane. "'We Dwell in Safety and Pursue Our Honest Callings': Free Blacks in New York City, 1783–1810." *Journal of American History* 75 (September 1988): 445–70.

Woodman, Harold D. "Sequel to Slavery: The New History Views the Postbellum South." *Journal of Southern History* 43 (November 1977): 523–54.

Wyatt-Brown, Bertram. "The Mask of Obedience: Male Slave Psychology in the Old South." *American Historical Review* 93 (December 1988): 1228–52.

Yanuck, Julius. "Thomas Ruffin and North Carolina Slave Law." *Journal of Southern History* 21 (November 1955): 456–75.

Index